To Mark:

May the Lord shower
precious words from this
devotional on you.
I love you!

Karrie 10-7

D0007052

WITH ALL MY STRENGTH

WITH ALL MY STRENGTH

DYNAMIC TIMES WITH GOD
DAILY DEVOTIONS FOR MEN

H. Norman Wright

Servant Publications
Ann Arbor, Michigan

Vine Books is an imprint of Servant Publications especially designed to serve evangelical Christians.

All scripture quotations, unless otherwise indicated, are taken from the HOLY BIBLE, NEW INTERNATIONAL VERSION. © 1973, 1978, 1984 by International Bible Society. Used by permission of Zondervan Publishing House. All rights reserved.

Excerpt reprinted from *What Makes a Man,* © 1992 by Bill McCartney. Used by permission of NavPress, Colorado Springs, CO. All rights reserved. For copies call (800) 366-7788. Permissions for excerpts from other books included in acknowledgments.

Published by Servant Publications
P.O. Box 8617
Ann Arbor, Michigan 48107

Cover design: Left Coast Design, Portland, OR

96 97 98 99 00 10 9 8 7 6 5 4 3 2 1

Printed in the United States of America
ISBN 0-89283-968-6

Library of Congress Cataloging-in-Publication Data

Wright, H. Norman
    With all my strength : dynamic times with God : devotions for men / H. Norman Wright.
        p.   cm.
    Includes index.
    ISBN 0-89283-968-6
    1. Men—Prayer—books and devotions —English.
2. Men—Religious life.   3. Devotional calendars.   I. Title.
BV4843.W75   1996
242'.642—dc20   96-13410
                                                    CIP

DEDICATION

This book is dedicated to my close friends of many years:

Dale Dukellis

Rex Johnson

Don Latra

Gary Oliver

Tim Thompson

Doug Weaver

Your support, encouragement, faithfulness, transparency, integrity, laughter, and prayers have made my life more complete. I am indeed fortunate to have you in my life.

And to my brother, Paul Fugleberg—your quiet and sensitive spirit, steadfastness, companionship, and love are deeply valued. Thanks for being you.

JANUARY 1

"Have nothing to do with godless myths and old wives' tales; rather, train yourself to be godly" (1 Timothy 4:7).

You know what it's like to sweat, don't you? You're playing an intense game of racquetball or working in the yard. At first small beads of water ooze from your pores. Then, as though a pump were turned on, the water pours down your face and body. Your shirt absorbs the perspiration, but soon it's so wet and sticky that it's in the way. So you strip it off. The harder you work or play, the more you sweat. And for most of us, the better we feel.

The word *train* that Paul uses here literally means *naked*. This is the same word from which we get our English word *gymnasium*. In the old Greek athletic contests, the athletes competed without clothing so they wouldn't be hampered by it. The word *train* actually meant "to exercise naked." And you know, whenever you train, there is sweat.

Do you catch what Paul is saying here? He's saying to train (exercise, work out) for the purpose of godliness. Paul is calling for spiritual sweat. As the Greeks rid themselves of clothing that got in their way, Paul is calling us to get rid of any habit, relationship, or practice that keeps us from being godly men. The writer of Hebrews puts it this way: "Therefore, since we are surrounded by such a great cloud of witnesses, let us throw off everything that hinders and the sin that so easily entangles, and let us run with perseverance the race marked out for us" (Heb 12:1).

After Paul said to "train," he said we need to labor and strive for it. Labor means "strenuous toil." The Christian life isn't an easy walk in the park. It takes effort, energy, sweat![1] One man put it this way: "The successful Christian life is a sweaty affair. No sweat, no sainthood."[2]

Is there anything holding you back from being godly? Ask the Lord to show you what you should do about that. Then put forth all your energy to train for godliness.

JANUARY 2

"It is God's will that you should be holy..."
(1 Thessalonians 4:3).

So... the Bible says we are to be holy. But what does that mean? How do you do whatever it takes to be holy? Perhaps a good place to begin is... with lust. Yes, lust—an issue we all struggle with in one way or another. Paul is saying that training ourselves to be godly (1 Tm 4:7) covers this area as well. In 1 Thessalonians 4:4-6, Paul says, "Each of you should learn to control his own body in a way that is holy and honorable, not in passionate lust like the heathen, who do not know God; and that in this matter no one should wrong his brother or take advantage of him. The Lord will punish men for all such sins, as we have already told you and warned you."

That's strong language, but it's important to heed. As Christians, we're called to be different from other men. We're called to purity in our sexual life. Impossible? No. A struggle? Yes. But that's why we need God's presence and power in our lives to enable us to use our sexual passion in a positive way.

How can we control raging hormones? Consider these steps.

- Be accountable to a small group or another man that you can be honest with and know will support you.
- Pray specifically for your own purity in thought and action.
- Memorize the Word of God. "I have hidden your word in my heart that I might not sin against you" (Ps 119:11). Memorize that passage today!
- Watch your thought life and your eyes! What we think about and focus our eyes on can fan that spark of lust into a raging fire.

Job had some counsel for us. He said, "I made a covenant with my eyes not to look lustfully at a girl!" (Jb 31:1). I bet you've never read that verse before, have you? It could mean avoiding that second look or keeping your eyes at eye level. If we don't, we experience what Proverbs states: "Can a man scoop fire into his lap without his clothes being burned?" (Prv 6:27).

A minister once said: "One look of recognition, one look of appreciation, and no more looks!"

Holiness—it takes on a whole new meaning when we apply it to everyday struggles, doesn't it? But it is possible.[3]

"Wounds from a friend are better than kisses from an enemy!"
(Proverbs 27:6, TLB)

"Give it to me straight, I can take it." Is there anyone in your life who will tell it to you like it is? Have you got someone who will level with you and with whom you can level? And the relationship is stronger because of the honesty? That's what Proverbs is talking about. We may not want to hear the truth, but we're better off because of what was said. Proverbs states: "A rebuke to a man of common sense is more effective than a hundred lashes on the back of a rebel" (17:10, TLB). Oh yeah, it feels good to have someone flatter you, but it can cause problems. "Flattery is a trap..." (Prv 29:5, TLB).

What we're talking about here is candor—being open and truthful so that the truth builds the relationship. You see, candor comes because of our care and love for the other person. We want the best for them. We have their well-being in mind. Ephesians 4:15 describes how we can share with another: "But, speaking the truth in love..." (NASB).

The wording here means that when you've spoken the truth your relationship is cemented together better than before. That's a healthy relationship. How many of those do you have? One? Several? If so, you're fortunate. Candor, mutual candor, is a sign of close friendship. You'll be a different person and so will the other when candor is present. You'll change. You'll grow. Again Proverbs states the result: "A friendly discussion is as stimulating as the sparks that fly when iron strikes iron" (27:17, TLB).

Keep in mind that your response to the candor of your friend (it could even be your wife!) will make a difference. Defensiveness kills candor. Responses like "Let me think about that" or "That's something for me to consider," keep a relationship going.

So... can you take it? Should you take it straight? Why not? Will you build better relationships with candor? Definitely. One last thought if you really want to have someone give it to you straight, take a look at God's Word.[4]

"The Lord is my shepherd, I shall not be in want. He makes me lie down in green pastures, he leads me beside quiet waters..." (Psalms 23:1-2).

Have you ever watched a marathon race? Better yet, have you ever experienced running those twenty-six miles under a hot baking sun or even a cold driving rain? Mile after mile the runners lift one foot, slam it down on the concrete, and do the same with the other foot. Have you ever wondered how many times each foot slams into that unyielding surface? Thousands upon thousands of times.

Sometimes microscopic cracks begin to appear in the outer layers of bone in the feet or legs. If the running continues and the lower body sustains the same degree of punishment, those tiny crevices enlarge. Soon they're large enough to create pain. There's a name for it: stress fracture.

You may think stress fractures are limited to the bones, but they're not. We pound our bodies in other ways. Our schedule begins to pile up, as do the bills; we take on a coaching job, learn to eat on the run (usually junk food), try to satisfy the boss, spouse, and church. Before long our nerves have these microscopic cracks beginning. We're on edge like a tightly wound rubber band just ready to snap at whatever gets in our way.

Your spirit and your heart can be stress fractured as well. It comes from taking on and doing too much by yourself. Whoever said we were called to go through life alone? That approach will fracture your life. There's a Shepherd waiting to help you. Why don't you let him?

He refreshes and restores my life (my self); He leads me in the paths of righteousness [uprightness and right standing with Him—not for my earning it, but] for His name's sake. Yes, though I walk through the [deep, sunless] valley of the shadow of death, I will fear *or* dread no evil; for You are with me; Your rod [to protect] and Your staff [to guide], they comfort me.   **Psalms 23:3-4, AMP**

Read this psalm aloud each day for a month. Then check your stress level.

"I went past the field of the sluggard, past the vineyard of the man who lacks judgment; thorns had come up everywhere, the ground was covered with weeds, and the stone wall was in ruins. I applied my heart to what I observed and learned a lesson from what I saw"
(Proverbs 24:30-32).

This is a strange verse, isn't it? The writer of Proverbs is talking about a person who is basically "inefficient." Some versions describe the person as a "sluggard." The *Amplified Bible* calls him "the lazy man." You may be thinking, *Just a minute here. That's not me, I'm an efficiency wizard. There's not a lazy bone in my body. You ought to see my smoke at work. They call me "Mr. Efficiency."* That's great. That's consistent with Scripture. Everything we do ought to be done for our Lord's sake.

But let's take a detour away from work and go to the home front. What does your garage look like? What about the work room, the backyard, or the "catch-all" drawer in the kitchen? If you're married, how would your wife rate you on efficiency around the homestead? Yeah, you're right. Bad question! But necessary to ask. Why? Simply because a number of men have MPP—Multiple Personality Problem. They're super-charged workhorses on the job, but at home they function like sluggards. And to make matters worse (much worse!), if their wives know they're giving it their all at the office, they will not be happy receiving only the leftovers at home.

So what's the answer? Consistent efficiency—at work and at home. Don't try to catch up or do it all at once. Space out the chores in an orderly fashion and watch the change—in you and your wife.

"To him who is able to keep you from falling and to present you before his glorious presence without fault and with great joy" (Jude 24).

It's embarrassing. There's no other word for it. You're just walking along and you either trip over your feet or miss a step and splat! You fall on your face. If any of your friends are around to see it, you know what you're going to hear about the rest of the day!

At many camps and conference grounds throughout the country there is a new activity. They call it The Wall. It's a fifty-foot simulated rock climb, a wall of wood with rock-shaped fingerholds jutting out all over. It's safe, though. You wear a harness around your waist that is attached to a rope that runs through a pulley. Someone holds onto the rope and secures it for you as you climb. If your fingers and hands tire and you happen to fall (which happens to many), the rope saves you.

It's a good metaphor for life, because we fall in other ways, too. Our hands have slipped from promises, commitments, and even convictions. Max Lucado describes what happens after we fall.

Now you are wiser. You have learned to go slowly. You are careful. You are cautious, but you are also confident. You trust the rope. You rely on the harness. And though you can't see your guide, you know him. You know he is strong. You know he is able to keep you from falling.

And you know you are only a few more steps from the top. So whatever you do, don't quit. Though your falls are great, his strength is greater. You will make it. You will see the summit. You will stand at the top. And when you get there, the first thing you'll do is join with all the others who have made the climb and sing this verse:

"To him who is able to keep you from falling..."[5]

"How can a young man keep his way pure? By living according to your word.... I have hidden your word in my heart that I might not sin against you" (Psalms 119:9-11).

This is personal—from me to you. I've got a confession to make. When I was a teenager I got into something—memorizing Scripture. And it helped me more times than I can remember. On several occasions when I was facing a temptation and struggling with a decision, guess what happened? Yeah, you can figure it out. A scripture I'd memorized just happened to "pop" into my mind right at that moment. And usually it was 1 Corinthians 10:13, "No temptation has seized you except what is common to man. And God is faithful; he will not let you be tempted beyond what you can bear. But when you are tempted, he will also provide a way out so that you can stand up under it." That passage was a lifesaver.

Over the decades of adulthood (I'm fifty-eight as I write this) I really didn't make any consistent attempt to memorize God's Word... until this past summer. A friend of mine at a family camp shared a session based on his new book, *Seeking Solid Ground*. It's all about Psalm 15. At the end he gently challenged us to memorize this psalm. It talks about how to get the most out of life.

I don't know why, but I decided to do it. One thing I found, the synapses of the brain cells at this age aren't quite as alive as they were forty years ago. It took more work, but just two or three minutes each morning and... it was mine. Sometimes when I wake up at night I quote it silently. I quote it when I'm driving. The words are reassuring. They keep me alert, on track for God. But why not—it's his Word.

So I wrote my friend the other day and said, "Thanks for the push." I'm working on a longer psalm now. Then a passage in Colossians. I don't want to stop. You can keep me accountable if you want to. Only one thing I ask. Give it a shot. You can do it. If you're not memorizing God's Word, you're missing out.

"The tongue of the wise commends knowledge, but the mouth of the fool gushes folly" (Proverbs 15:2).

Trivia question: How many times are the words *tongue, mouth, lips,* and *words* mentioned in Proverbs? The answer is coming later, but suffice it to say, this book is the finest guide we have ever had on how to communicate. In practical advice it surpasses all the other books in the Bible. Consider then the following guide on what not to say:

- How about boasting? "Like clouds and wind without rain is a man who boasts of gifts he does not give" (Prv 25:14). It's the kind of talking that is useless, ridiculous, and can be profane. Paul admonishes us: "Do not let any unwholesome talk come out of your mouths, but only what is helpful for building others up... that it may benefit those who listen" (Eph 4:29).
- How about flattery? "He who rebukes a man will in the end gain more favor than he who has a flattering tongue" (Prv 28:23). We know how to butter up someone, especially when we want something. Flattery is all about: using insincere compliments to deceive someone.
- How about being verbose and running off at the mouth? Look at Proverbs 10:19 (TLB). "Don't talk so much. You keep putting your foot in your mouth. Be sensible and turn off the flow!" That's graphic! You've met people like this. They fill the air with words—empty words of no significance. They don't know the meaning of listening.
- One last thing to avoid—angry, argumentative words. "An angry man stirs up dissension, and a hot-tempered one commits many sins" (Prv 29:22). Strife implies rigidity, stubbornness, and unhealthy anger. Purposeful, constructive, resolvable arguments are healthy. But many arguments are not conducted in this spirit.

If you would like to read some other powerful passages in Proverbs on communication and anger, here they are: Proverbs 14:16-17; Proverbs 15:4; Proverbs 17:14, 22, 24-25. And those are just for starters. As you read, which verses do you think would strengthen your life if you applied them?

By the way, would you believe the answer to my trivia question is "over 150"!

JANUARY 9

"Listen to me, you who pursue righteousness and who seek the Lord: Look to the rock from which you were cut and to the quarry from which you were hewn; look to Abraham, your father, and to Sarah, who gave you birth. When I called him he was but one, and I blessed him and made him many. The Lord will surely comfort Zion and will look with compassion on all her ruins; he will make her deserts like Eden, her wastelands like the garden of the Lord. Joy and glad-ness will be found in her, thanksgiving and the sound of singing" (Isaiah 51:1-3).

How do you resemble your father and mother? Do you resemble them physically? Do you have a similar temperament or personality? Do you have the same mannerisms? As you get older, do you catch yourself doing and saying things your dad did? It's common for that to happen.

Isaiah the prophet told a nation to look back at Abraham and Sarah and the heritage they passed on. There's a heritage passed on to all of us, whether we want it or not. Sometimes the only way you can understand yourself is to understand those who raised you. There's good and bad in us, and so there was in our parents. Sometimes why we do what we do is based on liking what our parents did or the opposite— reacting against it.

Some men don't want to look at their dads because they weren't really fathers to them. Perhaps you've been blamed for being the way you are because of your dad. It could be you're praised for who you are because of him.

Isaiah pointed the people back to their roots, to parents who were imperfect but also did much good as well. He said that by doing so they would find joy and gladness.

We have a choice. We can focus on what our parents didn't do, what they did wrong, or what they did correctly. There's a different result for each choice. What will your choice be?[6]

"For though a righteous man falls seven times, he rises again, but the wicked are brought down by calamity" (Proverbs 24:16).

Doesn't it get to you? Some people seem to get all the breaks. Whatever they do turns to gold. They're *always* successful. You do what they do, but it doesn't come out the same. They know the right people, have the right connections, or just "happen" to be in the right place at the right time, right? Well, not exactly, and not usually. It's easy for us to see someone else's success. What we rarely see is their failures or even their humiliations.

Most people who are successful have been knocked down again and again like a prize fighter. But they bounce back with the words "next time."

You probably take your telephone for granted. You use it every day at home, in the car, and you may carry one around in your back pocket. Thank Alexander Graham Bell for that convenience. But this man knew what it was like to be dumped on. He spent years going back and forth throughout New England trying to raise enough seed money to get his new invention off the ground. Mostly what he got was laughter and ridicule. But he kept saying, "Next time I'll get the funding." And he did!

If you're a father, you've probably gone to Disneyland or Disney World. Seems like those theme parks have always been around, right? But did you know they almost didn't exist? Years ago a man had an idea for a cartoon called "Steamboat Willie." He kept going around Hollywood trying to entice people to believe in his idea. He was bankrupt. Other people saw him as a failure. But Walt Disney kept at it! He said, "Next time." And the rest is a legend. Steamboat Willie became Mickey Mouse!

We've all failed. And that's all right. Failure brings about growth and change. It only stops us when we see it as the final chapter in life. If we see it as a detour, we can learn from it and go on.

"Call to me and I will answer you and tell you great and unsearch-able things you do not know" (Jeremiah 33:3).

"It's impossible. I'd never be able to share my faith with someone. I just can't witness."

"Me, coach that team of little tigers? You've got to be kidding. It's impossible."

Impossible—it's one of the most popular words in our language today—the great escape, the ultimate excuse, the absolute final foot-stomping refusal. Who can argue with it? The only problem is, the word is usually employed before we ever make an attempt to do what we call "impossible."

One hundred years ago no one would have believed you could jump from a great height and have a canopy of cloth blossom open above you that would carry you to the ground gently and safely. But it happened. The parachute came into being because someone was willing to try again and again and again. Sure, a number of attempts failed, but no one cried out, "It's impossible." They went back to the drawing board, came up with a solution, and today parachutes are used even for sport.

Several years ago a boy was born in southern California. When he graduated from high school he had a 3.5 grade-point average, was a top cross-country track star, and was skillful in using a welding torch. By the age of five he could tie his shoes and use a computer. That's not really spectacular unless you have no hands or arms. Yet this armless, legless young man didn't know the meaning of the word *impossible*.

What seems to be impossible to you? Is it really impossible? Maybe there's a different way to try it. And even if you try something once and it doesn't work, it doesn't mean you have to quit. You can use it as a learning experience.

As believers we're called to do the impossible, and why shouldn't we? After all, we worship and serve the Lord of the Impossible!

"Fathers, do not exasperate your children; instead, bring them up in the training and instruction of the Lord" (Ephesians 6:4).

A re you a father? If so, this is for you. If not, it's still for you. You may be a substitute father someday. God's Word has some simple and practical guidelines for dads. The first is a "do not." In a very loose translation, it means, "Don't be a big pain in the neck," don't provoke your children to anger so they end up seething with resentment and irritation. The *New English Bible* says, "You fathers, again, must not goad your children to resentment."

How might a dad goad his children? Criticism is one way. Focusing exclusively on what a child has done wrong (or hasn't done) can break his or her spirit. Criticism comes in many packages, including words, tone of voice, a silent stare, or body language.

Being overly strict and controlling is a sure way to create rebellion in a son or daughter. Irritability can deaden any atmosphere. No one enjoys a grouch! And it's sure not a scriptural calling!

Fortunately, Scripture tells dads what *to* do. Bringing a child up in the training and instruction of the Lord can be summed up in three words—*tenderness, discipline*, and *instruction*.

"Bring them up" can be translated "kindly cherish." Your words of love and your gentle touch—your *tenderness*—will send a message of love to both your wife and your children.

Discipline is not the same as punishment. Discipline's purpose is to create change for the better. And it's not a job to be relegated to your wife. Wise discipline takes into account the uniqueness of each child and adapts its response accordingly.

Instruction can be translated "to place before the mind." But keep in mind that your children *watch* your actions to see if they jibe with what you say. We teach by word and by example. We teach by what we watch and read and by being involved in their activities. But more than anything else, we teach by praying and worshiping with our children.

Being a father is not a chore—it's a challenge and a blessing![7]

"A desire accomplished is sweet to a soul" (Proverbs 13:19a, NKJV).

Accomplishments. Most of us like to be able to list a few. Even when we were kids we liked to have ribbons, trophies, or awards to show we'd made it. But to accomplish something, you've got to stick with it against the pain and the odds.

How does a guy who started out as a dishwasher at seventeen, right out of high school, get to be CEO of that same restaurant chain at thirty-five? By hard work. He didn't give up. He attracted attention because of his devotion.

How does a couple make it to their fiftieth wedding anniversary? (And that's some accomplishment in today's world!) They stick with it.

To accomplish anything, you have to do it completely. You don't leave loose ends. You don't complete it to a 97 percent level and never get back to what's left. You're thorough. Webster defines accomplishment this way: "Done through to the end, complete, omitting nothing; accurate; very exact."[8]

When you do something in this way it will reflect a pattern of excellence.

In what area of your life do you need to follow through more thoroughly? If you need some help figuring that out, ask a friend. Ask one of your children. Better yet, ask your wife! And next time you tackle a task, keep this in mind: "Whatever you do work at it with all your heart, as working for the Lord, not for men, since you know that you will receive an inheritance from the Lord as a reward. It is the Lord Christ you are serving" (Col 3:23-24).

Your accomplishments can draw someone to your Lord. That's an excellent reason to be thorough.

"Again I tell you, it is easier for a camel to go through the eye of a needle than for a rich man to enter the kingdom of God" (Matthew 19:24).

For years pack animals have been used to carry the excess baggage people take with them on a trip. If you've ever been backpacking on a hunting or fishing trip into the high country, you're glad to have those mules or burros along to carry all the gear. And if you're fortunate, you've got a guide along who knows how to load and unload the animals and does it for you. It's a lot of work. To add to it, sometimes the animal is in a foul mood and either kicks you or tries to take a bite out of you.

In the Far East, camels are the mainstay for the desert traveler. And in Jesus' day they were very common. His statement in today's verse has more significance to it than meets the eye. One of the gates in the Old Jerusalem wall was actually called the *Needle's Eye Gate*. It was very narrow, just barely wide enough for a camel. The problem was the baggage. It wouldn't fit. The merchants had to downsize their camels. They had to unload them, walk through the gate with the camel, bring the baggage through and, if they had further to go, load the beast back up. Only when the camel was unloaded could it get through the gate. It had to get rid of its baggage.

Jesus said, "Enter through the narrow gate. For wide is the gate and broad is the road that leads to destruction, and many enter through it" (Mt 7:13).

Are you carrying any baggage or burdens that make it difficult for you to enter the narrow gate? Like the camel, something may need to be stripped off. Take a look at your load. Something may need to be off-loaded before you can get through.[9]

JANUARY 15

"In all this, Job did not sin by charging God with wrongdoing"
(Job 1:22).

Every day counselors and psychologists listen to people's stories. So do bartenders and manicurists. Those stories seem to have one thing in common—bad news. Really bad news. Sometimes the story is a continuing saga of one bad item after another. You wonder how some people are able to make it.

Some of the losses people experience are right up there with Job. Remember him? He was the man who lost most of his money, his herds of livestock, his crops, and his servants. And then he lost not one but all ten of his children. Usually the loss of one child tears a family apart. But ten! And finally his health crumbled. He didn't deserve all this. He was an honest, God-fearing man. He was a man of integrity.

But Job survived. Have you ever wondered how? Could there be something he did that could help us today? Take a look. "He replied, 'Shall we accept good from God, and not trouble?'... In all this, Job did not sin in what he said" (Jb 2:10).

Job accepted the fact that God was in control. He acknowledged God's sovereignty. He didn't lash out in anger at God or curse him. He accepted something that's difficult for most people to accept today: God is who he is. He's in charge, even if we don't understand why things happen the way they do. "I know that my Redeemer lives, and that in the end he will stand upon the earth. And after my skin has been destroyed, yet in my flesh I will see God" (Jb 19:25-26).

Job said his hope was in the future. We know that one day there would be a resurrection, and all problems will be over. No doubt that hope of the future helped him handle the present (see Job 42:2-4).

Job did something that's vital to successful living. Basically he said, "God, I don't understand." He quit trying to figure it out himself. He looked to the only one who could bring him to that place. That's not a bad plan to follow when life seems to be one bad-news day after another.

"If it is possible, as far as it depends on you, live at peace with everyone" (Romans 12:18).

Heavenly Father of peace and love,

I ask for you to bring your peace to our world.

Take away from our cities the violence of gang war, from our nations the suspicions and mistrust of one another, from our world the domination and exploitation of the powerful over those who are weak.

Give us the wisdom, strength, and grace to overcome the suspicious attitudes and prejudices that we have carried and nurtured for years. Instead, help us show the love and acceptance that you have extended to all of us.

Father, send your peace to our city and our nation. Help those in public office to set aside their political ambitions and humble themselves in private before you.

May we learn to live in peace with those at work, on the expressway, in the check-out line, with the cantankerous neighbor, the difficult relative, and our family members.

Help me to get rid of any bitterness or unforgiveness. Father, I need control over my impulses, my desires, my tongue, my eyes, and my temper. Help me not to retreat into silence and solitude when others need to talk. Help me to lower my voice rather than raise it when I don't agree. Take away the worries that I choose to feed in my mind. Help me to feed my faith in you rather than my own doubts. I pray for a pure heart in my motives and my ambitions. Help me to be more content with what I have, and to thank you for it, rather than focusing on what I don't have.

I pray for inner peace and I thank you for Jesus, your Son.

I pray in his name.

Amen.

"And a voice from heaven said, 'This is my Son, whom I love; with him I am well pleased'" (Matthew 3:17).

Some men strive to be macho. But the world's standard of a man is a perversion of what it means to be masculine. If you want a model of masculinity, think about this portrait of a balanced man.

Jesus' personality had several facets, but he did not hide them from anyone. He could chase the corrupters out of his temple in righteous anger, displaying his manhood in what might be called "masculine" ways—and yet later he wept over Jerusalem, displaying what is considered a "feminine" side.

He met the challenge of the enemy and faced them in open debate; and yet he could hold children on his knees in a moment of tenderness and express how precious they were to him and the kingdom of God.

On more than one occasion, he lashed out with a sharp verbal lance, even calling the religious leaders a bunch of "vipers," thus taking the wind right out of them and leaving them dumbfounded; and yet he dealt mercifully with a frantic father who honestly confessed his inability to believe that Jesus could heal his son, touching the boy in tenderness, compassion, and power—making him whole.

He had all the legions of heaven on his side and could have, in one master stroke of his manliness, wiped out his enemies. Yet he stood mute before the Roman court, refusing to give dignity to a mob.

Here is the Son of God, Jesus, the Man, who was not asexual, but who never used his sexuality to prove his manhood.

Here is the king of the universe, sweating blood during the deep revulsion he felt in Gethsemane concerning the death that faced him, and yet pressing on to take that death on the cross without wilting.

There is no greater picture of the "whole man"—a man who was "masculine" in terms of strength, muscle, sinew, and courage, and yet was not ashamed to show his "feminine" side in terms of tears, compassion, gentleness, and peace.[10]

"Now I want you to know, brothers, that what has happened to me has really served to advance the gospel. As a result, it has become clear throughout the whole palace guard and to everyone else that I am in chains for Christ. Because of my chains, most of the brothers in the Lord have been encouraged to speak the word of God more courageously and fearlessly" (Philippians 1:12-14).

Archaeologists have an interesting job. They look for stuff that everyone else has forgotten about. Old—really old—stuff. Especially bones. They love to find the bones of animals that lived thousands of years ago.

You're full of bones, too. You've probably never counted them or seen one up close unless you broke one. You need all your bones, but there are three "bones" that are more important than the others. These are the ones that will get you through life, especially when the tough times roll. Do you know which three I'm talking about? The backbone, the wishbone, and the funny bone.

Your backbone stands for the strength and courage you need to make it through life. Paul the apostle showed backbone when he described his plight in 2 Corinthians 11:24-25—he was beaten, stoned, shipwrecked, and the list goes on. But he made it, and so can you.

Your wishbone is linked to your dreams and goals. Paul had a dream of spreading the gospel. The above verse describes how that was being realized. Is your wishbone working? Are you working toward making your goals a reality? Or has your wishbone been buried and begun to petrify? Don't wait for an archaeologist to find it. Bring it to life and let God guide your dreams.

Last but not least, your funny bone may keep the other bones going, especially when life is at its most difficult. Let it do its job. Keep a sense of humor alive and well. Let it do its job. The joy you experience will enrich your life.[11]

"But Jesus immediately said to them: 'Take courage! It is I. Don't be afraid'" (Matthew 14:27).

We're a lot like the disciples, aren't we? We spend time with Jesus, experience his strength, and then how quickly we forget. You remember what happened in Matthew 14? Jesus healed the sick. and fed the multitudes. Then he went away to pray. So the disciples took off in a boat, but in the evening a storm arose. In the midst of the thrashing waves and intense wind, Jesus walked toward his friends on the water. They saw him and thought he was a ghost. Jesus responded immediately, "It is I. Take courage. Don't be afraid." Then good old impulsive Peter got out of the boat, started toward Jesus, realized what he was doing, and panicked. One author gave an interesting analysis of what happened and its application for all of us.

1. *Uncertain circumstances*—Almost every time I deal with fear, I face uncertain circumstances—just like the disciples did. My situation seems unfamiliar. My boat is rocking. My favorite Captain does not seem to be on board. My future is unknown.

2. *Wrong conclusions*—In the middle of my panic, I often look at the obvious instead of the supernatural. Instead of seeing Jesus supernaturally at work in the middle of my storm, I see all kinds of ghosts, represented by my personal fears. Sometimes I voice my fears loudly as the disciples did. Other times I feel angry and powerless. "Where is Jesus when I need him most?"

3. *Impulsive conduct*—Peter's "jump out of the boat" behavior reminds me of myself. Sometimes I cry, "Lord, if you are *really* here, in the middle of my panic and my frightening situation, prove yourself supernaturally. I mean, *do* something so I know it's you!"

4. *Desperate call*—When I, like Peter, step out in trust, I sometimes take my eyes off Jesus and focus on my terrorizing circumstances. The "winds of fear" look much worse than they did before I tried to trust him. I cry, "Lord, save me!"

5. *Immediate calm*—*Without delay* he reaches out to me and says, "You of little faith...why did you doubt?" And in the security of his compassionate gaze and warm, affirming grip, my heart begins the measured, careful journey toward accepting his perfect love.[12]

"Blessed is the man who does not walk in the counsel of the wicked or stand in the way of sinners or sit in the seat of mockers" (Psalms 1:1).

"That's righteous." Remember that phrase? People used to use it to describe something good, positive, or outstanding. Psalm 1 describes something God wants from us, that will benefit us and change our society. It's called the righteous life, the godly life. But in our society, how does this happen?

First, the psalmist tells us what *not* to do and then what *to* do. In verse 1 you find the conditions for spiritual erosion. "Walk" suggests hanging around too closely to those who are living a lifestyle counter to Scripture. The phrase here implies the idea of a person who does not imitate what the wicked do. It's a calling to live differently, to be different.

"Standing" implies an even closer relationship with those living an ungodly lifestyle. When you get too close to the fire, you get burned. And once you get this close you can end up with the final condition, which is "sitting" with them. Actually this word suggests a permanent stay. You remain there. From walking to standing you finally slip into the lifestyle of the unrighteous.

Fortunately, the psalmist tells us what to do to avoid this. It's basic. It's simple. It's life-changing. In a nutshell, occupy yourself with God's Word. It gives you direction, guidance, insight, strength, and can serve as a deterrent to getting involved in the wrong lifestyle.

How? First, meditate on it—think, think, think. Discover what it really means. Second, memorize it. "How can a young man keep his way pure? By living according to your word.... I have hidden your word in my heart that I might not sin against you" (Ps 119:9, 11).

Immersing ourselves in God's Word works. Just check with someone who's tried it. He'll tell you the good news.

"Man shall not live by bread alone, but on every word that proceeds from the mouth of God" (Matthew 4:4, NKJV).

There is a whole range of eating disorders today: overeating, eating the wrong stuff, undereating, not eating, anorexia, bulimia, etc. They all have their own set of problems.

Usually we think of eating disorders associated with women, but men engage in anorexia and bulimia just like women. Some men are actually diet freaks. But usually men manifest eating disorders in a different way—spiritually!

Anorexia is body emaciation because of a physical aversion to food and eating. Bulimia is the binge-and-purge disorder. Listen to how Steve Farrar describes these two disorders in the spiritual realm.

Spiritual anorexia is an aversion to feeding from the Word of God. It is impossible for a man to stand and fight in spiritual warfare if he is spiritually malnourished. This is why the enemy will do whatever is necessary to keep us from reading and meditating on the Scriptures. Jesus put it this way in his dialogue with Satan: "Man shall not live by bread alone, but on every word that proceeds from the mouth of God."

If a man is not consistently taking in the Scriptures, then he will be weak and sickly and easily overcome by temptation. A man may believe in the Bible and even revere it, but if a man is not feeding from the Bible, he is easy prey for the enemy. That's why the enemy attempts to disrupt the appointments that we make to meet with the Lord and his Word.

As dangerous as spiritual anorexia is, there is another disorder that is even more dangerous. Bulimia is an eating disorder that is commonly known as the binge-and-purge syndrome.

Spiritual bulimia is knowing the Word of God without *doing* it. Or as James described, it is *hearing* the Word of God without doing it. Spiritual bulimia is characteristic of those who binge on truth: it can be through books, tapes, good Bible teaching, listening to a favorite communicator on the radio. That's why the spiritual bulimic appears to be so righteous. There's just one problem. The bulimic knows the truth, but he doesn't apply it.[13]

When we're undernourished physically, the answer is to eat and digest food. When we're undernourished spiritually, the answer is to eat and digest more of the Word.

"Be joyful always; pray continually; give thanks in all circumstances, for this is God's will for you in Christ Jesus" (1 Thessalonians 5:16-18).

Dr. Lloyd Ogilvie addressed the problem of whether prayer is always answered in his insightful daily devotional *God's Best for My Life.*

"If I thought" said John Baillie, "that God were going to grant me all my prayers simply for the asking, without even passing them under His own gracious review, without even bringing to bear upon them His own greater wisdom, I think there would be very few prayers that I would dare to pray."

All prayers are answered, but not always the way we had hoped or in the time we anticipated. We often judge the efficacy of prayer by how much it produces the results we prayed for. We make God our celestial errand-boy.

Because God can see what we cannot see, and know dimensions which we can never understand, He works out our answers according to a higher plan than we can conceive. We are to tell Him our needs and then leave them with Him. It's only in retrospect that we can see the narrowness of our vision and can see that His answer was far better than what we could ever have anticipated.

Prayer is not just the place and time we tell God what to do, but the experience in which He molds our lives. In the quiet meditative prayer, we begin to see things from a different point of view and are given the power to wait for the unfolding of God's plan.

Elton Trueblood was right: "Prayer is not some slick device according to which, when we say the right words, we are sure of the outcome. The promise, fundamentally, is not that the Father always does precisely as we ask, but rather that He always *hears.*" James Denney said, "A refusal is the answer if it is so given that God and the soul henceforth understand one another."[14]

JANUARY 23

There it is again!

A twinge of pain?
Forget it. It will go away.
In the business of my day.
I've places to go and things to do...
A round of meetings with entrepreneurs.
Planes to catch and taxis to hail,
I have life by the tail.
But what is this painful wail?
From the depths of me I ache.
It greets me when I wake.
Even in a crowded room of people
I can hear a haunting toll from the church bell steeple.
There's nothing wrong with me.
I'm a success, as anyone can see.
I—I hurt. I feel an emptiness.
This feeling, is it loneliness?
Loneliness?
I'm married with children, three.
Yet at times I feel so alone.
Maybe it's time to come down from my throne.
It's not good for a man to be alone.[15]

To be alone was the first thing God said was not good. Sometimes you can be with a lot of people and still feel lonely.

If you feel this way, reach out to a friend, to your wife, to God. If you don't feel this way, reach out anyway. Someone else is lonely and needs you.

"He who is slow to anger is better than the mighty, and he who rules his [own] spirit than he who takes a city" (Proverbs 16:32, AMP).

A book was recently published titled *Anger Kills*. Strong words, but true. Anger out of control can kill us and others. When we get angry our body prepares for action. Did you know that when you're angry your blood clots much more quickly than normal, additional adrenaline is released, and your muscles tense up?

Your blood pressure may increase from 130 to 230 and your heart beats faster—often up to 220 beats per minute or higher. People have had strokes and heart attacks during a fit of anger because of the increased blood pressure.

What happens if your anger is not released? Your body remains ready for action with your heart beating rapidly, blood pressure up, and blood chemical changes taking place. The results can be physically harmful.

Look at the result of anger in the life of Nabal (see 1 Samuel 25). David sent some of his men to Nabal, who was very wealthy. They wanted some food, but instead Nabal gave them a rebuke and sent them away. Upon hearing this David gathered his men together and set out to fight Nabal. But Abigail, Nabal's wife, heard what her husband had done, and gathering together a large store of food she went out, met David and his men, and appeased them by her gift of food.

> And Abigail came to Nabal; and behold, he was holding a feast in his house, like the feast of a king; and *his* heart was merry, for he was very drunk; so she told him nothing at all until morning light. But in the morning, when the wine was gone out of Nabal, and his wife told him these things, his heart died within him, and he became [paralyzed, helpless as] a stone. And about ten days after that the Lord smote Nabal and he died.
> 1 Samuel 25:36-38, AMP

The phrase, *his heart died within him,* in the original could mean he had a stroke or a heart attack. Why did this happen? Nabal probably reacted to his wife's disclosure with intense anger.

Think about that the next time you're angry!

"Drink water from your own cistern,
running water from your own well.
Should your springs overflow in the streets,
your streams of water in the public squares?
Let them be yours alone,
never to be shared with strangers.
May your fountain be blessed,
and may you rejoice in the wife of your youth.
A loving doe, a graceful deer—
may her breasts satisfy you always,
may you ever be captivated by her love." **Proverbs 5:15-19**

In his book *A Celebration of Sex*, Douglas Rosenau offers the following insight into this passage.

We could paraphrase this for wives:

Rejoice in the husband of your youth.
A gentle stag, a strong deer—
may his hands and mouth satisfy you always,
may you ever be captivated by his love.

The Bible often uses water as a very powerful and fitting metaphor for cleansing, healing, and rejuvenating. There are beautiful images like "streams in the desert," "water of life," and "beside the still waters." What a tremendous portrayal of the dynamic nature of lovemaking to compare it to a cistern, a well, a stream, and a fountain of water. It is like a cool, refreshing drink from your own safe supply.

In one way, your sex life is like a cistern in which you have stored many amorous memories and a sexy repertoire of arousing activities. You can dip into it again and again in your fantasy life and lovemaking for excitement and fun. In another way, making love is like a stream or spring of water. Sex in marriage has an ever-changing, renewing quality to it.

A routine sex life is not God's design. Renew your minds and attitudes, and get sexy and playful. You can make love four times a week for the next fifty years and still never plumb the surprising depths of this mysterious sexual "stream" of becoming one flesh.

I appreciate the words *rejoice, satisfy,* and *captivated* in the Proverbs passage. Pleasure and fun are an intended part of making love. It is important for mates to enjoy playing together. We can rejoice with the mate of our youth. Our creativity, imagination, and love allow us to remain ever enthralled sexually with the lover of our youth. We can be ever satisfied and captivated.[16]

"He whose walk is blameless and who does what is righteous, who speaks the truth from his heart... will never be shaken" (Psalms 15:2).

We need men of integrity today, but it's a costly virtue. You can count on it. What will it cost you? Just a few things like time, effort, money, and perhaps even popularity and respect from the people around you. Integrity isn't popular. It makes some people uncomfortable.

The word *integrity* means to be "sound, complete, without blemish, crack, or defect." In the construction business the concept of integrity refers to building codes that ensure the building will end up being safe. To have integrity the building has to be properly designed, comply with all the building codes, be safe, and be able to function in accordance with its purpose. Webster's dictionary has a simple word for it—*honesty.*

"So," you're probably asking, "what's in it for me? How will integrity make my life better?" Let God's Word answer that for you. "The integrity of the upright guides them, but the unfaithful are destroyed by their duplicity" (Prv 11:3).

Integrity gives you a solid footing. "The man of integrity walks securely, but he who takes crooked paths will be found out" (Prv 10:9).

Integrity gives you something that lasts. "The days of the blameless are known to the Lord, and their inheritance will endure forever" (Ps 37:18).

Integrity provides a blessing for your children. "The righteous man leads a blameless life; blessed are his children after him" (Prv 20:7).

Integrity gives a poor man riches. "Better a poor man whose walk is blameless than a fool whose lips are perverse" (Prv 19:1).

Integrity pleases God. "I know, my God, that you test the heart and are pleased with integrity" (1 Chr 29:17a).

Integrity makes you more like Jesus. "...'Teacher,' they said, 'we know you are a man of integrity and that you teach the way of God in accordance with the truth. You aren't swayed by men, because you pay no attention to who they are...'" (Mt 22:16b).[17]

Get used to the word *integrity.* It's the hallmark of a righteous man.

"After he left there, he came upon Jehonadab son of Recab, who was on his way to meet him. Jehu greeted him and said, 'Are you in accord with me, as I am with you?'

"'I am,' Jehonadab answered.

"'If so,' said Jehu, 'give me your hand.' So he did, and Jehu helped him up into the chariot. Jehu said, 'Come with me and see my zeal for the Lord.' Then he had him ride along in his chariot" (2 Kings 10:15-16).

What a verse for a devotional! Jehu was like a lot of men today— he loved to drive. Put him into our world and he'd be racing funny cars, off-road vehicles, or tearing down the street in a Corvette.

Driving a car is where it's at for some men. They seem to come alive behind the wheel. With a gleam in their eye, they put their foot to the pedal and take off. Speed limits and stop signs? Hey, those are for the other guys.

That was Jehu. Look at the description of his driving. "The lookout reported, 'He has reached them, but he isn't coming back either. The driving is like that of Jehu son of Nimshi—he drives like a madman'" (2 Kgs 9:20).

Do you relate to that description? Do your family members begin to tremble when you get behind the wheel? What does your driving say about your faith, your relationship with the Lord? How fast do you drive? If you speed a bit, why not enhance your enjoyment by singing while you drive? If you don't know what to sing, here are some suggestions.

At 50 mph..."God Will Take Care of You"
At 60 mph..."Guide Me, O Thou Great Jehovah"
At 70 mph..."Nearer, My God, to Thee"
At 80 mph..."Nearer, Still Nearer!"
At 90 mph..."This World Is Not My Home"
At 100 mph..."Lord, I'm Coming Home"
Over 100..."Precious Memories"

Remember that the way you drive and how you respond to other drivers says a lot about your relationship with the Lord.[18]

"A man's heart plans his way, but the Lord directs his steps"
(Proverbs 16:9, NKJV).

If you struggle to discover God's will for your life, perhaps you're not going about it in the best way. Dr. Lloyd Ogilvie shares an interesting perspective on this issue.

Dr. James Dobson, in his helpful book *God's Will*, tells a penetrating story of Rev. Everett Howard, a veteran missionary to the Cape Verde Islands for twenty-six years. His call to the mission field has implications for all of us.

After finishing college and dental school, Howard was still uncertain about God's will for his life. One night he went into the sanctuary of the church where his father was serving as pastor. He knelt down at the altar and took a piece of paper on which he wrote all the things he was ready to do for God. He signed his name at the bottom and waited for some sign of God's affirmation and presence, but nothing happened. He took his paper again, thinking he might have left something out—still no response from the Lord. He waited and waited. Then it happened. He felt the Lord speaking within him. The Lord told him to tear up the sheet.

"You're going about it all wrong," He said gently. "Son, I want you to take a blank piece of paper, sign it on the bottom, and let Me fill it in."

Howard responded, and God guided a spectacular missionary career from that day forward.

God is not as interested in our commitment to what we decide to do for Him as He is in what we will allow Him to do through us. Our task is not to list our accomplishments or our plans for service, but to give Him a blank sheet and let Him fill it in.[19]

JANUARY 29

"The Lord has sought out for Himself a man after His own heart..." (1 Samuel 13:14, NASB).

When Christ gave His farewell message to His disciples in the Upper Room (Jn 13), He knew His death was at hand. What was the most important message Christ wanted to leave with them? He told them what would identify them as followers. Interestingly, it was not an absence of mistakes or weaknesses, the number of things they abstained from, or their net worth. Instead, it was an emotion, expressed in behavior.

"A new commandment I give to you, that you love one another, even as I have loved you, that you also love one another. By this all men will know that you are My disciples, if you have love for one another" (Jn 13:34-35). Yes, He calls them to have love. Not the ability to be witty and clever, nor to win debates. Instead Jesus names the emotion of love.

God has designed us in such a way that our emotions influence almost every aspect of our lives. God speaks to us through our emotions. Emotions are to our personality what gasoline is to a car. They are the source of our passion and intensity. They help us to monitor our needs, make us aware of good and evil, provide motivation and energy.

When God told Saul that his kingdom would not endure, God showed His priorities. Through Samuel God said, "Your kingdom shall not endure. The Lord has sought out for Himself a man after His own heart, and the Lord has appointed him as ruler over His people, because you have not kept what the Lord commanded you" (1 Sm 13:14).

Notice God's primary criterion. He did not seek someone "after his own head." No, God sought someone after his own *heart*. David was that man. Yes, David made many mistakes. He was flawed and fallible, much as you and I are (a lot like I am). But David had one quality God admired greatly. David was a passionate man who had a heart for God.[20]

JANUARY 30

"Cast all your anxieties on him for he cares for you" (1 Peter 5:7, RSV).

You're driving along on the expressway with the nearest exit three miles away. Your car's engine misses a beat and then another. You notice that little light on the dash that says the word "empty." The gas tank is almost bone dry and you've been running on fumes. Your engine misses another beat and the car jerks. Your body tenses up. You slow down to conserve gas (a lot of good that will do now), and you pray for one more gallon of gas to appear miraculously in the tank.

It's interesting to see how many people purposely run around town with the gas tank of their car on empty. It's as though they enjoy flirting with disaster. Well, a car isn't the only thing that can try to run on empty. We men do it in our personal lives as well. Spiritually we may be running around with our tanks just bordering on empty. When nothing is left in the spiritual tank, we can make some major mistakes. This is a time when our resistance is low and temptation hits. We all know the result.

We can flirt with spiritual emptiness when we fail to fill up. Sometimes we just go through the motions when we attend church, talk to God, and read Scripture. Instead of merely attending church, we need to go there and worship the Living God. Worship is focusing on God as the center of our lives instead of on ourselves. Instead of just talking to God, listen to him. Instead of reading the Scriptures, study and memorize them.

You don't have to run on empty.

You don't have to run out of gas.

Like everything else in life, you have a choice.[21]

"When others are happy, be happy with them. If they are sad, share their sorrow. Work happily together. Don't try to act big. Don't try to get into the good graces of important people, but enjoy the company of ordinary folks. And don't think you know it all! Never pay back evil for evil. Do things in such a way that everyone can see you are honest clear through. Don't quarrel with anyone. Be at peace with everyone, just as much as possible. Dear friend, never avenge yourselves. Leave that to God, for he has said that he will repay those who deserve it. [Don't take the law into your own hands]" (Romans 12:15-19, TLB).

The words you've just read above were not created as a United Nations manifesto. Nor were they new policies to live by created by the current administration in the capital.

These words were inspired by God and given to each of us as a way of getting along with others.

Can you imagine what would happen if:

- Everyone at your place of employment made a commitment to live by these guidelines within the company as well as when interacting with customers. Furthermore, you all sat down for lengthy discussion on how you could put these principles into practice in simple ways.

- Your entire family decided to memorize this passage and each evening for a month evaluated how everyone was doing in applying its principles. They agreed to pray for each other and to implement the teaching in their own lives.

You may be saying, "Yes! Yes! Yes! If all these people would live by this teaching, it would be great. This is the way to go. Now how do we get them to do it?"

Thought you'd never ask. It's simple. Do it yourself. Live it. Show it in your life consistently. Go into partnership with the Holy Spirit as your source of power. You know the words. You know the source. The other people need a model, an example of the Scripture in action... and you're it!

"A glad heart makes a cheerful countenance, but by sorrow of heart the spirit is broken" (Proverbs 15:13, AMP).

Being around some men is a downer. They're not much fun. They're full of gloom. They have no joy, no laughter, no life. Sure, life is tough, but there is also a lot to smile about, a lot to laugh at. Did you ever wonder what made Jesus laugh? Probably a lot of the same humorous things we enjoy, and quite possibly there are some things we laugh at that he wouldn't.

Humor is everywhere. Look at the misprints in church bulletins or on signs, such as, "This being Easter Sunday, we will ask Mrs. Jones to come forward and lay an egg on the church altar," or "Due to the Rector's illness, this week's healing services will be discontinued until further notice."

What about some of the rules and regulations that are outdated but still on the books? In Seattle, it's illegal "to carry a concealed weapon of more than six feet in length." In the state of Oklahoma, there's a law that says, "Any vehicle involved in an accident which results in the death of another person shall stop and give his name and address to the person struck." How would you like to see these enforced?[1]

How do other people view you? Are you someone who can laugh easily, who exudes joy? Or are you a gloom machine? God is the author of smiles, joy, and laughter. He wants us to experience these gifts, express them, and infect other people with their positive potential. It's one of his prescriptions designed to make life bearable.

Think about these words of Elton Trueblood.

The Christian is joyful, not because he is blind to injustice and suffering, but because he is convinced that these, in the light of the divine sovereignty, are never ultimate.... The humor of the Christian is not a way of denying the tears, but rather a way of affirming something which is deeper than tears.[2]

A man of strength has a cheerful heart.

"Let us fix our eyes on Jesus, the author and perfecter of our faith, who for the joy set before him endured the cross, scorning its shame, and sat down at the right hand of the throne of God" (Hebrews 12:2).

When God called Moses to lead the Israelites out of Egypt, Moses argued with him. Really argued. Debated. In essence he said, "God, you don't know what you're talking about! You don't know what you're asking me to do."

Have you ever done that with God?

Exodus 3 and 4 record Moses' arguments, which seemed perfectly logical to him.

"God, I'm not much at all" (3:11). Have you ever felt that way or said that to God?

"You know, I won't have anything to say that's going to impact anyone" (3:13). Has that thought ever kept you quiet? It keeps a lot of men from speaking out for their faith, sharing in church, or praying out loud with their wives. We need to let God be the judge of what we say as well as the source of our words.

"I'm not a convincing speaker" (4:1). You won't know until you try.

"I'm just not a speaker. Look, I'm slow—in speech and tongue" (4:10). If that's true for you, does it really have to be a problem? With God's help and practice, who knows what you can do?

"Anyone else can do better than I" (4:13). You really don't know that. Give God an opportunity to use you.

When God put out a call to Jeremiah, his response was, "Oh, Lord God...I can't do that! I'm far too young! I'm only a youth!" (Jer 1:6, TLB). God answered with, "Don't say that...for you will go wherever I send you and speak whatever I tell you to" (Jer 1:7, TLB). That's quite a promise.

Both Moses and Jeremiah had one way of looking at things—through their own eyes. When they began to look at circumstances through God's eyes, it's remarkable to see what they accomplished.

FEBRUARY 3

"...for all have sinned and fall short of the glory of God"
(Romans 3:23).

Some of the most famous incidents in the history of our country have been acts of treason. Books have been written and movies made recounting the incidents and their effect upon our country. Some people are still referred to as "that traitor." Treason has been defined as "a betrayal of trust or faith; violation of the allegiance owed to one's sovereign."[3]

We are all guilty of treason. Every one of us. That's not a pleasant thought, is it? But it's true, and we're all aware of what most countries do to traitors, aren't we? Public hangings and firing squads are still the norm in some countries. The treason we've committed is called sin. Everyone has violated God's law.

Have you ever thought of the many ways we describe sin today? Consider these words: *unlawful, lawlessness, ungodliness, disobedience.* Each word is formed by negating another word. When you sin you fall short of the mark. That's exactly what the word means in Greek— missing the mark.

We're all aware of sin in our society. It's all around us. And sin is treason against who God is, what he stands for, and his law. Once you've committed treason, you cannot *not* be a traitor, and rarely are you given a pardon. It's different, though, with God: "For the wages of sin is death, but the gift of God is eternal life in Christ" (Rom 6:23). What a reprieve! The result is eternal life. Undeserved, but given anyway! The only reason anyone would ever do something like that is because of love.

> For God so loved the world that He gave His one and only Son, that whoever believes in Him shall not perish but have eternal life.
>
> **John 3:16**

Not only are we forgiven, not only has the slate been wiped clean by God, but he still wants us for himself... forever![4]

"But I tell you the truth: It is for your good that I am going away. Unless I go away, the Counselor will not come to you; but if I go, I will send him to you" (John 16:7-8).

You've got a power source for your life that will outlast any Delco or Energizer battery. It is more intense than the power pack of a nuclear submarine. But it is not just a power source, it is an actual person. That's right, a person, not an "it." Too many people think of the Holy Spirit as an "it." Scripture calls him "the Spirit of truth" and reminds us that "The world cannot accept him, because it neither sees him nor knows him. But you know him, for he lives with you and will be in you" (Jn 14:17).

The Holy Spirit has knowledge (see 1 Corinthians 2:11), a will (see 1 Corinthians 12:11), a mind (see Romans 8:27), and affections (see Romans 15:30). You can lie to him (see Acts 5:3-4), insult him (see Hebrews 10:20), and grieve for him (see Ephesians 4:30).

John calls him the helper. He is God inside of you to help you be a man of integrity. You may think you have to handle that business transaction, that irritating business associate, or that alluring temptation by yourself, but you don't. The Holy Spirit is there—all the time.

He has a job to do. His job description is quite varied, too.

- *He comforts anyone who is a Christian.* "When I go away, I will send the Helper to you" (Jn 16:7). Have you felt the comforting hands of God when your life seemed shattered? That was he.

- *He convicts those who don't know him.* "When the Helper comes, He will prove to the people of the world about sin, about being right with God, and about judgment" (Jn 16:8). Remember that time of conviction when you didn't belong to him? Or when something prodded you about what you had said or done? That was he.

- *He conveys the truth.* "When the Spirit of Truth comes, he will lead you into all truth" (Jn 16:13). Ever had a new spiritual insight or have Scripture speak to your heart? That was the Holy Spirit.

Let this power source, this person, run all of your life.[5]

"I have told you these things, so that in me you may have peace. In this world you will have trouble. But take heart! I have overcome the world" (John 16:33).

Hardship comes in several packages. One is physical suffering. "My life is consumed by anguish and my years by groaning; my strength fails because of my affliction, and my bones grow weak" (Ps 31:10). The older we get, the more we identify with David in this passage. It may not have hit you yet, but because of age, illness, or accident we'll become limited in our physical abilities. David's body went through some changes as he got older. Let's face it. Even if we take care of ourselves, decay and deterioration will set in. How will you handle it?

Hardship also happens because of people. They can cause some of the greatest grief in your life. If anyone knew this, David did. "Because of all my enemies, I am the utter contempt of my neighbors; I am a dread to my friends—those who see me on the street flee from me. I am forgotten by them as though I were dead; I have become like broken pottery. For I hear the slander of many; there is terror on every side; they conspire against me and plot to take my life" (Ps 31:11-13).

Sound familiar? Maybe you've been there, or perhaps that's where you are now. How do you handle people like this? Whether our problems are caused by our physical limitations or by other people, how we handle these problems of life say a lot about us.

Some men get sullen, grouchy, cantankerous, depressed, or withdrawn. Other men accept what can't be changed, change what they can, adjust, adapt, and learn from each hardship.

Which man makes it in life? Continues to grow? Really reflects Jesus Christ in his life?

Which one are you?

FEBRUARY 6

"Yet I will rejoice in the Lord, I will be joyful in God my Savior. The Sovereign Lord is my strength; he makes my feet like the feet of a deer, he enables me to go on the heights" (Habakkuk 3:18-19).

You get in your car, put the key in the ignition, turn it, and... nothing. The battery is dead, drained. There is not an ounce of electricity left to turn it over. You're not going anywhere.

Some mornings you may feel like that battery—drained and dead. The alarm goes off and you're supposed to roll out of bed. But you never make it. You don't have what it takes. You're a depleted, disengaged, dead battery.

Why do batteries die? Sometimes they've simply lived out their life expectancy. They've given all they were meant to, and now there's nothing left to recharge them. Others die because someone left the car lights on, which drained the battery of its strength.

We're a lot like a car battery. We keep running and running without stopping to rest and recharge. All too soon we can't function. We've run out of strength.

If you want strength, go to the power source, your Lord God. The phrase "I will rejoice in the Lord" really means "to leap for joy and spin around in exultation." Not too many of us do this literally but perhaps it wouldn't be a bad idea.

Do you know the difference between the words *joy* and *happiness* as they're used here? The latter is based on having no problems or concerns. Joy means having faith in God, no matter what happens. When you trust in God rather than in your circumstances, you discover that God will give you the strength you need. And this strength will keep you moving ahead. Go to your power source—go to God.

"Here is my servant whom I have chosen, the one I love, in whom I delight...." (Matthew 12:18).

It's doubtful that you were raised in a home with servants. Not too many of us were. But if you were, you remember that those servants had one job to perform—serve. That's what the Bible calls us to do. In some positions of serving we are recognized and appreciated. In others we feel taken for granted. If that's the way you feel at times, remember that someone else who came to serve was unappreciated as well.

One of the more than one hundred names and titles of Jesus was Servant. This role was a fulfillment of the prophecy in Isaiah (see Isaiah 52:13; 53:11-12).

All through the New Testament we have examples of transformed people who called themselves servants. In Romans 1:1, Paul introduced himself as a servant of Jesus Christ. In 2 Peter 1:1, Peter introduced himself as a servant of Jesus Christ. Judas, the brother of Jesus, said the same, as did John in Revelation. Why, then, aren't we more ready to serve, as followers of Christ?

Perhaps it's because we don't live in a world that values the servant role. We'd rather get than give, take than share, grasp than release. Let's face it, many of us men do reflect this tendency. We have to be taught to be other-centered. It's all too natural to be self-centered.

Perhaps we're afraid of what being a servant might cost us. You can focus on the risks, or you could focus on service as a privilege and a learning experience.[6]

Colonel James Irwin, a former astronaut who became a lunar pedestrian, shares that while walking on the moon he realized that when he would return to earth many would consider him an international celebrity. Realizing his role as a Christian, he records: "As I was returning to earth, I realized that I was a servant, not a celebrity. I am here as God's servant on Planet Earth to share what I have experienced, that others might know the glory of God."

If Christ, Lord of the universe, became a Servant for us, can we do any less for him?[7]

How can each one in your family or at work be more of a servant today? Why not discuss how to put it into action?[8]

"A wife of noble character who can find? She is worth far more than rubies. Her husband has full confidence in her and lacks nothing of value" (Proverbs 31:10-11).

One of my favorite books is *The Mystery of Marriage* by Mike Mason. Here are a few of his statements to help you think about your marriage.

A marriage is not a joining of two worlds, but an abandoning of two worlds in order that one new one might be formed.

In this sense, the call to be married bears comparison with Jesus' advice to the rich young man to sell all his possessions and to follow Him. It is a vocation to total abandonment. For most people, in fact, marriage is the single most wholehearted step they will ever take toward a fulfillment of Jesus' command to love one's neighbor as oneself. For every marriage partner begins as a neighbor, and often enough a neighbor who has been left beaten and wounded on the road of love, whom all the rest of the world has in a sense passed by.

The marriage vows give glory to God. While it is true that a man and a woman on their wedding day take a step toward a unique fulfillment of the commandment of love, it is even more true to say of matrimony that it is a sacramental outpouring of God's grace enabling such love to take place. The human couple indicates humbly a willingness to give themselves to this love; but it is the Lord Who makes love possible in the first place, and therefore it is He Who promises that His gift of love will not be taken away.

Marriage, even under the very best of circumstances, is a crisis—one of the major crises of life—and it is a dangerous thing not to be aware of this. Whether it turns out to be a healthy, challenging, and constructive crisis or a disastrous nightmare depends largely upon how willing the partners are to be changed, how malleable they are.[9]

FEBRUARY 9

"The law of the Lord is perfect, reviving the soul. The statutes of the Lord are trustworthy, making wise the simple. The precepts of the Lord are right, giving joy to the heart. The commands of the Lord are radiant, giving light to the eyes. The fear of the Lord is pure, enduring forever. The ordinances of the Lord are sure and altogether righteous. They are more precious than gold, than much pure gold; they are sweeter than honey, than honey from the comb. By them is your servant warned; in keeping them there is great reward" (Psalms 19:7-11).

Rules... and more rules. Have you ever read the section in the newspaper that tells you what laws were passed in your state capital that day? We live in a culture that wants as much freedom as possible, yet we enact so many rules. It's unnerving at times. Sometimes it seems like there are rules for the rules.

Rules and laws are there for a reason. We need boundaries. Granted, sometimes some of our laws are ridiculous, but God's laws never are. What are some of God's rules or laws that you resist? Some of us resist only in our minds, some of us flagrantly break God's laws, while others of us devise clever schemes to get around them, believing we'll never get caught. But God's laws are not given to restrict our lives and freedom. Their purpose is to give us a better life.

Television newscaster Ted Koppel shocked a number of people in his address to a graduating class at Duke University some years ago when he said,

> We have actually convinced ourselves that slogans will save us. Shoot up if you must, but use a clean needle. Enjoy sex whenever and with whomever you wish, but wear a condom. No! The answer is No! Not because it isn't cool or smart or because you might end up in jail or dying in an AIDS ward.... In its purest form, truth is not a polite tap on the shoulder. It is a howling reproach. What Moses brought down from Mount Sinai were not the Ten Suggestions.[10]

Are you treating some of God's laws as suggestions, or do you see that He has given them to us for our benefit?

"A man who refuses to admit his mistakes can never be successful. But if he confesses and forsakes them, he gets another chance" (Proverbs 28:13, TLB).

Blame—you know what it is, don't you? You point your finger at another person to get the focus off yourself. And there's a lot to blame out there. Look at the people you have to deal with. Just look at the crazy drivers on the road. No wonder you lose your temper.

Blame is not a new response. It started in the Garden.

> And he said, "Who told you that you were naked? Have you eaten from the tree that I commanded you not to eat from?" The man said, "The woman you put here with me—she gave me some fruit from the tree, and I ate it." Then the Lord God said to the woman, "What is this you have done?" The woman said, "The serpent deceived me, and I ate."

Genesis 3:11-13

We blame people, circumstances, and even God. Most often, the blaming statements aren't too original. Read through this list and note which ones you may have used.

1. Well, I didn't start this. It wasn't my fault. It's what they said.
2. What I did could have been worse. Besides, they provoked me.
3. If my wife hadn't said what she did, there wouldn't have been any problem.
4. Everybody at work was doing it, so I couldn't be the odd one.
5. I only spoke to you the way you spoke to me.
6. No one let me know that I was supposed to be there. You just think you did.

Blame neither builds relationships nor resolves differences. It pushes people apart. And it's a great way to get into an endless argument.

There is a better way to handle a mistake. Try saying,

1. You're right.
2. I am responsible.
3. I'm sorry.
4. I will be different the next time.

"Then the Lord God said, 'It is not good for the man to be alone'"
(Genesis 2:18, NASB).

Intimacy is the foundation for both love and friendship. It's a close emotional bond that involves mutual sharing and understanding.

Please note the word *mutual*. Each person in an intimate relationship wants to know the other's deepest dreams, wishes, concerns, hopes, and fears, while at the same time being an open book himself. Intimacy leads to deep feelings of closeness, warmth, and trust. Intimacy eliminates the pain of loneliness and the pain of being strangers with one another. If you're going to have intimacy in your relationship, you must have the confidence to expose the private, vulnerable portion of your life. Intimacy means you cannot remain isolated from each other.

But sometimes intimacy hurts. Vulnerability carries with it the risk of being painfully real with another person. When a man relates closely to others, he discovers a greater awareness of himself. His fears can be dissolved and a healthy level of self-acceptance has an opportunity to develop.

Some men approach intimacy with reservation, saying, "If I do start to confront my fear of intimacy and open up, I need several things to keep myself going. I need to see there are more benefits in opening up than in staying closed. I need to see it's safe to open up. I don't want any negative value judgments about what I'm sharing. Nor do I want others telling me their opinion of what I think or feel inside. I need others to tell me it's okay to do this."

Men, be encouraged that others like you are hesitant about developing intimacy in relationships. It is a slow journey. It takes work and time and it involves a level of discomfort. It means learning more and more about your feelings. And it may involve participating in a small group of men who are willing to embark upon this same journey with you.

One man who made this journey stated, "What was there to be afraid of in the first place? There are other things in life more terrifying than intimacy, and I've faced them. I guess I created my fear in the first place."

Now that you have a clearer idea of what true intimacy entails, how do you think your partner would rate the level of intimacy in your relationship?

FEBRUARY 12

"… who speaks the truth from his heart…" (Psalms 15:2b).

The heart is an important organ. We make reference to it all the time. When we're scared we say, "My heart almost stopped with fright." If we know someone who's generous we describe him as "having a big heart." When we describe a person as having a broken heart, we are talking about grief. When we were kids, to emphasize the fact that we were telling the truth, we'd say, "Cross my heart and hope to die."

The heart is also referred to when we talk about convictions, "I know deep down in my heart." When we say, "That person has a good heart," we could be talking about a person's character or ability to keep commitments. When David in Psalm 15 says, "and speaks truth in his heart," he's saying a man of character is truthful and can be depended on to speak the truth regardless. There's the key word—*regardless*—regardless of how much it costs him.

Regardless of how much it makes him look bad.

Regardless of how much difficulty he gets into.

Regardless of how much others don't like to hear the truth.

Telling the truth is rare today. Who can you count on to consistently tell the truth? Anyone? If you are that person, you'll be different from others. But you'll also be trusted. Telling the truth benefits you, but more than that, it's a way to bring honor and glory to God in today's society![11]

"So let us then definitely aim for and eagerly pursue what makes for harmony and for mutual upbuilding [edification and development] of one another" (Romans 14:19, AMP).

Do you want your marriage to last forever? Here's how.

People in long-term marriages tend to take each other for granted. The most common of the "takens" include:

You will always be here for me.

You will always love me.

You will always be able to provide for me.

You will always be the same.

We will always be together.

Making these assumptions in a marriage is living more in Fantasyland than on Reality Ridge. People who take things for granted are seldom appreciative of the everyday blessings in their lives. After a time, they come to believe life owes them these little gifts. They seldom say thank you for anything.

When you take someone for granted you demean him or her. You send the unspoken message, "You are not worth much to me." You also rob this person of the gift of human appreciation. And to be loved and appreciated gives all of us a reason to live each day. When that gift is withdrawn or denied over the years, your spirits wither and die. People may endure this hardship and stay married forever, but they are only serving a sentence. In long-term marriages where one or both spouses are continually taken for granted, a wall of indifference arises between husband and wife. The longer the marriage, the higher the wall and the greater the human isolation. The way out of this woodpile is simple but crucial:

Start saying thank you and showing appreciation for anything and everything.

Be more consciously tuned in to what is going on around you.

Become more giving and affirming.

Specialize in the many little things that mean a lot: Bring each other flowers, take long walks in the country, lie on the floor in front of the fireplace, prepare breakfast in bed for each other, hold hands in public and walk in the rain, send caring and funny cards to each other in the mail, buy each other small gifts for no apparent reason.

Remember: A thirty-five-year marriage does not guarantee year number thirty-six. Take nothing for granted just because you have it today.[12]

"Husbands, love your wives, just as Christ loved the church and gave himself up for her" (Ephesians 5:25).

If you're married, here are today's Ten Commandments for loving your wife. They should bring a smile to her face.

1. *Silence is not always golden,* especially between husband and wife. Ask your wife when she'd like to set aside time just to talk.

2. *When you love your wife, you take her feelings and viewpoints seriously,* even when they differ from your own. When you disagree, tell her, "I see things differently, but maybe I can learn from you." Believe it!

3. *Tell your wife how much you value her.* "A wife of noble character, who can find? She is worth far more than rubies" (Prv 31:10).

4. *Don't stop at complimenting your wife once.* Look for something else nice to tell her.

5. *The best way to tell your wife about something you* don't *like is to tell her about something you* do *like.* For example: "I really like it when you try out new recipes on me."

6. *When your wife lets you know you've hurt or offended her, think about your goal and choose your response.* Will you be defensive? Resentful? Humble? Sorrowful? If your goal is to be close again, the choice is clear.

7. *Be your wife's companion.* When your wife is upset, exhausted, or overwhelmed, do you know what she needs most of all? Usually it's simple companionship. She doesn't want to feel alone. Be there for her. Your presence, patience, and prayers will help her feel loved.

8. *If you love someone you will be loyal to her no matter what the cost.* You will always believe in her, always expect the best of her, and always stand your ground in defending her (1 Cor 13:7, author's paraphrase).

9. *Complaining about your wife won't improve your marriage.* Instead, tell her what you like about your marriage and make positive suggestions that include action on your part as well as hers.

10. *Don't suffocate your wife with possessiveness.* Remember that God is the one who owns us; He has merely entrusted your wife to your care. Ask her how she would like you to care for her in new and different ways, then follow through.[13]

"Therefore I tell you, do not worry about your life, what you will eat or drink; or about your body, what you will wear. Is not life more important than food, and the body more important than clothes?... But seek first his kingdom and his righteousness, and all these things will be given to you as well" (Matthew 6:25, 33).

During the Great Depression of the thirties, the unemployment rate in this country soared out of sight. Men and women waited for hours just to get a loaf of bread or a bowl of soup. Jobs that seemed secure disappeared overnight.

Today, as in the thirties, job security seems to be a thing of the past. Executives, managers, and engineers, as well as factory workers, are at risk of losing their jobs. How secure is your job? If you were to lose it tomorrow, how would you or your family survive? How would you feel about yourself as a man? When a job is gone we seem to hear other implied messages behind the loss. Have you ever had these thoughts?

They don't need me anymore.

Someone else can do it better.

It could be I'm too old.

I can't cut it anymore.

Some men live in constant fear of these messages, even when their job is secure. So, to keep it that way, they work harder, longer, and strive to be better than anyone else. They give 110 percent at the office, which leaves a deficit for home. And once you give the appearance of working so diligently and sacrificially, the management begins to expect that of you. It's all because we live in fear and use our work as our source of security. We forget that our security, no matter what job we have, is not in our work. Our security is in God. If we do our job secure in him, we'll work better anyway and enjoy it more.

Sure, you can worry about it, but that's as much of a choice as following today's Scriptures. Don't you think one is a much better choice than the other?

"But clothe yourself with the Lord Jesus Christ..." (Romans 13:14a, AMP).

O God, our Father, we thank you that you sent your Son Jesus Christ into this world to be our Savior and our Lord.

We thank you that he took our body and our flesh and blood upon himself, and so showed us that this body of ours is fit to be your dwelling place.

We thank you that he did our work, that he earned a living, that he served the public, and so showed us that even the smallest tasks are not beneath your majesty and can be done for you.

We thank you that he lived in an ordinary home, that he knew the problems of living together, that he experienced the rough and smooth of family life, and so showed us that any home, however humble, can be a place where in the ordinary routine of daily life we can make all life an act of worship to you.

Lord Jesus, come again to us this day.

Come into our hearts, and so cleanse them, that we being pure in heart may see God our Father.

Come into our minds, and so enlighten and illumine them that we may know you who are the way, the truth, and the life.

Touch our lips, that we may speak no word which would hurt another or grieve you.

Touch our eyes, that they may never linger on any forbidden thing.

Touch our hands, that they may become useful with service to the needs of others.

When we are sad, comfort us; when we are tired, refresh us; when we are lonely, cheer us; when we are tempted, strengthen us; when we are perplexed, guide us; when we are happy, make our joy doubly dear.

O God, our Father, help us so to live that, whenever your call comes for us, at morning, at midday or at evening, it may find us ready, our work completed and our hearts at peace with you, so that we may enter at last with joy into your nearer presence and into life eternal; through Jesus Christ our Lord. Amen.[14]

"Husbands, love your wives, just as Christ loved the church and gave himself up for her" (Ephesians 5:25).

Commitment is costly. There's no other way to see it, especially if you're married.

In March 1990, Dr. Robertson McQuilken announced his resignation as president of Columbia Bible College in order to care for his beloved wife, Muriel, who was suffering from the advanced stages of Alzheimer's disease. In his resignation letter he wrote:

"My dear wife, Muriel, has been in failing mental health for about eight years. So far I have been able to carry both her ever-growing needs and my leadership responsibilities at CBC. But recently it has become apparent that Muriel is contented most of the time she is with me and almost none of the time I am away from her. It is not just discontent. She is filled with fear— even terror—that she has lost me and always goes in search of me when I leave home. Then she may be full of anger when she cannot get to me. So it is clear to me that she needs me now, full-time.

"Perhaps it would help you to understand if I shared with you what I shared at the time of the announcement of my resignation in chapel. The decision was made, in a way, forty-two years ago when I promised to care for Muriel 'in sickness and in health… till death do us part.' So, as I told the students and faculty, as a man of my word, integrity has something to do with it. But so does fairness. She has cared for me fully and sacrificially all these years; if I cared for her for the next forty years I would not be out of debt. Duty, however, can be grim and stoic. But there is more; I love Muriel. She is a delight to me—her childlike dependence and confidence in me, her warm love, occasional flashes of that wit I used to relish so, her happy spirit and tough resilience in the face of her continual distressing frustration. I do not have to care for her, I get to! It is a high honor to care for so wonderful a person."[15]

FEBRUARY 18

"Get rid of all bitterness, rage and anger, brawling and slander, along with every form of malice. Be kind and compassionate to one another, forgiving each other, just as in Christ God forgave you" *(Ephesians 4:31-32).*

Getting along with others—whether in your church, place of employment, or your family—is not always the easiest task. It not only takes work, it requires the absence of four different spirits.

The *competitive spirit.* Whenever there are several people involved in any task, it's important to learn to work together. You get much more accomplished when you function as partners rather than competitors. This is difficult for men, because many of us were raised to be competitors and we live in a competitive society. When you're competitive you look out for yourself, disparage the successes of others, and focus on winning rather than on serving others. It's possible, however, to do your best and live a life of excellence without it being at the expense of others.

The *critical spirit* destroys not only others but the person possessing it. Often it comes from either being overly critical of ourselves, or being a perfectionist. No matter the reason, it's not a good way to live. God's Word says, "Therefore let us stop passing judgment on one another. Instead, make up your mind not to put any stumbling block or obstacle in your brother's way" (Rom 14:13).

Some men struggle with a *vain spirit.* We're enamored with ourselves, and our calling in life seems to be to impress others. Our goal is to capture people's attention and live off their applause. When this spirit overtakes us it's difficult to reflect the presence of Jesus in our lives. The two can't live together.

The last spirit is very destructive. It's the *adversarial spirit.* When we're at odds with another person and feelings linger, bitterness and resentment come into play. Perhaps you've resented your parents, your wife, or your coworkers for years. God's Word tells us there's a better way to live. Go back and read today's Scripture again. Let the spirit of these two verses indwell your heart and run your life.[16]

FEBRUARY 19

"For God so loved the world..." (John 3:16).

I f you would like to be loved and accepted in a consistent way, there is only One who can do that: God. Note what the Scriptures say about him. Spend time reading and rereading these verses.

- He is the loving, concerned Father who is interested in the intimate details of our lives (see Matthew 6:25-34).
- He is the Father who never gives up on us (see Luke 15:3-32).
- He is the God who sent his Son to die for us though we were undeserving (see Romans 5:8).
- He stands with us in good and bad circumstances (see Hebrews 13:5).
- He is the ever-active Creator of our universe. He died to heal our sickness, pain, and grief (see Isaiah 53:3-6).
- He has broken the power of death (see Luke 24:6-7).
- He gives all races and sexes equal status (see Galatians 3:28).
- He is available to us through prayer (see John 14:13, 14).
- He is aware of our needs (see Isaiah 65:24).
- He created us for an eternal relationship with him (see John 3:16).
- He values us (see Luke 7:28).
- He doesn't condemn us (see Romans 8:1).
- He values and causes our growth (see 1 Corinthians 10:13).
- He comforts us (see 2 Corinthians 1:3-5).
- He strengthens us through his Spirit (see Ephesians 3:16).
- He cleanses us from sin (see Hebrews 10:17-18).
- He is for us (see Romans 8:31).
- He is always available to us (see Romans 8:38-39).
- He is a God of hope (see Romans 15:13).
- He helps us in temptation (see Hebrews 2:17-18).
- He provides a way to escape temptation (see 1 Corinthians 10:13).
- He is at work in us (see Philippians 2:13).
- He wants us to be free (see Galatians 5:1).
- He is the Lord of time and eternity (see Revelation 1:18).

"So God created man in his own image, in the image of God he created him; male and female he created them" (Genesis 1:27).

Have you ever talked to God about sex? If not, why not? It's his creation. Thank him for it in a prayer, perhaps like this one.

Thank you, O Redeemer,
for letting me express love through sex.
Thank you for making it possible
for things to be right with sex—
that there can be beauty and wonder
between woman and man.

You have given us a model for love in Jesus.
He lived and laughed and accepted his humanity.
He resisted sexual temptations
which were every bit as real as mine.
He taught about the relationship of husband and wife
by showing love for his bride the church.

Thank you that he gives me
the power to resist temptations also.
Thank you that real sexual freedom
comes in being bound to the true man Jesus.

Everywhere there are signs that point to the sex god:
Books declare that sex is our savior;
Songs are sung as prayers to sex;
Pictures show its airbrushed incarnations;
Advertisers hawk its perfume and after-shave libations.
Help me know that sex is not salvation.
Help me see instead that there is salvation for sex.
For the exciting sensations of erotic love,
I offer you my thanks.

Lord, you replace sexual boredom with joy;
you point past sexual slavery to the hope of purity;
you enable sexual lovers to be friends;
you teach how to replace lust-making with lovemaking.

continued on next page

Would I have any hope for sexual responsibility
without the power you give?

Would I ever be a covenent keeper
without the fidelity you inspire?

Thank you, Lord, for a love that stays when the bed is made.
Help me to keep my marriage bed undefiled—
to see it as an altar of grace and pleasure.
Keep sex good in my life,
through your redeeming love.
Teach me to say:
"Thank God for sex!"[17]

"Grace and peace to you from God our Father and the Lord Jesus Christ" (Ephesians 1:2).

If someone asked you to explain the grace of God, what would you say? Basically, grace is the unmerited favor of God. He gives us what we don't deserve.

There are four aspects of grace. The first is described in the word *prevenient* and it means "beforehand." God's grace is extended to you before you ever ask. It means God's acceptance is given before you feel acceptable, forgiveness is offered before you ask, and God chose you before you chose to respond. That's grace. Jesus said, "You did not choose Me, but I chose you" (Jn 15:16). "But God demonstrates his own love for us in this: While we were still sinners, Christ died for us" (Rom 5:8).

Sometimes after a man accepts the Lord he will say, "I found God!" It may seem that way, but it's just the opposite. God chose the man. This is grace as well.

Second, God's grace is an *initiative* grace on His part. He is always pursuing a deeper relationship with us, even if we're in a holding pattern.

> No longer will they build houses and others live in them, or plant and others eat. For as the days of a tree, so will be the days of my people; my chosen ones will long enjoy the works of their hands. They will not toil in vain or bear children doomed to misfortune; for they will be a people blessed by the Lord, they and their descendants with them. Before they call I will answer; while they are still speaking I will hear. **Isaiah 65:22-24**

Third, God's grace is *inexhaustible*. You can't drain the supply. You can't even diminish it. The container is always full. And fourth, to top it all off, God's grace is *all-sufficient*, not partial, but all! Jesus said to Paul at his time of need, "My grace is sufficient for you." The word *sufficient* means "fitting." What God will give you is an exact fit.

So, with this in mind go out and do what you have to do today with a new sense of assurance and power. That's what grace can do for you![18]

"So when you, a mere man, pass judgment on them and yet do the same things, do you think you will escape God's judgment?" (Romans 2:3).

The former pastor of the church I attend, Dr. Lloyd Ogilvie, had this insight to share about judging others.

A father paced the bedroom floor while his daughter took what he thought was far too long to say good night to her boyfriend in the living room below. "I don't see why it takes that young man so long to say good night. I don't know about this younger generation!" he said.

"Oh, come to bed," his wife said. "Weren't you young once?"

"Yes, I was, and that's just why I'm worried and can't come to bed!"...

The humor of this story enables us to consider a very serious truth. The overworried father's statement expressed real insight into himself. His judgment of his daughter and her young man was based on his own memories of what he had done in living rooms a generation before. The problem was that he had projected these memories into worry in the present. His judgment did not fit the new situation but was based on his own concern.

Judgments often are exposures of our own needs. The things we judge in others are often the things which are troubling us deeply within. Righteous indignation may be caused by something not so righteous in us. Something we have done or wished we had had the courage to do, something unresolved or unforgiven, something hidden or unhealed will cause the judgment of someone else.

Whenever we are overly critical we should ask ourselves, "Why does that bother you?" There are some things which need to be questioned in loving concern for another person, but when our judgments are rash or emotional or severe, it usually indicates that part of the problem is still within us.[19]

"I can do everything through him who gives me strength"
(Philippians 4:13).

It's been one of those days, a bad day, a furball day, a rotten day. The kind of day where nothing seems to go well: people are late, they don't follow through, dinner is cold, everyone seems to want something from you with no real appreciation, the expressway is a joke, and nothing you do seems to turn out right! You're irritated and discouraged. You may even be a bit depressed.

When days like this occur, sometimes we compound the problem by making one major mistake—we try to fix everything by ourselves. We take on the role of the Lone Ranger and tough it out alone. But even the Lone Ranger was smart enough to have a partner, Tonto.

This is the time to say, "God, help me," and he will. One of the best ways to handle these days is to dwell on God's Word. Read these passages out loud during your dark days. Reflect on what each one is saying, and then note the differences.

"I have set the Lord always before me; because he is at my right hand, I will not be shaken" (Ps 16:8).

"You, O Lord, keep my lamp burning; my God turns my darkness into light" (Ps 18:28).

"The Lord is my light and my salvation; whom shall I fear? The Lord is the stronghold of my life; of whom shall I be afraid?" (Ps 27:1).

"God is our refuge and strength, an ever present help in trouble" (Ps 46:1).

"Create in me a pure heart, O God, and renew a steadfast spirit within me" (Ps 51:10).

"Cast your cares upon the Lord, and he will sustain you; he will never let the righteous fall" (Ps 55:22).

"My soul finds rest in God alone; my salvation comes from him" (Ps 62:1).

FEBRUARY 24

"Always keep on praying" (1 Thessalonians 5:17, TLB).

Here is another thought about praying together as a couple.

Prayer is an awareness of the presence of a holy and loving God in one's life, and an awareness of God's relations to one's husband or wife. Prayer is listening to God, a valuable lesson in learning to listen to one another. In prayer one searches the interior life for blocks to personal surrender to God, evaluating one's conduct in the quiet of prayerful meditation. At times prayer may be rich with confession and self-humbling, or with renunciation and higher resolve to fulfill God's best. Praying together shuts out the petty elements of daily conflict and anxiety, permitting a couple to gain a higher perspective upon their lives, allowing their spirits to be elevated to a consideration of eternal values and enduring relationships. Prayer helps a couple sort out unworthy objects of concern and helps them to concentrate on the nobler goals of life. All the threatening things that trouble a pair can find relief in the presence of God; humbling themselves before Him, they humble themselves before one another—an invaluable therapy. In this way the couple comes to honest estimates of themselves and one another. Unbecoming self-assurance and stubborn independence give way before the recognition of their inadequacy to meet divine standards of life; thus, two people are led to seek God's help and the support of each other.[20]

Scripture also tells us to pray:

As for me, far be it from me that I should sin against the Lord by ending my prayers for you; and I will continue to teach you those things which are good and right. **1 Samuel 12:23, TLB**

You haven't tried this before, [but begin now]. Ask, using my name, and you will receive, and your cup of joy will overflow. **John 16:24, TLB**

Admit your faults to one another and pray for each other so that you may be healed. The earnest prayer of a righteous man has great power and wonderful results. **James 5:16, TLB**

FEBRUARY 25

"On the last and greatest day of the Feast, Jesus stood and said in a loud voice, 'If anyone is thirsty, let him come to me and drink. Whoever believes in me, as the Scripture has said, streams of living water will flow from within him'" (John 7:37-38).

You've been walking across the desert for two days now. Your car broke down and you had no other choice but to walk to civilization. You know it will take at least four days to get there. The quart of water you started out with is gone. Your mouth feels as dry as the desert you're walking on and your tongue has swelled. The gritty sand feels like rocks between your teeth.

All of a sudden you see a well. You run up to it and pump the handle. Soon there's a flow, but it's not water... it's sand. Then you notice this sign: "Two feet over and two feet down you'll find a jug of water buried. Dig it up and use the water to prime the pump. Drink all the water you want, but when you are done, be sure you fill the jug again for the next person and then bury it!"

You dig down, one foot, eighteen inches, and then your hand hits the jug. You bring it up and hear the water sloshing around. What do you do? Your mouth and throat are crying out for water. But the well could provide enough for you to drink to your heart's content, fill your containers, and make it to safety. But what if you prime the pump with water and it doesn't work?

What would you do? It's a risk, isn't it? That's what life is all about. That's what faith is all about, too. It's trusting the sign writer. It's following the instructions. It's living on the edge. God wants us to be faithful. Hebrews 11:6 says, "And without faith it is impossible to please God, because anyone who comes to him must believe that he exists and that he rewards those who earnestly seek him."[21]

FEBRUARY 26

"You have made known to me the path of life; you will fill me with joy in your presence, with eternal pleasures at your right hand" *(Psalms 16:11).*

P leasure is an interesting word. The dictionary defines it as "a pleased feeling; enjoyment; delight; satisfaction; something that gives these. Gratification of the senses; sensual satisfaction."[22]

Slogans use the word incorrectly. Tobacco companies say, "Come to where the pleasure is." A chewing gum company says, "Double your pleasure, double your fun."

The ads work. We all want to be satisfied. Some pleasures are all right. Some violate other people. Some violate us and lead to addiction.

Have you ever thought about what gives you the *most* pleasure and what gives you the *least* pleasure in what you do? When your pursuit of pleasure is in balance and stays within boundaries, it's all right. You're still in control of it. But many men become slaves to their pleasures. It becomes the number-one drive in their world.

You're not the only one to struggle with this balance. It's always been a temptation. Just look at Solomon. This king went overboard in his desire for pleasure and so did his kingdom. He didn't know the meaning of the word *moderation.* He lost it and the nation was destroyed.

A nation may not be destroyed today by your pursuit of pleasure, but your family can be and so can your career. God is not against pleasure; he provides it. Ask him what kind of pleasure he has in store for you.

Delight yourself in the Lord and he will give you the desires of your heart.
Psalms 37:4

Who satisfies your desires with good things so that your youth is renewed like the eagle's. **Psalms 103:5**

The pleasures God provides are not like those fleeting pleasures promised by commercials. He really satisfies!

FEBRUARY 27

"He who listens to a life-giving rebuke will be at home among the wise. He who ignores discipline despises himself, but whoever heeds correction gains understanding" (Proverbs 15:31-32).

How do you handle it when someone takes you to task? You know, they criticize you or make "constructive suggestions." Do you enjoy it? Probably not. Does it make you feel better? Probably not. Do you usually say, "You're right. Thanks for telling me"? Probably not. But you know what? We need all the help we can get, even though most of the time we resist it.

The Bible talks about the word *reproof.* It's a Hebrew word which means "to correct or to convince." It's not always other people who correct us. It could be God's Word. A slight course correction now can prevent disaster later on. If an airliner is off course by just half a degree (which isn't much to begin with), several hundred miles later it's way off course. It's the same way with our lives. But too often we do what Solomon talks about in Proverbs 1:23-24: "If you had responded to my rebuke, I would have poured out my heart to you and made my thoughts known to you. But since you rejected me when I called and no one gave heed when I stretched out my hand ..." In verse 24 the word *refuse* means a direct digging in of the heels and saying, "Don't confuse me with the facts. My mind is made up." We call this stubbornness. It's ironic that so often when someone else says we're stubborn, we respond with, "No, I'm not!"

When Solomon says, "No one pays attention," it's as though others are ignoring what is said or, worse yet, are totally insensitive.

Verse 25 says, "Since you ignored all my advice and would not accept my rebuke..."

Two problems jump out here. Neglecting counsel implies indifference, which is like saying, "Hey, don't bother me. I don't care!" This attitude certainly doesn't build close and loving relationships.

And when it says, "... did not want my reproof," what word comes to mind? You're right—defensiveness. The defensive person says, "You're wrong. I'm right, and I won't consider it."

So, when someone gives you a reproof, what is your response going to be? You have a choice. Reread Proverbs 15:31. It offers some pretty good advice.

"Now when Joshua was near Jericho, he looked up and saw a man standing in front of him with a drawn sword in his hand. Joshua went up to him and asked, 'Are you for us or for our enemies?'

"'Neither,' he replied, 'but as commander of the army of the Lord I have now come.' Then Joshua fell facedown to the ground in rev-erence, and asked him, 'What message does my Lord have for his servant?' The commander of the Lord's army replied, 'Take off your sandals, for the place where you are standing is holy.' And Joshua did so" (Joshua 5:13-15).

Joshua's mentor, Moses, was dead. There was no more help from that direction. Joshua was the newly appointed commander of the Jewish army of Israel. They were ready to go to battle to claim the Promised Land, but the results were uncertain. Then Joshua sees this imposing figure with a sword. When Joshua challenges him, he is confronted by the commander of the Lord's army.

If you had been Joshua, how would you have responded? Joshua's response gives us a model of what to do. He threw himself on the ground in worship. He probably had a sense of relief, as well, and thought, "Now God is going to give me the battle plan! Yes! Now we can overwhelm our enemy." Right? Wrong! Not at all.

Joshua was told something quite simple: Recognize that God is holy. Surrender yourself to him. Humble yourself before him.

It's the same for us today. Our battles are different, but they are, in some ways, the same. There's an enemy out there to fight. Before you engage him, go to God and be humble before him. That's the secret source of strength. Then you can face your enemies.[23]

FEBRUARY 29

"And he said to them, 'Where is your faith?'" (Luke 8:25, NASB).

Perhaps you've had days when you wonder where your faith is. It seems to be lost, and you wonder how to get it back. Martyn Lloyd-Jones had something to say about this.

Faith is not something that acts automatically, faith is not something that acts magically. We seem to think that faith is something that acts automatically. Many people, it seems to me, conceive of faith as if it were something similar to those thermostats which you have in connection with a heating apparatus: you set your thermostat at a given level and it acts automatically. If the temperature is tending to rise above that, the thermostat comes into operation and brings it down; if you use your hot water and the temperature is lowered, the thermostat comes into operation and sends it up, etc. You do not have to do anything about it, the thermostat acts automatically and brings the temperature back to the desired level automatically.

Now there are many people who seem to think that faith acts like that. They assume that it does not matter what happens to them, that faith will operate and all will be well. Faith, however, is not something that acts magically or automatically. If it did, these men would never have been in trouble, faith would have come into operation, and they would have been calm and quiet and all could have been well. But faith is not like that and those are utter fallacies with respect to it.

What is faith? Let us look at it positively. The principle taught here is that faith is an activity, it is something that has to be exercised. It does not come into operation itself, you and I have to put it into operation. It is a form of activity.[24]

Remind yourself of what Scripture says. Study a passage and act on it. Follow through. Believe that God will help you. That's faith!

"I know that there is nothing better for men than to be happy and do good while they live. That everyone may eat and drink, and find satisfaction in all his toil—this is the gift of God" (Ecclesiastes 3:12-13).

These interesting verses from the Book of Ecclesiastes talk about four gifts God has given to us.

The first gift is the ability to rejoice and enjoy life. To what extent are you enjoying your life right now? Is there something to rejoice in that you are now overlooking? Perhaps someone else—a family member or friend—could help you discover what that is.

Being a Christian means that we have the capability of enjoying life *regardless*. That's an important word. *Regardless* of what is or isn't happening, we can rejoice and be happy. The writer of Proverbs said, "All the days of the despondent afflicted are made evil [by anxious thoughts and foreboding], but he who has a glad heart has a continual feast [regardless of circumstances]" (15:15, AMP).

The second gift is the ability to do good independently from what others do for us. God helps us develop a heart of generosity and helpfulness toward others. *Regardless!* There's that word again. You see, if you wait for someone else to do good before acting, you're letting them control what you do. That puts a new light on it! You don't have to explain to others why you're generous and helpful, nor do you have to do it in a way that gains recognition. Do it for the sake of the kingdom.

The third gift is the appetite to eat and drink—yes! The ability to enjoy our food. If that sounds basic and mundane, just remember that it's one of God's gifts.

The fourth gift is the ability to see good in all our labor. Do you see it that way? Some of our work is boring and routine, but do you look for the purpose in all that you do?

There's a purpose in all of God's gifts. As you live through today, reflect on the four gifts we've just discussed. It could make a big difference in how you view all of life.

MARCH 2

"Some people like to make cutting remarks, but the words of the wise soothe and heal" (Proverbs 12:18, TLB).

Frustration! That teeth-grinding, steering-wheel-pounding feeling! We've all been there and done that. But think about these facts:

1. *Frustration is a normal response.* But you have a choice about how far your frustration will go and how you will deal with it.

2. *Anger is also a normal response.* God created us with the capacity to experience anger.

3. *You will at times become irritated, disappointed, and frustrated with other people.*

4. *Accepting and recognizing your frustration and anger is healthy.* Denying or repressing them can be disastrous.

A common myth is that "frustration always has to upset us." That's not true. If another person is doing something that bothers you, you may feel frustrated, but you can control both your inner and outer responses.

Frustration doesn't have to lead to an angry reaction. You are free to decide how you will respond to it.

Two events during the 1976 Olympic games in Montreal illustrate the contrast between these two responses to frustration. In the two-man sailing event, the team from Britain came in fourteenth in a field of sixteen. The two British sailors were so frustrated by their performance that they set fire to their yacht and waded ashore while it went up in flames. Their response to frustration was destructive and costly.

Olneus Charles, a distance runner from Haiti, also experienced frustration in the Montreal Olympics. He was lapped nine times in the ten-thousand meter race and came in dead last, five minutes behind everyone else. But he didn't become discouraged or quit. He chose not to let his frustrating experience get the best of him. He was glad to complete the race for his country.

Here are three smart tactics for handling frustration. First, commit Proverbs 12:18 to memory. Then delay your response; slow down and take a few breaths. Finally, plan your response to frustration in advance. You will be able to change only if you plan to change.

Go for it! The results can be very constructive.

MARCH 3

"And the Lord spoke to Moses face to face, as a man speaks to his friend..." (Exodus 33:11, AMP).

Remember the story of Gale Sayers and Brian Piccolo? Gary Oliver describes it so well in his book, *Real Men Have Feelings, Too.*

Both were running backs with the Chicago Bears; Sayers was black and Piccolo was white. When they became roommates for away games in 1967 it was a first for race relations in the NFL.

Between 1967 and 1969 their relationship developed into one of the most memorable in the history of professional sports. During the '69 season Brian Piccolo developed cancer. Though he fought as hard as he could to complete the season, he was in the hospital more than on the football field.

Sayers and Piccolo and their wives had planned to attend the annual Professional Football Writers' Banquet in New York where Sayers was to receive the George S. Halas award as "the most courageous player in professional football," but Brian Piccolo was too ill to attend. As the strong and athletic Sayers stood to receive the award, tears began to flow that he couldn't hold back. He said: "You flatter me by giving me this award, but I tell you here and now that I accept it for Brian Piccolo. Brian Piccolo is the man of courage who should receive the George S. Halas Award. I love Brian Piccolo and I'd like you to love him. Tonight, when you hit your knees, ask God to love him too."

Healthy men are men who aren't afraid to need other men. Real men aren't afraid of what people will say about them if they have close male friends. Godly men aren't afraid to risk learning how to love another man.[1]

Do you have a male friend you can talk to, face-to-face? You know, heart to heart, from the gut? If so, you're fortunate. If not, it's a worthwhile goal to develop such a relationship. Sure, it takes time, some risks, listening, sharing, and honesty. But the sense of fulfillment can't be described.

"Whatever you do, work at it with all your heart, as working for the Lord, not for men" (Colossians 3:23).

Sixty thousand people in one stadium. They all paid good money to attend this game. Look at them: row after row jammed together for the next three hours. They're not the players in the game, they're the spectators. They're there to watch and enjoy their favorite sport. They cheer, yell, boo, and second-guess the coaches and players. If they were out there on the field they'd do it differently. But they're not out there in the game; they're in the stands. They wouldn't dare get out of the stands and go on the field. They'd get kicked out. They're supposed to be in the stands. But spectators do make a difference at times. Their enthusiastic cheering encourages the players. The money they spend for the tickets helps to pay the bills for the team. They may take pictures of their hero and wear a shirt with the team name on it. But that's all they do. They're spectators.

There's another place where we have a lot of spectators—in church. People file in, take their places in the pews, sing rather than cheer, pray rather than stomp their feet, and sit and listen quietly to a message. Then when it's over, they get up and leave.

But wait. Where was the team, the players? They're supposed to be there, too. Guess what? They were. But they were sitting in the wrong place—the pews. The players had turned into spectators. In the church it's all right to climb out of the stands to get on the playing field. Not only is it all right, it's a necessity. Christianity is not a spectator sport. It's for players only. There's a game being played and the stakes are high—eternal life. But others won't know about it unless the players play the game. What about you? Are you in the game or just watching?

"I became greater by far than anyone in Jerusalem before me. In all this my wisdom stayed with me" (Ecclesiastes 2:9).

Your name is printed on the program for everyone to see. So are your accomplishments. In fact, not only are your family and your company aware of what you've accomplished, so is everyone else at the convention—two thousand delegates all in the same field you're in. And because of that, all sorts of doors and opportunities are now open to you.

Your company just offered you a new position. It comes with more money, status, responsibility, two secretaries, a spacious office with windows. You've arrived! Life is full of perks with this new position.

The pursuit of position in our society is accepted as normal. We all want to move up the ladder. Each rung gets us closer to the top. But as we climb we need to ask ourselves several questions. What rung of the ladder does God want us on?

If you become the "best" in your field, how will you feel when someone else takes your place? Keep in mind that if you aren't available for that position, you'd be replaced immediately! We are called to live a life of excellence. That's great. But that doesn't always mean we'll get the best position.

What's the cost of striving for that position? Solomon went after prestige, power, and position, and he knew what it was like to reach the top. He couldn't go any higher. He was top dog. He was even greater than his own father. But it cost him—not just the nation but also his son Rehoboam. Scripture says, "He (Rehoboam) did evil because he had not set his heart on seeking the Lord" (2 Chr 12:14). That's a high price to pay for being on top.

"In this same way, husbands ought to love their wives as their own bodies. He who loves his wife loves himself. After all, no one ever hated his own body, but he feeds and cares for it, just as Christ does the church—for we are members of his body" (Ephesians 5:28-31).

Do you want to know how to love your wife? Those forty-nine words in Ephesians sum it up. A husband loves his wife as himself. Her body is his body. Her comfort is his comfort. Her need for care and concern is his. Richard Selzer explains it this way.

Her young husband is in the room. He stands on the opposite side of the bed, and together they seem to do well in the evening lamplight, isolated from me, private. Who are they, I ask myself, he and this wry-mouth I have made, who gaze at and touch each other so generously, greedily? The young woman speaks. "Will my mouth always be like this?" she asks. "Yes," I say, "it will. It is because the nerve was cut." She nods and is silent. But the young man smiles. "I like it," he says. "It is kind of cute...." Unmindful, he bends to kiss her crooked mouth, and I, so close, can see how he twists his own lips to accommodate to hers, to show her that their kiss still works.[2]

That's love. That's care. That's adapting and sacrificing.

Love in everyday living means not only noticing that your wife may be very different in personality and temperament, but accepting it—praising her uniqueness and learning how she will help you become a more complete and fulfilled man because of it![3]

Love means that if you give yourself extra energy, you give her the same. Love means that if you give yourself some leisure time, you give her your time as well. Kent Hughes gives a great summary of Ephesians 5:

What a challenge Ephesians 5 presents us—*sacrificial* love (love is like death!), *sanctifying* love (love that elevates), and *self-love* (loving your wife as much as you love your own body). If it calls for anything, it calls for some holy sweat![4]

"And whatever you do, whether in word or deed, do it all in the name of the Lord Jesus, giving thanks to God the Father through him" (Colossians 3:17).

Some people are like animals. Have you ever watched a humming-bird or a bumblebee? They're quite similar. They're active, busy, and never spend very much time in one place. They hop from one flower to another. It seems like they dabble in one and then another and another.

There are men and women who fit this pattern. They jump from one thing to another, never settling in for any length of time. They dabble with activities and beliefs, never concentrating on any one thing. Have you ever listed all the various activities or causes you're involved with? Ask yourself why you do what you do. What are the results? It may help to gain a better perspective on your life.

Dabblers engage in quantity rather than quality. Some remind me of the college student who signed up for forty different courses in one semester. When asked if he were crazy, his answer was, "I just want to have a varied education. I go to class for fifteen minutes then leave and go to another one. I've got it worked out so I can hit every class and pick up a little from each one." A little is right! There was no depth of learning, no thorough education, just a frantic pace.

Does all that you do bring satisfaction to you?

Does all that you do bring honor and glory to God?

Are you living your life the way God wants or are you exhausted trying to live up to the demands and expectations of others? Are you at peace with the way you go about living your life? Doing less, when it is done thoroughly and enjoyed, will bring you more satisfaction, and may reflect upon the Lord in a better way, too.[5]

"I keep asking that the God of our Lord Jesus Christ, the glorious Father, may give you the Spirit of wisdom and revelation, so that you may know him better" (Ephesians 1:17).

"It's right in front of your nose. Are you blind? Can't you see it?" Most kids hear that from their parents at some time or another, and it's true. You can be looking at something and not see it. It happens to us men, too.

William Randolph Hearst, the world-renowned newspaper publisher, invested a fortune in collecting great works of art. You can still see some of them at Hearst Castle in California. One day he heard about a piece of artwork that was very valuable. He wanted to find it and add it to his collection. His art agent searched all over the world in the various art galleries and couldn't locate it. Months later he did find it...in one of Randolph Hearst's own warehouses. It had been stored there, right under his nose, but he couldn't see it!

It happens to us, too. Some Christians are continually searching for something more in life. They're just not fulfilled. They just don't understand who they are and what they have in Christ.

Paul knew about this. That's why he prayed what he did in the above verse. He wanted us to understand the fullness of our inheritance. It is difficult for us to imagine or fully comprehend all that God has done for us. There will always be some part of what we have been given that will remain a mystery. But sometimes we don't stop to think about all that we have. And when we do we can say, "It is there right in front of me."6

"Praise be to the God and Father of our Lord Jesus Christ, who has blessed us in the heavenly realms with every spiritual blessing in Christ" (Ephesians 1:3).

You're at work and a coworker comes up to you and says, "What's this stuff I hear about you being a Christian? Are you? What do you have being a Christian that you didn't have before?" So, what do you say?

You might say, "It's not too pleasant to think about when I wasn't a Christian. I was in bondage to evil, spiritually dead, and had no hope whatsoever! (see Romans 3:10-12; 1 John 5:19; Romans 1:18; Ephesians 2:1; 4:17-18; Ephesians 2:12). I decided that kind of life wasn't for me. The benefits of being a Christian are so much better. Do you want to hear about them?" Your coworker didn't realize what he was in for, so he might stammer and say, "Sure, why not?" That's your opportunity to share the gospel with him.

"When I became a believer my life with God changed. It took a lot longer for my attitudes and behavior to change, but instantly here's what I received. I became a new creation in Jesus Christ. All these changes are stated in the Word of God. They're not just my idea. I actually became fully alive, and would you believe I now possess the righteousness of Jesus Christ? That's right, the righteousness of the Son of God and I'm going to share in everything he receives (see 2 Corinthians 5:17; Ephesians 2:5; Romans 6:22; 2 Corinthians 5:21; Romans 8:16-17).

"How's that for some benefits? Aren't you glad you asked me that question? So, what about you? Does that sound like something you'd like, too?"

"Finally, all of you, live in harmony with one another; be sympathetic, love as brothers, be compassionate and humble. Do not repay evil with evil or insult with insult, but with blessing, because to this you were called so that you may inherit a blessing" (1 Peter 3:8-9).

Some men have a real gift when it comes to the fine art of insults. That's not unusual, because men's style of humor is different from women's. We use gentle insults, poke fun at one another, emphasize each other's goofs and mistakes, and throw in some sarcasm from time to time. Men enjoy putting each other down. There's nothing wrong with any of this—when it's in fun, when it's mutual, and when it's between men. Often it occurs because we care for these men. They are our friends.

Sometimes, though, our tendency to use insults and put-downs seeps into our family life. Then it becomes destructive. It's easy to fall into this trap because we know our family members better than anyone else. They make easy targets. Within a family, insults and sarcasm hurt. You may make a wisecrack to your teenage daughter that seems funny to you. You laugh and so do her siblings, but she runs off crying to her room. You may wonder, "What did I say?" Keep this question in mind: Can my insult or sarcastic comment fit in with the passage from 1 Peter above? Use that as your guide. It will help.

Often we learn sarcasm from the sitcoms and comedy shows we watch. Put-downs and comments that hurt seem to be an accepted part of our culture. But as Christians this culture is not to be our culture. If sarcasm and insults seem to be the norm in your family, the most powerful way to change that is to have every family member memorize the passage above from 1 Peter. Make it a family project and note the changes that take place when you put those verses into practice.

"My son, do not forget my teaching, but keep my commands in your heart, for they will prolong your life many years and bring you prosperity" (Proverbs 3:1-2).

The frog sat in the cool water enjoying himself. He was happy swimming around. He was also oblivious to the fact that underneath the pan was a Bunsen burner with a flame so small the water was being heated at .017 of a degree Fahrenheit per second. The water temperature was rising so gradually that the frog wasn't even aware of the change. The minutes went by and then about two-and-a-half hours later the frog was dead. He boiled to death, never even knowing what had happened to him, it was so gradual.

Changes can happen to us in the same way. There can be an erosion in our lives that is so subtle it's like the slippage of a hillside that loses a few grains of soil a minute. A year later there is no hill.

Deterioration is all around us. A building suddenly crumbles and people are injured and killed. "What went wrong today?" we ask. It didn't just happen today. It started to give way years ago, but it was so slight that no one noticed.

Character doesn't erode overnight.

Morals don't change suddenly.

A marriage doesn't "suddenly" fall apart.

Children don't "go wild" out of the blue.

A company doesn't "suddenly" go bankrupt.

Enough said?

"So, if you think you are standing firm, be careful that you don't fall!" (1 Corinthians 10:12).

Years ago the television viewing audience was captivated by the cop show *Hill Street Blues*. After their morning briefing and just before they hit the streets, the sergeant would say to the officers, "Let's be careful out there." He was warning them to keep their guard up because the unpredictable could and would happen.

That was good advice for those police officers.

It's good advice for us as well.

You are faced with a number of issues in the world that are just begging you to leave behind your Christian values and standards. Some of the temptations are very enticing.

Scripture warns us again and again.

"Be on your guard." Be on your guard, Jesus said, against hypocrisy (see Matthew 16:6-12), against greed (see Luke 12:15), against persecution from others (see Matthew 10:17), against false teaching (see Mark 13:22-23), and above all, against spiritual slackness and unreadiness for the Lord's return (see Mark 13:32-37). "Be careful," he said in Luke 21:34, "or your hearts will be weighed down with dissipation, drunkenness, and the anxieties of life."

The same caution is repeated throughout the Scriptures. Listen to these warnings: "Be careful that you don't fall" (1 Cor 10:12). "Be careful to do what is right" (Rom 12:17). "Be careful, then, how you live" (Eph 5:15). "Be careful that none of you be found to have fallen short" (Heb 4:1). "Only be careful, and watch yourselves" (Dt 4:9). "Be careful to do what the Lord your God has commanded you" (Dt 5:32). "Be careful that you do not forget the Lord" (Dt 6:12). "Be careful to obey all that is written in the Book" (Jos 23:6). "Give careful thought to your ways" (Hg 1:5-7).

There's a reason for all the warnings. We need to be reminded of them constantly. If you're struggling with an issue, read these passages out loud every morning for a month. Before long you'll know them from memory. That's the best safeguard.[7]

MARCH 13

"Each of you should learn to control his own body in a way that is holy and honorable" (1 Thessalonians 4:4).

Just when you think you're in control of your life and you've got all the walls up against attack, something breaks through. It's embarrassing when you've got your guard up and something slips by. Defensive lines in football face this constantly. A runner slips by and is off to the goal line. A boxer is told by his trainer time and time again, "Don't let your guard down."

Even countries let their guard down from time to time. On May 29, 1987, Russia was celebrating "Border Guards' Day." They prided themselves on their ability to let no one in or out. That is, until Matthias Rust, a West German computer analyst, took off from Helsinki in a single-engine Cessna and flew through four hundred miles of heavily guarded airspace. He not only passed borders, he buzzed through them.

The "impenetrable" borders weren't impenetrable. The guards weren't guarding, and you can bet some heads rolled. Especially as this little plane buzzed Leningrad, barely cleared the walls of the Kremlin, and landed in Red Square a few feet from the tomb. Adding insult to injury, the whole world knew about it! Red Square turned into red faces and some made a trip to the Siberian salt mines. This teenager gained fame and a four-year trip to a society labor camp. But he caught the Russian nation with their guard down.

Have you ever been caught with your guard down? It doesn't just happen to football players, boxers, and border guards. It happens to us, too, if we're not careful. Hear the warning of Scripture. Heed the learning of Scripture. Be careful out there.

"Why, you do not even know what will happen tomorrow. What is your life? You are a mist that appears for a little while and then vanishes. Instead, you ought to say, 'If it is the Lord's will, we will live and do this or that'" (James 4:14-15).

What happened in the yesterdays of your life? Think about it for a minute. In the past twenty years, what are the three most significant events of your life? How did they impact you? How did they affect you spiritually? Sometimes it pays to stop and take stock of the past in order to keep on course in the present.

Sometimes we get caught up in remembering the past a bit too much and get stuck there. We spend too much time experiencing those past good times, especially if the present is kind of ho-hum. It's safer to stay in the past, especially when you read the passage in James above.

James has an unnerving message for each of us: Life in the future is uncertain. That's basically it. What we have to look forward to is not the certainty of the events of the past, but the inevitability of the unexpected occurring in the future. In fact, the best-case scenario could occur as easily as the worst-case scenario. Life is uncertain. That's nothing new. It has always been that way.

Life is short and challenging. We're not to live in fear of the future or to constantly ask "What if?" That attitude can rob us of our joy. The way Chuck Swindoll puts James 4:14-15 in perspective is great.

LIFE IS CHALLENGING. Because it is short, life is packed with challenging possibilities. Because it is uncertain it's filled with challenging adjustments. I'm convinced that's much of what Jesus meant when He promised us an abundant life. Abundant with challenges, running over with possibilities, filled with opportunities to adapt, shift, alter, and change. Come to think of it, that's the secret of staying young. It is also the path that leads to optimism and motivation.[8]

"Here I am! I stand at the door and knock. If anyone hears my voice and opens the door I will come in and eat with him, and he with me" (Revelation 3:20).

Heavenly Father,

You stood at the door of my heart and knocked. I am thankful that I opened the door to let you in. But I need you to walk through all the rooms of my life and fill them with your presence.

Give me ears that hear you calling me to live for you in a world that has gone deaf to your voice. May I not only hear but respond to your summons, even though it may be costly. Help me to hear the silent cries of suffering in the vacant eyes of the abused in families and in the shuffling walk of the homeless on the streets of my city. And may I act with a heart of compassion.

Give me an open mind to hear something new from my family, my coworkers, and my pastor. Don't let my past experiences keep me frozen against the newness of today and tomorrow. Give me the courage to change my mind and be a man of unpopular conviction when necessary.

Give me open eyes to see the greatness of what you have created as well as the needs of the lost who have not heard about Jesus. Lift the covering from my eyes and forgive me for my self-imposed blindness to the concerns around me. Help me to see the person who needs the door opened, the sack lifted, the wave of recognition, and the "well done" touch on the shoulder.

Give me open hands to lift the hurting and tired, to share the blessing that you have given to me.

Give me an open heart to be receptive to who you want me to be and to do all you want me to do.

I praise you for being a giving God.

In Jesus' name.

Amen.

"You shall not commit adultery" (Exodus 20:14).

One of the best books written for couples on the sexual relationship is Doug Rosenau's *A Celebration of Sex*. Hear what he has to say about the above verse.

A great marital partnership has room for only two people in it. Commitment is vital to intimate companionship, and the creation of good boundaries is irreplaceable for a fantastic marriage and sex life.

Adulterate means "to contaminate by adding a foreign substance or watering down a product." You can adulterate your marital companionship in many ways other than by having a sexual affair. You can adulterate your marriage by overcommitting to work, children, or church.

God's injunction of "thou shalt not commit adultery" is often portrayed in terms of a protective fence that guards the beautiful marital and sexual garden. So often we look at fences as something to jump so we can get to greener grass. Actually, the no-adultery fence is there so you can have the intimacy to create an unbelievable relationship within that enclosure—a deeper level of emotional and sexual connecting that can occur and flourish only in an intimate marriage. It protects you from contaminating elements that can threaten the quality of your companionship.

The more important commitments to your mate come in a series of daily choices. Every day when you say, "I have my mate," and refuse to entertain thoughts about someone else, you are reaffirming your commitment. You are allowing sex to be relational and setting good boundaries as you choose to control your sexual impulses and preserve sexual integrity.

These little commitment choices to preserve and deepen intimacy pop up in all areas of marriage. It could mean calling off a lunch with a colleague, deciding whether to have that third child, going to a bed and breakfast for weekend renewal, leaving work early, or buying that funny card and leaving it in the car for your spouse. It can be going to that marriage seminar, reading a book on sexual technique, apologizing for that unkind remark, or working harder to correct a personal character defect.

These choices are not always huge and obvious, but they create the glue that keeps a marriage and sexual relationship together. Daily you have to choose not to adulterate and water down your companionship.[9]

"And now, brothers, we want you to know about the grace that God has given the Macedonian churches. Out of the most severe trial, their overflowing joy and their extreme poverty welled up in rich generosity. For I testify that they gave as much as they were able, and even beyond their ability. Entirely on their own, they urgently pleaded with us for the privilege of sharing in this service to the saints. And they did not do as we expected, but they gave themselves first to the Lord and then to us in keeping with God's will" (2 Corinthians 8:1-5).

It's good to be seen as a giver by your family members. And in giving to your church it's good to be seen as a giver by God. Some men are known as givers, and some aren't. But that doesn't mean the unknown ones are not givers. Some of the most generous men keep it private.

This passage in 2 Corinthians has several suggestions regarding the way we are to give. The first is anonymity. No one needs to know what you give. Sometimes we run into people who are very quick to let you know they tithe a huge amount. You don't have to wonder why they tell you either.

The second is to give voluntarily. Sometimes we may resent having to give. Or we may hold on to our money until December 31 before giving it. But the money, or anything we have, isn't ours to begin with. It all belongs to God.

> Each man should give what he has decided in his heart to give, not reluctantly or under compulsion, for God loves a cheerful giver.
>
> **2 Corinthians 9:7**

The third suggestion is to give generously. Paul described the people in Macedonia as overflowing in their generosity. This doesn't have to be just with money, but with time and ability as well. Generosity means determining what you are going to give and then... giving even more. And the way to develop generosity as a natural part of your life is to give generously. It becomes a good habit.

"You, my brothers, were called to be free. But do not use your freedom to indulge the sinful nature; rather, serve one another in love" *(Galatians 5:13).*

"Who me?"

"I didn't do it."

"You asked for it."

"I didn't mean to."

"It was their fault. It would never have happened if he…"

Blame the perpetual projection of responsibility onto the other guy. One of the best lines I've heard was an accident report which said, "No one was to blame for the accident, but it never would have happened if the other driver had been alert."

People get away with a lot. An FBI agent embezzled $2,000 from the government and blew it all in one afternoon of gambling. He was fired. But then he was reinstated. Why? The court ruled that he had a gambling addiction and was protected under federal law because of his "handicap."

Or, what about the man who applied for a job as a park attendant? The park ran a background check, and guess what they discovered? This man had been convicted more than thirty times for indecent exposure and flashing. Naturally he was turned down. But he followed the new American pastime and sued the park service. After all, he had never flashed in a park, only in libraries and laundromats. You know the outcome. The officials hired him because he had been a victim of job discrimination. Blaming is the way many people avoid personal responsibility.

Blame cripples the atmosphere in the workplace. It tears apart churches. And too many couples follow the pattern of Adam and Eve and put the responsibility for problems onto one another.

Proverbs suggests a better way to live than blaming people. It goes like this:

A man who refuses to admit his mistakes can never be successful. But if he confesses and forsakes them, he gets another chance.

Proverbs 28:13 TLB[10]

MARCH 19

"Trust in Him at all times, O people; pour out your heart before Him; God is a refuge for us" (Psalms 62:8, NASB).

Do you ever get angry? Ridiculous question, isn't it? We all do. Some people show it, others stow it. Some people use it, others abuse it. Some people see it as a tool from Satan, others see it for what it is... a gift from God. You probably never heard it put that way before. But it is a gift. We need the emotion of anger. We need it to counter injustice.

We tend to view anger as a problem, but the problem is in how we use it and express it. Often our anger is a cover-up for other feelings like hurt, fear, and frustration. When you're angry, ask yourself if you're frustrated or hurt or afraid. Then deal with the real issue.

God's Word can help you use your anger wisely. "Better a patient man than a warrior, a man who controls his temper than one who takes a city" (Prv 16:32). Following the advice of this verse helps you focus and direct the power and energy of your anger. "The end of a matter is better than its beginning, and patience is better than pride. Do not be quickly provoked in your spirit, for anger resides in the lap of fools" (Eccl 7:8-9). If you take time to consider the issue at hand you can make progress, even if you're starting to get upset.

One other suggestion: Pray about your anger. How? Like this:

Dear Lord, Thank you for creating me in your image with the ability to experience and express the emotion of anger. I know sin has damaged and distorted anger in my life. I thank you that you have promised to be at work within me both to will and to work for your good pleasure. I thank you that you can cause all things to work together for good and that I can do all things through you because you give me strength. I ask you to help me to change my anger patterns. Help me to experience and express this emotion in ways that are good and that bring honor and glory to you. Amen.[11]

"Instead, speaking the truth in love, we will in all things grow up into him who is the Head, that is, Christ.... Therefore each of you must put off falsehood and speak truthfully to his neighbor, for we are all members of one body" (Ephesians 4:15, 25).

God's Word calls men and women to be people of truth. But it's not just for his benefit, it's for ours as well. John Trent and Rick Hicks suggest four benefits you'll receive by being truthful.

First, you won't have to put forth the energy to maintain a facade. Putting up a false image to fool other people and get what you want puts pressure and strain on you. When people interact with you, they want a situation where "what they see is what they get."

Second, you will have freedom from being found out. When you tell the truth, you don't have to remember what you said for fear of contradicting yourself. Politicians live with this fear, or at least they should! We've seen too many people who say one thing before they're elected and then change later on. That doesn't sit well with us.

Third, you will have freedom from guilt. Unfortunately, some people have practiced lying so much that their conscience is damaged and they're not sure where lies and truth part company. But most of us know what guilt feels like. It's miserable. Perhaps David described it best when he said, "When I kept silent, my bones wasted away through my groaning all day long. For day and night your hand was heavy upon me; my strength was sapped as in the heat of summer" (Ps 32:3-4). When there's a clear conscience, there's peace of mind, too.

The last benefit is that our truthfulness honors God. "Sing to him, sing praise to him; tell of all his wonderful acts" (1 Chr 16:9). God wants truthful hearts. He helps us speak the truth and then when we do we're actually drawing attention to him and his character.

Telling the truth benefits everybody.[12]

"The fruit of the Spirit is... peace" (Galatians 5:22); "And the peace of God... will guard your hearts and your minds in Christ Jesus" (Philippians 4:7).

Here is a slightly different way to look at peace. Perhaps you can relate to it.

J.L. Glass has written a humorous article, titled "Five Ways to Have a Nervous Breakdown." He lists the ways as follows:

1. *Try to figure out the answer before the problem arises.* "Most of the bridges we cross are never built, because they are unnecessary." We carry tomorrow's load along with today's. Matthew 6:34 says: "Do not worry about tomorrow, for tomorrow will worry about itself."

2. *Try to relive the past.* As we trust him (God) for the future, we must trust him with the past. And he can use the most checkered past imaginable for his good. (See Romans 8:28).

3. *Try to avoid making decisions.* Doing this is like deciding whether to allow weeds to grow in our gardens. While we're deciding, they're growing. Decisions will be made in our delay.... Choice "is a man's most godlike characteristic."

4. *Demand more of yourself than you can produce.* Unrealistic demands result in "beating our heads against stone walls. We don't change the walls. We just damage ourselves." Romans 12:3 says, "Do not think of yourself more highly than you ought, but rather think of yourself with sober judgment."

5. *Believe everything Satan tells you.* Jesus described Satan as the "father of lies" (Jn 8:44). He's a master of disguise, masquerading as an angel of light. But our Lord declared that his sheep follow him because they "know his voice" (Jn 10:4). They have listened to it in his Word.[13]

"I saw that wisdom is better than folly, just as light is better than darkness" (Ecclesiastes 2:13).

Do you know what real success is? Listen to the world's view.

Aristotle Onassis, tycoon: "It's not a question of money. After you reach a certain point, money becomes unimportant. What matters is success. The sensible thing would be for me to stop now. But I can't. I have to keep aiming higher and higher—just for the thrill."

Barbra Streisand, recording artist: "Success for me is having ten honeydew melons and eating only the top half of each one."

Ted Turner, media mogul: "Well, I think it's kind of an empty bag, to tell you the truth, but you have to really get there to really know that. I've always said I was more an adventurer than I was a businessman. I mainly did CNN just to see if it would work. And the same with the super-station... just out of personal curiosity to see if it could be done."[14]

Dr. Gary Rossberg has a much better perspective.

Success is not just a matter of money, power, and ego, but also issues of the heart—like compassion, kindness, bravery, generosity, love.

It's an issue of character, not performance.

It's an issue of being the person God designed you to be, not how much salary you can pull down in a year.

It's an issue of who you really are, not how many notches you can rack up on your résumé or the shape of your car's hood ornament.

There's a shift now in our culture—Success hasn't cut it. But significance has more meaning.

Who makes us significant? I believe it is a Person. Not your boss, kids, parents, or even you. What makes you and me significant is the Person of Jesus Christ. He created us in order to glorify Himself. That's our job in life, to bring honor and glory to Him. He is the One who makes us significant."[15]

"Am I now trying to win the approval of men, or of God? Or am I trying to please men? If I were still trying to please men, I would not be a servant of Christ" (Gal 1:10).

"Let no debt remain outstanding, except the continuing debt to love one another, for he who loves his fellowman has fulfilled the law" (Romans 13:8).

How are you and your bank getting along? You know, the place where you go and deposit your weekly check, and then turn around and draw it out again along with some additional funds.

How would you feel if you were at a restaurant with some friends and the loan officer of your bank walked by, said hello, and suggested you stop in to talk about your account? What would be your comfort level? Your guilt level? It's interesting the amount of tension that can arise when you're in the presence of somebody to whom you owe money.

One of the greatest sources of tension happens when money is loaned between family members. Perhaps you loaned your brother-in-law some money to help him save up for the downpayment on his house. The next time you see him he drives up in a new BMW purchased with a down payment from the money you loaned him! It sticks in your throat, doesn't it? You feel ripped off and you'd like him to pay back every cent right now!

Friendships have been lost over the loaning of money.

Families have been torn apart over loaning money.

Bankruptcies have occurred over the borrowing of funds.

Keep this in mind: When you owe on your credit cards, you've become a servant to the one you owe. Does that make you feel comfortable? Proverbs states it even more strongly: "The rich rule over the poor, and the borrower is servant to the lender" (22:7).

When you're tempted to borrow, to put it on the credit card, to explain how desperately you have to have this item—wait. Delay. Pray. And look at your current bills. It may take longer to obtain something, but you'll have a greater sense of freedom in the long run.

MARCH 24

"What good is it for a man to gain the whole world, and yet lose or forfeit his very self?" (Luke 9:25).

An interesting paraphrase of this verse is "What good is it for a man to gain the whole world and lose his children?" Even generations ago there was concern over putting career above family. In 1923, Edgar Guest wrote the following.

I have known of a number of wealthy men who were not successes as fathers. They made money rapidly; their factories were marvels of organization; their money investments were sound and made with excellent judgment, and their contributions to public service were useful and willingly made. All this took time and thought. At the finish there was a fortune on the one hand, and a worthless and dissolute son on the other. WHY? Too much time spent in making money implies too little time spent with the boy.

When these children were youngsters romping on the floor, if someone had come to any one of those fathers and offered him a million dollars for his lad he would have spurned the offer and kicked the proposer out of doors. Had someone offered him ten million dollars in cash for the privilege of making a drunkard out of his son, the answer would have been the same. Had someone offered to buy from him for a fortune the privilege of playing with the boy, of going on picnics and fishing trips and outings, and being with him a part of every day, he would have refused the proposition without giving it a second thought.

Yet that is exactly the bargain those men made, and which many men are still making. They are coining their lives into fortunes and automobile factories and great industries, but their boys are growing up as they may. These men probably will succeed in business; but they will be failures as fathers. To me it seems that a little less industry and a little more comradeship with the boy is more desirable.

Not so much of me in the bank, and more of me and of my best in the lad, is what I should like to have to show at the end of my career.

To be the father of a great son is what I should call success.... This is what I conceive my job to be.[16]

These words are as applicable today as when they were written.

"Lord, who may go and find refuge and shelter in your tabernacle up on your holy hill?" (Psalms 15:1, TLB).

Have you ever seen someone who appears to "have it made" and wished you were him or her? We look at people who have money, position, security, fame, and wonder, "Why them? Why not me? I've got what it takes. They just lucked out." The only problem is... we tend to see their "up" times and not the downs. Their life could be an elevator ride just like yours. A lot of men have ridden the elevator of life... like David, the writer of many of the psalms as well as a man "after God's own heart." Think about his life for a moment.

At one point he was the classic example of a gladiator as he stood up to the giant Goliath and gave him a major migraine. But he also covered up two major sins—murder and adultery. A king rewarded him for his military exploits by giving him his daughter to marry. Later on she ridiculed and belittled him in front of his friends as his marriage crumbled.

David experienced the delight of becoming a parent but also the devastation of having a baby die. To make matters worse, he faced a corporate takeover attempt—not by rivals, but by two of his grown children who tried to topple his kingdom and kill him. He had a close friendship with a man who stood up for David at the risk of his life, but other friends who dropped him when he needed them most. His employer tried to make him a wall ornament with a spear—not once but twice. He was hunted like a common criminal in the wilderness.

He stepped from the up elevator to the down elevator again and again.

Yet no matter how down he was, no matter how desperate he was, no matter how devastated and discouraged he was, he never lost his inner core of strength. His source of strength was not himself and his abilities. It was God. David's repeated response, in spite of what was going down, was, "Yet will I trust you."[17]

MARCH 26

"There is no fear in love. But perfect love drives out fear, because fear has to do with punishment. The one who fears is not made perfect in love. We love because he first loved us" (1 John 4:18-19).

Have you ever tried to control a cat? It's a losing battle. There's just no way to accomplish that feat. Cats have incorrigible character disorders!

Some men don't seem to get the message about control. They can't control everything, but they keep trying. Why? Because they must be in control of every aspect of their lives. They push, pull, persuade, manipulate, and withdraw. Yes, withdraw. Silence and withdrawal are great ways to control others.

What is it that prompts this lifestyle? *Control is a camouflage for fear.* Who wants to be afraid or even admit that you are? Not me. Not you. Fear makes you feel vulnerable. If others knew you were afraid they would take advantage of you. So be the opposite and hide your fear by going on the offensive.

Control is a cover-up for insecurity. A secure man doesn't need to always be in control. He can defer to others, ask their advice, be comfortable when someone else leads. To feel safe we go overboard by trying to control everything and everyone. There's an emptiness within us when we're insecure, but we're like a bucket with a hole in it. We can never get filled up enough, but we keep trying through control.

Control is also a cover-up for low self-esteem. When we feel down on ourselves, worthless, lacking, we don't want others to know about it. And we may even blame them for helping to create the problem. What better way to overcome this than by making others pay through control? But you know, we're fooling ourselves. Control never fulfills, it never solves the basic problem. It simply perpetuates it. It never draws others closer, rather, it pushes them away.

Give God the reins of your life. Let him control you. When God is in control of your life, you'll be amazed at how much better your relationships with others will be.

"'Come, follow me,' Jesus said, 'and I will make you fishers of men'" (Matthew 4:19).

"I have absolute confidence in you. I believe you have the ability and the wisdom to do what I'm asking you to do. Go for it!" Great words of encouragement, aren't they? Well, this is a statement made to every believer by Jesus. He is saying, "Tell others about me. You can do it."

Many Christians hesitate, however. It's a bit scary to tell others about Christ. But there are three "I will" statements in Scripture that can give us courage.

"*I will make you fishers of men.*" Luke 5:10 says, "Do not be afraid. From now on you will catch men" (NKJV). The Aramaic word for *catch* means "to take alive." This passage defines our call to become fishermen—of people—and tells us that Christ will help us do that. But what will I say? you ask. That brings us to the second "I will."

"*I will give you a mouth and wisdom.*" Luke 21:13-15 tells us that God will give us the words when we need them. "It will turn out for you as an occasion for testimony. Therefore, settle it in your hearts not to meditate beforehand on what you will answer, for I will give you a mouth and wisdom which all your adversaries will not be able to contradict or resist." Isn't that some promise! You don't have to struggle to assemble a bunch of pat phrases ahead of time. Ask him for both opportunities as well as the words to say and believe that he will give them.

The third "I will" is a word of encouragement and alarm. "Whoever acknowledges me before men, *I will also acknowledge him before my Father* in heaven. But whoever disowns me before men, *I will disown him before my Father* in heaven" (Mt 10:32-33).

Jesus doesn't want us to be silent about him. Being silent is just as much a form of denial as Peter's spoken words "I do not know him." The more we confess him to others, the more he attests to the fact that we belong to him.

He empowers us to share and then proclaims we are his. He has confidence in us. When you think about it, doesn't that make it a whole lot easier to share your faith?[18]

MARCH 28

"There is a time for everything, and a season for every activity under heaven." (Ecclesiastes 3:1).

You're probably quite conscious of time. Most of us are. Our lives are regulated by it. When you get up, eat, begin work, leave for church... it's all regulated by time. Some of us control it and others are controlled by it.

What would it be like to live in a society where there was no such thing as time? No seconds, minutes, or hours. You wouldn't have to keep checking your wrist to see what time it was. Unfortunately, this wouldn't work. We'd have chaos. And we'd use the stars and the sun to create some other time framework.

Do you struggle with time? You know, do you usually run late? Do you feel your stomach muscles tighten up when you're running behind? Or does irritation creep in when your wife keeps you waiting for twenty minutes?

There are a few things to remember about time.

Time is limited. You have 1,440 minutes a day—no more, no less. Every day is the same. No twenty-three hour days or twenty-five, only twenty-four.

Once you use time, it's gone. Forever. There's no retrieval system.

Time needs to be used wisely. As one man put it, "The great use of life is to spend it for something that will outlast it."[19]

How do you use your time? Wait a minute. Let's correct that. It's not our time. It's God's. He's given it to us. So how are you using God's time?

"Be kind and compassionate to one another, forgiving each other, just as in Christ God forgave you" (Ephesians 4:32).

What makes a marriage work today? Affection is a key component.

Being consistently affectionate—and not just at those times when one is interested in sex—is a must in a marriage. Sometimes nothing is shared verbally. It can be sitting side by side and touching gently or moving close enough that you barely touch while you watch the sun dipping over a mountain with reddish clouds capturing your attention. It could be reaching out and holding hands in public. It can be doing something thoughtful, unrequested and noticed only by your wife.

Affection is demonstrated in many ways and displays. Years ago I heard the story of a couple who had been invited to a potluck dinner. The wife was not known for her cooking ability, but she decided to make a custard pie. As they drove to the dinner, they knew they were in trouble for they smelled the scorched crust. Then when they turned a corner, the contents of the pie shifted dramatically from one side of the pie shell to the other. He could see her anxiety rising by the moment.

When they arrived, they placed the pie on the dessert table. The guests were serving themselves salad and then went back for the main course. Just before they could move on to the desserts, the husband marched up to the table, looked over the number of homemade desserts and snatched up his wife's pie. As others looked at him, he announced, "There are so many desserts here and my wife so rarely makes my favorite dessert, I'm claiming this for myself. I ate light on all the other courses so now I can be a glutton."

And a glutton he was. Later his wife said, "He sat by the door eating what he could, mushing up the rest so no one else would bug him for a piece, and slipping chunks to the hosts' Rottweiler when no one was looking. He saw me looking at him and gave me a big wink. What he did made my evening. My husband, who doesn't always say much, communicated more love with what he did than with what any words could ever say."[20]

Are you this kind of man?

"How long, O Lord? Will you forget me forever? How long will you hide your face from me?" (Psalms 13:1).

There are times when we have the same response as the psalmist. We feel forgotten because of the way our lives are going, especially when we fall flat on our faces.

Have you ever fallen flat on your face? Literally? You're walking down some stairs and miss the last step or trip over a threshold you didn't see and—splat! You're on your face. This happens to some people more publicly than to others. I think of the Olympic competitions in speed skating and track. A few years back the US runner Mary Decker had trained for years to get to the Olympics, but she fell during the competition. It's one thing to fall when you're by yourself, but it's a little different when you're in front of 60,000 people in the stands and over 45 million on TV. Years of training and one slip spelled defeat. There is agony in defeat. It hurts. We lose face. Just think of all the candidates who run for office and lose.[21]

Perhaps you've fallen flat on your face in a figurative way. You feel defeated. But God is in the business of raising men from the ashes of defeat. He gives us more than one chance. Peter Drucker has helped numerous men and companies to rise up again from apparent failure. Here is what he suggests after you fall down.

• Watch what you focus on. Pick the future rather than the past.

• Instead of concentrating on the problems, go after opportunities.

• Choose your own direction.

• Aim for something that's going to make a difference.

Perhaps the answer to defeat (and to the psalmist's question) is found in this passage: "How precious it is, Lord, to realize that you are thinking about me constantly! I can't even count how many times a day your thoughts turn towards me. And when I waken in the morning, you are still thinking of me!" (Ps 139:17-18, TLB).[22]

"The Lord God took the man and put him in the Garden of Eden to work it and take care of it" (Genesis 2:15).

The term *junkie* has come to be associated with drug users or people addicted to a substance. They allow the substance not only to dominate their life, but to give them a high, a feeling of euphoria. Many men today are work junkies. They use work for a "rush" of feeling, for their sole source of identity, for determining their sense of adequacy. They've taken something God gave as a blessing to men before the Fall and distorted it.

What about you? What part does work play in your life? Perhaps these questions can help you evaluate the place of work in your life.

Do you spend a lot of time thinking about the satisfaction you're receiving from your job, or what you wish would happen?

Can you articulate clearly what you need out of your job compared to what you want from your job?

In what way is your job furthering the kingdom of God here on earth? If your job were taken away from you for the next six months, how would you feel about yourself?

If someone asked you to explain how you experience God's pleasure in your work, what would you say?

Remember Eric Liddell in the Oscar-winning movie, *Chariots of Fire?* Everything Liddell did was for the glory of God. His sister felt he was neglecting his calling as a missionary to China, and one day she was upset with him because he missed a missions meeting. Eric said to her, "Jennie, you've got to understand. I believe God made me for a purpose—for China. But he also made me fast! And when I run, I feel his pleasure."

Can you say that about what you do?

"And whatever you do, whether in word or deed, do it all in the name of the Lord Jesus, giving thanks to God the Father through him" (Colossians 3:17).

"**I** almost made it. Not quite, but almost."

"I'm almost finished."

"I was just a bit behind but it should be good enough—for now." Some people live by the "almost" creed. They never quite get in line with the program. They're just a step behind everyone else.

It's easy to do this with our Christian walk. "I almost lived for the Lord today" or "I was almost a loving husband this weekend" or "I almost made it to church Sunday, but you know, we got home late Saturday night after water skiing all day and, well, you know how it goes." We become proficient at creating and using excuses. In short, we become "almost Christians." As Tim Hansel puts it,

> What would [it] have been like if Jesus had done the same thing? What if God had almost revealed himself in Jesus Christ? What if Christ were almost born and almost lived and almost died? What if he would have said, "Ask and it will almost be given you; seek and you will almost find; knock and it will almost be opened to you?" What if he would have said, "Come to me, all who labor and are heavy-laden, and I will almost give you rest?" And what if Jesus had told his disciples, "For whoever would save his life will lose it, and whosoever loses his life for my sake will almost find it?"[1]

Are you living your life as an "almost disciple"? It's easy to do, especially in our prayer life. We "almost" believe but not enough to live by faith. *Almost*—just a simple word when it stands by itself. But put it with our faith and, well, it just doesn't belong there. It belongs with incompleteness. The life and work of Jesus were complete, definite, and thorough. And that means the benefits of his life, death, and resurrection for you are complete—not "almost."

"Come, follow me," Jesus said (Mark 1:17).

Years ago Tim Hansel wrote some thoughts that challenge your ideas about what it means to follow Christ.

When God chose to reveal himself uniquely, he did it through a person, through a lifestyle—because he knew then, as now, that what we are is far more potent than what we say. Two thousand years ago God declared unambiguously in the life of Jesus Christ that human flesh is a good conductor of divine electricity—and, as far as I understand, he hasn't changed his mind.

The great problem with Jesus' message is not that it cannot be understood, but that it can. The difficulty is not what translation we should read, but whether or not we can translate what we know into a lifestyle.

Almost Christianity will reveal itself in countless subtle ways. I know many who claim that "with Christ *all* things are possible"—except to help them lose weight. I know those who extol the benefits of quiet time—but don't have enough time for contemplation themselves. Others lecture on the resurrection—and try to do everything on their own power. I know people who give sermons on the Lordship of Christ—but who can't slow down, because they think the world would collapse without their activities. Some people applaud the security we have in Christ—but are unwilling to take any chances. And still others glorify the freedom that is ours—but are still enslaved to their work.

It is merely my contention that we are living in an age, not unlike other ages, that demands first of all a deep, quality relationship with Jesus Christ. This era's pace of life has changed so radically that it demands we take a solid look at our lifestyles, including both work and leisure. We cannot afford to simply try to keep up with the new pace. But we must constantly remind ourselves that we are a part of the permanent, and that we are called to be holy, which means to be different and to have a distinct identity in Christ.[2]

"Unless the Lord builds the house, its builders labor in vain. Unless the Lord watches over the city, the watchmen stand guard in vain" (Psalms 127:1).

Work! Work! Work! Now and then you meet someone who reminds you of a hamster frantically running around inside the wheel in its cage. For some reason they believe that unless you live life in a frantic frenzy you're wasting time. *Hurry* is their byword. But why shouldn't it be? Our society is fast-paced. Everything in our society has to be instant: instant success, instant happiness, instant sex. Computer technology is changing so fast you just get your new system up and it's outdated.

Sometimes we Christians fall into the same trap. We become frantic in wanting our Christian life or our church to be perfect and complete. Ever met a Christian workaholic? They never stop, and through guilt and the misuse of Scripture they try to get you to hop on their frantic treadmill.

It's not very relaxing or enjoyable to be around frantic people, even if they are Christians. We weren't called to live like this. Tim Hansel puts it well:

> We are called to be faithful, not frantic. If we are to meet the challenges of today, there must be integrity between our words and our lives, and more reliance on the source of our purpose.

> "Unless the Lord builds the house, those who build it labor in vain.
> Unless the Lord watches over the city, the watchman stays awake in vain.
> It is in vain that you rise up early and go late to rest,
> eating the bread of anxious toil; for he gives to his beloved sleep."
>
> **Psalms 127:1-2**

Almost Christianity reveals itself in feverish work, excessive hurry, and exhaustion. I believe that the Enemy has done an effective job of convincing us that unless a person is worn to a frazzle, running here and there, he or she cannot possibly be a dedicated, sacrificing, spiritual Christian. Perhaps the Seven Deadly Sins have recruited another member—Overwork.

We need to remember that our strength lies not in hurried efforts and ceaseless long hours, but in our quietness and confidence.

The world today says, "Enough is not enough."

Christ answers softly, "Enough is enough."[3]

APRIL 4

"Rejoice with those who rejoice; mourn with those who mourn" *(Romans 12:15).*

You may not agree with what's written here. If not, good! That means you're thinking. Here it is. *Men and women tend to handle their losses differently.* Let's see if you fit the pattern.

The difference is that women talk their way through things and men think their way through things. Women lighten their load by sharing the weight. They talk about it with somebody. It stands to reason that women are going to spend more time with other people when they have something important to deal with.

Men, thinking alone, never really get at what is troubling them because they're not talking, not explaining, not asking questions, not using someone else to figure out their own feelings. Of course, they can't do that unless they are going to fully share all of what they are thinking, and men just don't do that with their friends. We men tend to think it's the manly thing to carry all the weight ourselves.

Well, what do you think? Is this you? Are you comfortable with the way you respond to loss?

We as men face another problem. Not too many people bother to really ask how we're feeling. And often when we tell them, they don't know how to handle it. So our silence is reinforced.

Years ago, I used to wonder if I should bring up my feelings about a newly experienced loss I felt over Matthew, my retarded son. But I learned to just come out with it, which helped both my wife, Joyce, and me.

Few people over the years ever asked how I felt when they learned our son was mentally retarded. Fortunately, when Matthew died, people asked me about my feelings as much as they did Joyce.

I've made the leap from silence to sharing. And you know what? I feel, yes, I feel a whole lot better. So will you.

APRIL 5

"Two men went up to the temple to pray, one a Pharisee and the other a tax collector. The Pharisee stood and prayed about himself: 'God, I thank you that I am not like other men—robbers, evildoers, adulterers—or even like this tax collector. I fast twice a week and give a tenth of all I get.' But the tax collector stood at a distance. He would not even look up to heaven, but beat his breast and said, 'God, have mercy on me, a sinner.' I tell you that this man, rather than the other, went home justified before God. For everyone who exalts himself will be humbled, and he who humbles himself will be exalted" (Luke 18:10-14).

There's a lesson here for us. Two men were praying. One was praying to God. The other? Who was he praying to? It sounded more like he was having a dialogue with himself. He wasn't dependent upon God, he was dependent upon himself. That's dangerous. God is deaf toward those prayers. Dr. Lloyd Ogilvie has quite an insight on these two men.

God does not hear a comparative prayer. The Pharisee took the wrong measurements, comparing himself with the tax collector. He was looking down on another human being rather than up to God. He grasped an opportunity to lift himself up by putting another down. But our status with God is not based on being better than others. We are to be all that God has gifted us to be. God has given us the only acceptable basis of comparison: Jesus Christ.

God does not hear the prayer that is based merely on externals. The Pharisee's prayer was built on the unstable foundation of *what he had done*, not *what he was*. Both what he did and abstained from doing were on the surface. He had accomplished it all himself. He had no dependence on God for his impeccable life.

Jesus wants us to understand how pride twists and distorts our capacity for self-scrutiny. Our minds were meant to be truth-gathering computers. But prayers such as that of the Pharisee make us ignore reality and forget things that are beneath the surface agenda of our conscious perceptions. Prayers such as this delude us into thinking that we can be right with God because of our own accomplishments and goodness.

The purpose of prayer is to see things as they are: ourselves as we really are, and God as He has revealed Himself to be. God wants us to come to grips with the true person inside us—our hopes and dreams, failures and sins, missed opportunities and potential.[4]

*"Young men, in the same way be submissive to those who are older.
All of you, clothe yourselves with humility toward one another,
because, 'God opposes the proud but gives grace to the humble.'
Humble yourselves, therefore under God's mighty hand, that he
may lift you up in due time. Cast all your anxiety on him because
he cares for you" (1 Peter 5:5-7).*

Most of us want to be successful. In fact, all men want to succeed
in some way. Why not? It's much better than tasting the fruits
of failure. Why do we work? Why do we play? Why do we compete?
After all, we do live in a success-saturated society. There are books,
classes, videos, cassettes, and seminars all promising to teach us some
new approach that will enable us to taste success.

The problem with success is the cost. Who counts it in advance?
The Executive Digest said, "The trouble with success is the formula is
the same as the one for a nervous breakdown." That's sobering,
uncomfortable, and too often true.

There's a way to gain success other than by pushing, striving, pro-
moting, and being slick and aggressive. It's a simple way. It's God's
way. You read it in the passage above. It involves authority, attitude,
and anxiety. Read it again. First of all, submit yourself to those who
know more than you. Listen to their advice, their wisdom, the lessons
they've learned, their guidance. Find a mentor and let this man help
shape your life.

Next, be humble, especially before God. Let him bring the success
to you in his way and in his time. It will happen. We can choose to pull
strings and manipulate or we can let God work. A humble attitude
doesn't offend or repulse other people, but attracts them because you
are different.

Finally, take the anxieties that will definitely come into your life and
throw them, cast them, relinquish them to God. Let him deal with
them.

Success is there waiting for you. So is God's plan. They do go hand
in hand![5]

APRIL 7

"When he had said this, Jesus called in a loud voice, 'Lazarus, come out!' The dead man came out, his hands and feet wrapped with strips of linen, and a cloth around his face. Jesus said to them, 'Take off the grave clothes and let him go'" (John 11:43-44).

Judson Edwards wrote a fascinating statement about a play, *Laughing with Lazarus*. Consider his words:

Eugene O'Neill's play *Laughing with Lazarus* begins with Jesus' raising of Lazarus from the dead and deals with the change this miracle makes in Lazarus' life. After he has been raised, Lazarus becomes fearless. Try as they might, the Jewish leaders cannot stifle his gladness. Laughter is his trademark, and everywhere he goes people are warmed and enlivened by his presence. Because he has learned that even the Final Enemy cannot defeat him, Lazarus is eternally infected with joy. It's a scenario we uptight Christians would do well to consider.

Sheer fiction you say? A figment of the playwright's imagination? Not really—for we are like Lazarus! We are the people who have been raised to walk in newness of life. We are the ones who insist that the hope of the resurrection affects us profoundly the moment we choose Jesus. Every last one of us who claims to be a Christian has an inheritance, the same joy Lazarus experienced after his miracle at Bethany. The same fearlessness. The same contagious freedom.

The only bucket of water hanging over the fire is our unbelief. At heart, you see, we are unbelievers. We refuse to accept all of the incredible implications of Calvary. We believe the lie that God is not for us. Though the prison door stands wide open, we huddle in self-imposed chains and refuse to claim our liberty. Unlike Lazarus, we refuse to leave the tomb. We cannot get our heart to believe that laughter is our birthright.

But, thank God, it is never too late! The door stands eternally open. And our joy and peace are the surest indicators we have walked through it.

So, if you want to know just how Christian you really are, don't listen to your creeds or your prayers. They come from your head and reflect your mind. Listen, instead, to your laughter. It comes from your soul and reflects your heart. Your laughter will tell you unfailingly of your faith in God.[6]

"But the fruit of the Spirit is love, joy, peace, patience, kindness, goodness, faithfulness" (Galatians 5:22).

Do you understand what joy is? Really understand? Most people don't. And yet, as followers of Christ it is one of our main benefits. It's available to all of us.

Some people think joy is a good feeling. But that's not joy.

To some joy comes from what happens to them. That's not joy, that's happiness. Happiness is based on circumstances that go our way. Joy is a choice, a sense of gladness. Here are some definitions of joy for you to consider.

"Joy does not depend on outer circumstances but on the reality of God."[7]

Joy is "believing the reasons to be excited about life are greater than the reasons to get discouraged and negative."[8]

> Joy at its highest meaning calls for the vertical, or spiritual, dimension that translates superficial happiness, productive adjustment, and self-help techniques into an encounter with God. Joy becomes the power of God's grace, the process of God's Spirit, and the presence of God's nature in our lives.
>
> In the biblical sense, joy then becomes a spiritual balance between expectations and achievements—the ability to approach problems objectively by accepting things as they are and working toward solution and adjustment. Assuming this stance, joy is a sense of imperturbable gladness that sings when rejected, praises when persecuted, and stands when attacked. (See Acts 16:25; Acts 5:41; 2 Chronicles 20:14-30.)
>
> It is seeking first the kingdom of God and His righteousness. It is knowing full well that all things we need—and can realistically handle—will be given to us as we live in the knowledge that God loves us.[9]

Do these definitions fit your beliefs about joy? Perhaps not. But when you begin to live your life based on this perspective of joy, things happen—good things.

"But we preach Christ crucified, to the Jews a stumbling block and to the Greeks foolishness, but to those who are called, both Jews and Greeks, Christ the power of God and the wisdom of God" (1 Corinthians 1:23-24, NKJV).

Power failure—the lights dim and then go out. The sounds of machinery, the refrigerator, or air conditioners come to a halt. An eerie silence hangs in the air. Usually it happens when there's an overload of usage by those tapping into the power source. It could be a short in the system or a transformer that wore out. Sometimes it's just a simple thing such as tripping over a cord and unplugging it from the wall socket. But no matter what the cause, a power outage is no fun. If it goes on for an extended time, food rots in the refrigerator, heat can rise along with tempers—your life is totally thrown off course.

Consider these two important questions. First, who's your power source? Is it you? Your spouse? Your friends? The Lord? Some of us go through life connected to a real power source and others run their lives on a portable battery pack of their own doing. And naturally they run out of juice after awhile. But when your source is the Lord, there's never any lack of potential power.

In Acts 2:32-33 we read, "God has raised this Jesus to life, and we are all witnesses of the fact. Exalted to the right hand of God, he has received from the Father the promised Holy Spirit and has poured out what you now see and hear."

He gives us the gift of power—the Holy Spirit.

But the second question is this: Are you plugged in? An electric saw won't work by running the blade back and forth by hand over wood. It's got to be connected.

We're connected when we pray, listen, and read the Word. Busy? Yes, we all are. We can pray lying down, sitting, standing, walking, or driving. We can read at any time just for a minute at a time. Those who begin their day with Jesus realize they are connected to a power source that won't overload or run out. That's a pretty good source.[10]

"You are awesome, O God, in your sanctuary; the God of Israel, whose power is in the skies" (Psalms 68:34-35).

Power—what a word! What a feeling! We come into the world looking for power. One of our first experiences in life is a power struggle between ourselves and our parents. One of our first words, if not *the* first one, is *no!* No! No! No! Why should we be surprised at that? The first couple here on earth engaged in a power struggle with God. God created us with free will—the ability to choose. Well, Adam did choose. And he messed it up for the rest of us because of his failure to follow God's way.

We equate power with security and control. We hear about power brokers. Books are written in the leadership arena telling you how to gain power, retain power, and use power. In the Christian world we even have a group of men called the Power Team, hunks with the strength of Hercules who go around bursting chains strapped to their bodies and giving their testimonies. The feeling of power can be addictive. It gives an adrenaline rush.

Listen to the ads that appeal to our desire for power. We buy into whatever they're selling because they promise to give us power.

The misuse of power in marriage usually manifests itself as domination. In fact, some men demand that their wives be submissive to them because Scripture says they're supposed to do this. How sad. Any time a man demands submission, he's lost it. He's failed. Instead of bringing up what his wife is supposed to do, all a man really needs to do is to follow God's instructions for *him*—love his wife as Christ loves the Church. Power isn't the problem unless you make it your god. Power isn't the problem unless you misuse it.

David gives perspective to this issue.

It is God who arms me with strength and makes my way perfect.

Psalms 18:32

The Lord is my light and my salvation—whom shall I fear? The Lord is the stronghold of my life—of whom shall I be afraid? **Psalms 27:1**

APRIL 11

"When Jesus had finished saying these things, the crowds were amazed at his teaching, because he taught as one who had authority, and not as their teachers of the law" (Matthew 7:28-29).

Tension. We don't enjoy it and we don't want it. We try our best to get rid of it. But then you go and become a Christian. You invite Jesus Christ into your life as Lord and Savior and set out to live for him, and what do you get? Tension. Or at least you should.

When Jesus taught the people in Matthew 5-7 he spoke out directly against the religious leaders of his day. In fact, in Matthew 6:8 he said, "Therefore, do not be like them"—don't be like the hypocrites. And therein lies the tension. The reason you will have tension if you follow Jesus is simple. We live in a society that has a multitude of different beliefs and values, most of them contrary to the teaching of Scripture. You're pressured at work, at play, and even in the family to fit in with the world. But Jesus is asking you to be a misfit. He's calling you to be different to the extent that others will notice the difference. And this will make them uncomfortable.

Take time to read Matthew 5:21-44 where Jesus says repeatedly, "You have heard... but I say to you..." It's the call not to fit in. It's the call to be different. It's the call that will increase the tension in your life. But it's a great calling. Ask yourself,

- "How do I fit in where it would be best not to fit in?"
- "In what way am I obviously different so it draws others to Jesus?"
- "In what way does God want me to be different this week?"

When God calls you to be different it's a good calling.

APRIL 12

"In the morning, O Lord, consider my sighing" (Psalms 5:3).

A re you a morning person, or are you married to one? You know what they're like. They wake up bright-eyed and bushy-tailed at 6:00 A.M. (or earlier). They're ready to face the day and can't wait to start talking, even before coffee!

Some of us are just not wired that well for morning. You may feel the day ought to begin at 10:00 A.M., not 6:00! Sometimes people who are early-morning "alerts" are insensitive to other people and need to heed the admonition of Proverbs: "If you shout a pleasant greeting to a friend too early in the morning, he will count it as a curse!" (27:14, TLB).

Whether you fit the 6:00 A.M. crew or the 10:00 A.M., keep in mind there is something good that can come out of the morning: time alone with God. That's what David did in the above psalm. And it's mentioned other times in Scripture as well.

"Evening, morning, and noon I cry out in distress, and he hears my voice" (Ps 55:17).

"But I cry to you for help, O Lord; in the morning my prayer comes before you" (Ps 88:13).

"Because of the Lord's great love we are not consumed, for his compassions never fail. They are new every morning; great is your faithfulness" (Lam 3:22-23).

Is there a better way to begin your day? Not really. If you're down and the day looks dim and dreary, you can make a choice to look up. You'll be amazed at what you see!

APRIL 13

"My tears have been my food day and night, while men say to me all day long, 'Where is your God?'" (Psalms 42:3).

"I'm at a loss for words." We will all say this sometime when we've heard some unbelievably shocking news. Our brains go into reverse, and we become tongue-tied. What do you say? What can you say? Sometimes nothing, nothing at all. It's probably good that your body and mind helped you at that time by shutting down and turning off. When we don't know what to say and we go ahead and say something anyway, it's usually the wrong thing. These are the occasions when we usually open mouth and insert foot.

When you hear tragic news from someone close to you or even experience a devastating loss yourself, sometimes there are no words to express the hurt and anguish. But when our words fail, there is something else that will express what we are experiencing even better—tears.

Tears are God's gift to all of us—men and women—to release our feelings. When Jesus arrived in Bethany following the death of Lazarus, he wept (see John 11:35). Ken Gire describes the scene beautifully in *Incredible Moments with the Savior.*

> On our way to Lazarus' tomb we stumble on still another question. Jesus approaches the gravesite with the full assurance that he will raise his friend from the dead. Why then does the sight of the tomb trouble him?
>
> Maybe the tomb in the garden is too graphic a reminder of Eden gone to seed. Of Paradise lost. And of the cold, dark tomb he would have to enter to regain it.
>
> In any case, it is remarkable that *our* plight could trouble *his* spirit; that *our* pain could summon *his* tears.
>
> The raising of Lazarus is the most daring and dramatic of all the Savior's healings. He courageously went into a den where hostility rages against him to snatch a friend from the jaws of death.
>
> It was an incredible moment.
>
> It revealed that Jesus was who he said he was—the resurrection and the life. But it revealed something else.
>
> The tears of God.
>
> And who's to say which is more incredible—a man who raises the dead...or a God who weeps?[11]

"Now when he saw the crowds, he went up on a mountainside and sat down. His disciples came to him, and he began to teach them, saying: Blessed are the poor in spirit, for theirs is the kingdom of heaven" (Matthew 5:1-3).

Have you ever wondered what would happen if Jesus were here today and gave the Sermon on the Mount in person? Picture him in the L.A. Coliseum or Mile High Stadium in Denver or the Super Dome with thousands of people waiting for him to teach. And teach he does. He says: "Blessed are the poor in spirit." What? That's not what we're taught to be in our society. You're right. We're not. That's okay. Many people have tried it society's way. It won't hurt to try it this way. *The Living Bible* spells it out in a practical way: "Humble men are very fortunate." Why? Because "the kingdom of heaven is given to them."

Jesus is asking every believer to be humble. But you can't be strong-willed if you plan to be humble. You can't promote yourself and call attention to your achievements if you're humble. You can't carry around your box score to show everyone how you've done if you're humble. You can't rely upon yourself if you're humble.

Poor in spirit also means that we admit we are lacking spiritually. We have a condition known as spiritual poverty. When we admit this and acknowledge our need of God, we find lasting, permanent happiness. When you put all of your trust in God, the kingdom of heaven is yours. Do you hear anyone else making such an offer?

"Now when he saw the crowds, he went up on a mountainside and sat down. His disciples came to him, and he began to teach them, saying,... 'Blessed are those who mourn, for they will be comforted'" (Matthew 5:1-2, 4)

"How can someone be blessed when they mourn? Sitting at a graveside with a long face hurts. It's the pits. What in the world was Jesus talking about anyway? It's one thing to be different, but I'm not going to go around in sackcloth and ashes!"

That's what one man thought this passage meant. But it's much more than that. *Mourn* is a heavy word. When you think of someone mourning, you think of an aching heart or a mind torn apart with anguish. There is a lot to mourn over in life because life is full of losses. The people who don't mourn are the ones who end up with problems. We mourn over our losses and the losses of others. We also mourn over the state of affairs of our country and the world.

Mourn also includes the idea of caring for the needs and hurts of others. We are called to weep with those who weep. Perhaps one way of translating this passage is, "You are fortunate when your heart is broken by all the suffering you see around you and by your own sinful condition. Out of this sorrow you will discover the fullness of life and the joy which comes from God."

So what have you mourned for recently? What do you need to mourn for? In what way can your compassion be used to minister to a hurting person? When you can truly mourn you will receive the benefits of this passage.

APRIL 16

"The earnest (heartfelt, continued) prayer of a righteous man makes tremendous power available—dynamic in its working" *(James 5:16b, AMP).*

O h God, I'm full of questions about myself today. I thank you in advance for hearing my confusion and my concern. I ask for wisdom and clarity as I talk with you about what is on my mind and heart. Lord, I just want to talk out loud with you and ask you:

Have I been living in the way you want me to live to fulfill the reason that I'm here? Have I been seeing the ways that you want me to serve you and others? Have I done anything that defeats my calling myself a Christian? Have I been lazy or neglectful or passive in any way that would frustrate others and cause them difficulty in their life? Have I failed you and those I love by the use of my thought life? Have I been honest in my work, and given my full energy and dedication to my employer? Have I cheated my family in any way by bringing home my work either in my briefcase or my mind? Have I been a peacemaker at home or work, or have I been more of a pain in the neck? Have I learned the fine art of rationalizing so well that I fail to see my faults and stagnation, stifling growth and change? Have I been rude to those I love rather than being loving?

Lord, these are hard questions for me to ask. Help me to answer honestly, to hear your clear answers, and then to be open to your Holy Spirit's work in me.

In Jesus' name,
Amen.

"My son, if you accept my words and store up my commands within you, turning your ear to wisdom and applying your heart to understanding, and if you call out for insight and cry aloud for understanding, and if you look for it as for silver and search for it as for hidden treasure, then you will understand the fear of the LORD and find the knowledge of God" (Proverbs 2:1-5).

Choices—your life is full of them. Have you ever read the entire Book of Proverbs? Have you studied its teachings in depth? If you do, it will help you handle the stresses and strains of everyday life because it talks about making choices.

Look again at the passage above. Notice the "ifs" and the "thens." An "If... then" structure in a sentence (Groan! Back to basic English class) is a conditional clause. And that's just what it means. The outcome depends on the person doing or taking certain steps. The result is not guaranteed. You have to choose what it says to do if you want the results. And choosing means you also accept the responsibility for your choice.

The way you and I turn out as adults is our choice. It's kind of ridiculous to see a forty-year-old man blaming his parents for the way he is now.

As you read through Proverbs, note your options. You can choose to be wise or you can act the fool. You can be angry or calm, be liked or disliked, be lazy or productive, tear down others or be an encourager, be righteous or evil, bring honor to your parents or disgrace, be pure or sleep around.

It's old wisdom that has never grown old. It changes lives. It could change yours.

"For where your treasure is, there your heart will be also" (Matthew 6:21).

Purity. Ethics. Commitments. Standards. Where do these begin? Scripture says they begin in our hearts. Consider some strong statements about this from Dr. Gary Oliver.

> Moral and ethical purity start in the heart. Only the passionate love of purity can save a person from impurity. That's why Proverbs tells us, "Above all else, guard your affections. For they influence everything else in your life." It goes on to warn us, "Spurn the careless kiss of a prostitute. Stay far from her. Look straight ahead; don't even turn your head to look. Watch your step. Stick to the path and be safe. Don't sidetrack; pull back your foot from danger" (Prv 4:23-27, TLB).
>
> Are there any prostitutes in your life? Hear me out before you answer. When most people think of a prostitute, they think of someone who sells herself for money. However, a prostitute can be any person, habit, or activity that promises short-term pleasure for a high price, that makes you forget the most important for the least important, that increases your vulnerability.
>
> Let me ask the question a different way. Are there any thoughts, habits, possessions, or activities in your life that are more important to you than God, that make you more vulnerable to compromise and sin? If so, giving in to that is like giving in to the careless kiss of a prostitute. Proverbs warns us to stay as far away from these things as possible.
>
> How do you do that? By looking for and focusing on all the potential pitfalls? No! The only solution is to set your mind on things above, to fix your eyes on Jesus. When Christ met Peter on the seashore after His resurrection, He didn't bawl him out for his lack of faith in denying Him. Three times He asked Peter the simple question, "Do you love Me?" A growing affection for our Lord Jesus Christ is the only antidote for the kind of apathy that leads down the primrose path to compromise.[12]

"This, then, is how you should pray: 'Our Father in heaven, hallowed be your name, your kingdom come, your will be done on earth as it is in heaven. Give us today our daily bread. Forgive us our debts, as we also have forgiven our debtors. And lead us not into temptation, but deliver us from the evil one'" (Matthew 6:9-13).

The Lord's Prayer, or the Disciple's Prayer, as it is also called, is often one of the first passages of Scripture that children memorize. It's one of the few passages of Scripture that many adults know. It's used in church services and either said or sung in unison. But that's not its purpose. That wasn't the reason it was given to the disciples. They didn't ask Jesus for a prayer to memorize or recite each day. They asked him to teach them to pray, and that is exactly what he did. What he gave them was a general pattern for all prayer.

There are six things this prayer teaches us to ask God for. One is that his name be honored. Second, that he bring his kingdom here to earth; third, that he do his will; fourth, that he provide for our daily needs; fifth, that he pardon our sins; and sixth, that he protect us from temptation. Did you catch that sixfold pattern? Read it again. Do your prayers fit this pattern? All of these requests contribute to the ultimate good of prayer—to bring glory to his name.

When you follow this pattern of prayer, remember that you are following Jesus' teaching and he will do whatever you ask in his name. You may want to write out some of your prayers. It's an easy way to develop this pattern of praying. Go ahead. Follow these six steps for prayer.[13]

"Now when he saw the crowds, he went up on a mountainside and sat down. His disciples came to him, and he began to teach them, saying, Blessed are the meek, for they will inherit the earth'" (Matthew 5:1-2, 5).

A mistranslation of this passage is, "Blessed are the wimps, for they shall be doormats and walked on." The word *meek* brings up that image. It's not a favorite word in our culture. A more correct definition of the word is "yieldedness." It's not easy to yield either. Have you ever watched two men approach an intersection with signs saying "yield to oncoming traffic"? Too often neither yields and they end up with fractured fenders. We see yielding as a negative. In reality to yield shows strength and control. It says, "Hey, I don't care what others think. No one has forced me to do this. I'm choosing it."

Yielding can actually put you in the driver's seat in many situations. A number of Bible versions use the word *gentle*. We use this term in many ways. We talk about gentle words. A horse that has been broken and tamed has been "gentled."

Chuck Swindoll offers a great description of what this beatitude means.

Gentleness includes such enviable qualities as having strength under control, being calm and peaceful when surrounded by a heated atmosphere, emitting a soothing effect on those who may be angry or otherwise beside themselves, and possessing tact and gracious courtesy that causes others to retain their self-esteem and dignity. Clearly, it includes a Christlikeness, since the same word is used to describe His own makeup:

"Come to Me, all who are weary and heavy laden, and I will give you rest. Take My yoke upon you, and learn from Me, for I am gentle and humble in heart; and YOU SHALL FIND REST FOR YOUR SOULS" (Mt 11:28-29).[14]

APRIL 21

"Good sense makes a man restrain his anger, and it is his glory to overlook a transgression or an offense" (Proverbs 19:11, AMP).

A nger can be used for either good or bad. Unfortunately, it's often used in a negative way in our families. Look at the Old Testament, for example:

Saul's anger toward David and Jonathan is an illustration of the destructive force of anger.

> And the women responded, as they laughed *and* frolicked, saying Saul has slain thousands, and David his ten thousands. And Saul was very angry, for the saying displeased him. **1 Samuel 18:7-8, AMP**

Jealousy and envy toward David progressed to anger and hatred, and not far behind was action—attempts to take David's life. Later Saul's anger turned toward his own son.

> Then Saul's anger was kindled against Jonathan, and he said to him, "You son of a perverse, rebellious woman, do not I know that you have chosen the son of Jesse to your shame, and to the shame of your mother who bore you?"... But Saul cast his spear at him to smite him, by which Jonathan knew that his father had determined to kill David.
> **1 Samuel 20:30, 33, AMP**

When a person allows himself to be governed by emotion instead of fact, he may react impulsively in ways that are decidedly destructive. Each year in the United States thousands of children are abused physically because a parent's anger got out of control. Many parents and spouses live with overwhelming regrets because of actions made in anger toward other family members.

When you're angry, take the four-step approach:

1. Delay—put Proverbs into practice.

2. Discover the cause—it's usually fear, hurt, or frustration.

3. Say what you're feeling in a calm voice.

4. Let the person know what you want. It works. Really, it does.

"Now when he saw the crowds, he went up on a mountainside and sat down. His disciples came to him, and he began to teach them, saying:... 'Blessed are the merciful, for they will be shown mercy'" (Matthew 5:1-2, 7).

You've seen it in movies and perhaps even in live television trials. It's the courtroom scene and the perpetrator has been convicted. There's only one thing left for him to do: to throw himself on the mercy of the court and hope they'll be lenient.

We have a misconception of what it means to show mercy. We think it's just a matter of showing some kindness to others. Cutting a bit of slack for someone who owes us, giving someone more time to pay off a debt, or giving a little more in the special missions offering to help the poor. This is our idea of being merciful. But that misses the mark.

The original word for mercy is a bit difficult to translate. We do know that it doesn't simply mean to feel sorry for someone in trouble. It's the ability to get inside the other person's skin and see life with their eyes and feel things with their feelings. Mercy will cost you. It's empathy—experiencing with another person what they are going through. You're with them. It means reaching out to others in need to the extent that it costs you. You get involved—that's the key word, *involved*. Listen to God's Word.

> If you have a friend who is in need of food and clothing, and you say to him, "Well, good-bye and God bless you; stay warm and eat hearty," and then don't give him clothes or food, what good does that do?
> **James 2:15-16, TLB**

> But if someone who is supposed to be a Christian has money enough to live well, and sees a brother in need, and won't help him–how can God's love be within him?
> **1 John 3:17, TLB**

Who needs you to get involved in their lives today?

APRIL 23

"Now when he saw the crowds, he went up on a mountainside and sat down. His disciples came to him, and he began to teach them, saying... 'Blessed are the pure in heart, for they will see God'" (Matthew 5: 1-2, 8).

This is a problem verse if we're honest about it. Who has a truly pure heart? How is it possible to have a pure heart? How can you tell if a person's heart is pure? It's not easy. We seem to have an array of masks in our closets that we put on, depending on the occasion. We fool people. We say what we think they want to hear.

Being pure in heart means your motives are clean, uncontaminated, with no corruption. Your motives aren't mixed. It means looking at what we do and trying to discover the purpose. It's having the same attitude, behavior, and speech at home and at work that we display at church. This is a big order. But that's what pure in heart is all about. It's being consistent.

Purity of heart means not wearing a mask. Jesus said,

Settle matters quickly with your adversary who is taking you to court. Do it while you are still with him on the way, or he may hand you over to the judge, and the judge may hand you over to the officer, and you may be thrown into prison. I tell you the truth, you will not get out until you have paid the last penny. You have heard that it was said, "Do not commit adultery." But I tell you that anyone who looks at a woman lustfully has already committed adultery with her in his heart. **Matthew 5:25-28**

No masks—no hidden agendas. Check your motives.

APRIL 24

"Now when he saw the crowds, he went up on a mountainside and sat down. His disciples came to him, and he began to teach them, saying,... 'Blessed are the peacemakers, for they will be called sons of God'" (Matthew 5:1-2, 9).

There are a number of misconceptions about what a peacemaker is. Some think that to be a peacemaker you should:

- avoid all arguments and conflict
- be passive and nonconfrontational
- be easygoing and let others always have their way.

Not quite.

The peace this passage is talking about doesn't happen because of avoidance tactics. Just the opposite. A peacemaker forces problems and settles them. In the last century one of the weapons used in the Old West was a revolver called "The Peacemaker." It served its purpose, but the peacemaking this passage talks about doesn't blow people away!

Look at God's Word and the emphasis on living in peace.

If it is possible, as far as it depends on you, live at peace with everyone.
Romans 12:18

Let us therefore make every effort to do what leads to peace and to mutual edification. **Romans 14:19**

To be a peacemaker you've got to be at peace with yourself. A peacemaker is a person who doesn't add fuel to the fire when there is a conflict. A peacemaker looks for the positive and brings it out. He looks for solution-oriented alternatives. He doesn't bait others to lure them into an argument. He knows how to arbitrate in order to settle disputes.

A peacemaker watches what he says: "Pleasant words are a honeycomb, sweet to the soul and healing to the bones" (Prv 16:24).

Could you be called a peacemaker? Think about it. Where are your peacemaking skills? What skills do you still need to make you a more effective peacemaker?

"Now when he saw the crowds, he went up on a mountainside and sat down. His disciples came to him, and he began to teach them, saying... 'Blessed are those who are persecuted because of righteousness, for theirs is the kingdom of heaven. Blessed are you when people insult you, persecute you and falsely say all kinds of evil against you because of me. Rejoice and be glad, because great is your reward in heaven, for in the same way they persecuted the prophets who were before you'" (Matthew 5:1-2, 10-12).

Persecuted? Today? Not likely. But if not, why not? Many men live their faith like they belong to the Secret Service. No one knows about it.

Being a Christian costs. Being a Christian in the business world today cuts counter to the values of our society. When you take a stand and follow what Scripture says in your work, you may hear:

"Hey, slow down. Don't work so hard. You're making the rest of us look bad."

"Take a two-hour lunch. If you don't the management may get suspicious."

"Everyone around here does it. Don't rock the boat. We've got a good thing going."

"This is convention time. Your wife will never know. These shows will turn you on."

"It's no big deal to pad that expense account. If you don't, how do we explain it?"

You're pressured to be one of the guys, to go along with the flow, to not disrupt the pattern. When you don't just go along, you'll feel the heat.

But that kind of persecution isn't much compared to what the first Christians had to endure. Their faith disrupted their work, their social lives, their home lives, and their families. Many of them were killed for their faith.

We're called to take a faithful, loving stand for our faith—not to be obnoxious about it. A simple statement of our beliefs and a consistent pattern of behavior will get through to others in time. In the meantime, expect to take some flack. The heat will go up. When it does, go back to this passage and read it again. There are some benefits to being persecuted for your faith. Keep those in mind.

APRIL 26

Yes, we're going to talk about money again. We can't afford not to. Most of us have never thought about, let alone developed, a "money lifestyle." We all have four choices regarding that lifestyle. Some choices have better consequences than others.

You can live *above* your means—that's easy. Anyone can do it. We look rich to other people. We accumulate as much as we want in goods... and pay more than we should in high interest rates. We indulge our insecurities with material goods. The problem is, it's never enough. It takes more... and more... and more. Question: How does this lifestyle glorify God?

Living *at* your means is a better choice, but still not a good one. It comes in one hand and goes out the other at the same rate. At least there's not much debt. But there are no savings, either. The focus is still on gathering rather than on planning for the future. Things occupy our thoughts. The problem is, there's not much room left for God. Question: How does this lifestyle glorify God?

Living *within* your means follows the scriptural teaching of being a good steward of what God has entrusted to you. The man who lives within his means thinks about today and the future. But more than that, he looks at how his money can be used for the kingdom of God. Tithing is a part of this man's life, even when he can't afford it. Question: How does this lifestyle glorify God?

Living *below* your means is not a typical choice. It requires unusual self-discipline and a deliberate choice not to move up. The gift of giving rather than acquiring is this man's joy. He simply uses only what's necessary.

So, there you have it.

Which of these four styles describes your life? And... is it by choice?[15]

APRIL 27

"The Lord God said, 'It is not good for the man to be alone. I will make a helper suitable for him.'... Then the Lord God made a woman from the rib he had taken out of the man, and he brought her to the man" (Genesis 2:18, 22).

You've probably had the experience of working long and hard on some project that turned out great. You stand back and say, "That's good. In fact, it's great. Just perfect. I did a good job." That's not pride, it's fact. It's a good feeling to know you did a quality job. You know a little about how God felt when he created the earth.

The first daylight burst forth and he said, "It is good."

Then there was land and sea and he said, "It is good."

When the land produced trees and plants he said, "It is good."

When two great lights were formed he said, "It is good."

When the sea creatures and birds were created he said, "It is good."

When the animals came into being he said, "It is good."

When man was created he said, "It is *not* good... for man to be alone."

Aloneness and isolation—not good. If you're married, you need your wife more than you realize. The greatest hurt in marriage today is to end up feeling like you're a married single. It hurts. It cuts.

Isolation has no place in marriage. It's the first step toward adultery. Couples need intimacy—verbal intimacy. Talking, listening, and sharing is a purpose of marriage. Dr. John Baucom makes an interesting observation about how we've moved away from intimacy:

> With the appearance of the two-bathroom home, Americans forgot how to cooperate. With the appearance of the two-car family, we forgot how to associate, and with the coming of the two-television home, we will forget how to communicate.[16]

If you have been given a special helper, ask her if there are times when she feels lonely and if so, what she would like you to do to help. Whatever she says, just reply with, "Thank you for letting me know. I'll begin to work on that." Your answer will do wonders to cure the loneliness.[17]

"Husbands, love your wives, just as Christ loved the church and gave himself up for her" (Ephesians 5:25).

If you're married, do you pray together as a couple? Perhaps you haven't had the opportunity to experience this yet, but you can learn to do so. It will take a while to develop a comfort level so don't give up. Charles and Martha Shedd have helped thousands of couples with their prayer lives.

We would sit on our rocking love seat. We would take turns telling each other things we'd like to pray about. Then holding hands we would pray each in our own way, silently.

This was the beginning of prayer together that lasted. Naturally, through the years we've learned to pray in every possible way, including aloud. Anytime, anywhere, every position, every setting, in everyday language. Seldom with "thee" or "thou." Plain talk, ordinary conversation. We interrupt, we laugh, we argue, we enjoy. We hurt together, cry together, wonder together. Together we tune our friendship to the Friend of friends.

Do we still pray silently together? Often. Some groanings of the spirit go better in silence.

"I've been feeling anxious lately and I don't know why. Will you listen while I tell you what I can? Then let's pray about the known and unknown in silence."

"This is one of my super days. So good. Yet somehow I can't find words to tell you. Let's thank the Lord together in the quiet."

Negatives, positives, woes, celebrations, shadowy things—all these, all kinds of things we share in prayer. Aloud we share what we can. Without the vocals we share those things not ready yet for words.

Why would this approach have the feel of the real? Almost from the first we knew we'd discovered an authentic new dimension.

In becoming best friends with each other, we were becoming best friends with the Lord.

And the more we sought his friendship, the more we were becoming best friends with each other.[18]

"Let the word of Christ dwell in you richly as you teach and admon-ish one another with all wisdom, and as you sing psalms, hymns and spiritual songs with gratitude in your hearts to God" (Colossians 3:16).

One of the best descriptions of the Bible you will ever find came from an old-time evangelist and baseball player by the name of Billy Sunday. He talked about entering the "Wonderful Temple" of the Bible.

I entered at the portico of Genesis, walked down through the Old Testament art galleries, where pictures of Noah, Abraham, Moses, Joseph, Isaac, Jacob and Daniel hung on the wall. I passed into the music room of Psalms, where the Spirit swept the key-board of nature until it seemed that every reed and pipe in God's great organ responded to the tuneful harp of David, the sweet singer of Israel. I entered the chamber of Ecclesiastes, where the voice of the preacher was heard; and into the conservatory of Sharon, where the Lily of the Valley's sweet-scented spices filled and per-fumed my life. I entered the business office of Proverbs, and then into the observatory room of the Prophets, where I saw telescopes of various sizes, pointed to far-off events, but all concentrated upon the bright and morning star. I entered the audience room of the King of Kings, and caught a vision of His glory from the standpoint of Matthew, Mark, Luke and John, passed into the Acts of the Apostles, where the Holy Spirit was doing His work in the formation of the infant church. Then into the correspondence room, where sat Paul, Peter, James, and John penning their epistles. I stepped into the throne room of Revelation, where towered the glittering peaks, and got a vision of the King sitting upon the throne in all His glory, and I cried:

> *"All hail the power of Jesus' name,*
> *Let angels prostrate fall,*
> *Bring forth the royal diadem,*
> *And crown him Lord of all."*[19]

"Six days you shall labor and do all your work..." (Exodus 20:9).

Are you a workaholic? You know, that person who is a blur as he rushes by, talking on the phone, checking his watch, and grabbing something to eat while running to catch a cab. Hustle and hassle is his life. It's a trap many of us fall into.

Workaholics work hard, but not all hard workers are workaholics. Hard workers work to gain a promotion, to earn more money, or to please someone. Workaholism differs in its approach or attitude toward work. Workaholics think about work when they are not working. **They love working!** They come from all classes, sexes, and occupations, and they all have the same passion—work. Many of them are very happy. The problem is that those around them are often unhappy. Workaholics are rarely at home, and when they are, they do not participate very much.

There are several standard characteristics of workaholics. They are intense, energetic, competitive, and driven. They enjoy what they do. They wake up in the morning and can't wait to get started. They drive themselves and compete with others. Often they compare with others the number of hours per week they work.

Workaholics also have strong self-doubts. You would not suspect this by looking at them, because they cover it well. They suspect they are inadequate, so they work hard to compensate. "The workaholic trades sweat for talent." He thinks the way to overcome these feelings of inadequacy is to do more.

Workaholics prefer work to leisure. There is no holiday or work season for them. Their homes may be a branch office or extension of their profession. Saving time is a goal, and they glance at their watches frequently. They sleep less, and their meals are functional (in other words, mealtimes are for eating, not socializing). They make schedules well in advance, punch the walk button several times at street corners, and plan, plan, plan.

It wears me out to read this description. How do they work in a wife, children, church, prayer, and... waiting on the Lord?

Is there a better way to live? Yes. It's called *balance:* enjoying life, enjoying yourself, and enjoying God.

"Your attitude should be the kind that was shown us by Jesus Christ, who, though he was God, did not demand and cling to his rights as God..." (Philippians 2:5-6, TLB).

The world's motto is "Look out for number one." Many people live by this phrase. They believe it's the only way if you plan to get ahead in this life, so they use this philosophy to fight and claw their way to the top. Bodies are strewn along the way, but they are just the casualties of war. Everyone wants to get to that top position, where you have the office with windows, your own parking space, personal secretary, private phone line. After all, rank has its privileges.

Have you met men like this? You know, the ones who have "arrived." They have status, they have power—and they let everyone know it. You feel overwhelmed by them because whatever they have they flaunt.

Jesus' example is such a sharp contrast to this pattern. If ever anyone had status, he did. If ever anyone had power, he did. If ever anyone had the right to say, "Listen to me and do what I say," he did. After all, he was and is the Son of God. But he didn't do it that way. He wanted to leave us a model to follow, an example that would confuse, irritate, and convict the world around us. It's called *servanthood,* and it goes counter to the world around us. If you follow Jesus' words to his disciples, you won't have to call attention to yourself. You will be noticed.

"But among you it is quite different. Anyone wanting to be a leader among you must be your servant. And if you want to be right at the top, you must serve like a slave. Your attitude must be like my own, for I, the Messiah did not come to be served, but to serve, and to give my life as a ransom for many" (Mt 20:26-28, TLB).[1]

MAY 2

"And let us run with perseverance the race marked out for us"
(Hebrews 12:1).

Many men are into running—some run in marathons, others are still competing in sprints and shorter races, while others spend their time running from the couch to the refrigerator during commercial breaks. Running can be enjoyable, but it's hard work. Are you aware that both feet leave the ground for an instant during each stride? There's a risk involved when your feet come down in unfamiliar territory.

If you decide to run, here's what to expect. Your heart will pound, you'll gasp for air, your lungs will feel tight, your mouth will dry up, and your muscles will ache. It's a grueling experience. Stand at the end of a marathon and watch the finishers. Some are dead on their feet.

If you decide to get into running, you're faced with a multitude of choices: what kind of running or race you want to be in, why you run, how long you run, how fast, and how much time you spend running. Once you select the race to run, you're stuck. You can't deviate from the prescribed course. If you want to run on flat land, don't go into cross-country running! You now have two goals—to finish the course and, hopefully, to place first.

We also run a spiritual race, based on the way we live. Some men run the race of life on a treadmill. They'll get exercise, but they don't go anywhere. Others run a race that destroys them. It's called the "rat race." It's easy to enter and difficult to get out of. Keep in mind that the only one who wins a rat race is a rat.

Hebrews 12 tells us that God has a different race for us to run, and when we run that race we're not running it alone. "But those who hope in the Lord will renew their strength. They will soar on wings like eagles; they will run and not grow weary, they will walk and not be faint" (Is 40:31).[2]

It doesn't matter how fast or how slow you run the race; it only matters that you finish.

*A certain man was preparing a banquet and invited many guests.
At the time of the banquet he sent his servant to tell those who had
been invited, "Come, for everything is now ready." But they all
alike began to make excuses. The first said, "I have just bought a
field, and I must go and see it. Please excuse me."... Then the master told his servant, "Go out to the roads and country lanes and
make them come in, so that my house will be full. I tell you not one
of those men who were invited will get a taste of my banquet" (Luke
14:16-18, 23-24).*

I t was party time. But no one wanted to come. They had more
excuses than you could imagine. Read them in verses 18-20. Talk
about flimsy excuses. The man was probably shocked, just like God is
shocked when he hears our excuses for not coming to his party.

One man couldn't come because he had to look at a field... after he
bought it?

Another couldn't come because he had to look at his oxen... after
he bought them?

And the man with the wife... he had all year, according to Jewish
custom, to tend to her with no responsibilities.

You've got to be kidding. Excuses? No, they just didn't want to
come. Lloyd Ogilvie has an interesting thought about it.

Jesus is telling us that the people's longing for the Messiah was not authentic. And in telling us this, He has drawn us into the parable. We find ourselves in those three reluctant guests. Do we really want the kingdom of
God if it means the absolute rule of the Lord in our lives? We talk a great
deal about our need for Christ in our lives. How much do we want Him?
Why are we so quick to make excuses when He invades our lives and wants
to take charge of our minds and hearts? Is it possible that we want our relationship with Him on our own terms? What's the real reason we stay away
from the feast?[3]

There's a party waiting. There's a feast waiting. The invitations have
gone out. What about it? Will you come?

"After David had finished talking with Saul, Jonathan became one in spirit with David" (1 Samuel 18:1).

If there were ever two men who had a close friendship, it was David and Jonathan. In fact, they are a great model for what it means to have a close friend. We need other men, and they need us. But real friendship is deeper than acquaintances (those we work with, work out with, or share a mutual fence with).

"One in spirit" means you're on the same wavelength. You connect, you relate well, and you share similar values and a similar view of life. When you're both Christians, you know the same God, want the same things for your life, and can open your hearts to each other in prayer.

Let's go further into the life of David and Jonathan. As we do, think about your male relationships. Do you have a friendship like they did?

There was an intense bonding of love: "And he [Jonathan] loved him [David] as himself" (1 Sm 18:1). It's difficult for some men to say they have love for another male friend. But if it's there, why not admit it?

Friendship involves a deep commitment to the other person and a willingness to be vulnerable. "And Jonathan made a covenant with David because he loved him as himself. Jonathan took off the robe he was wearing and gave it to David, along with his tunic, and even his sword, his bow and his belt" (1 Sm 18:3-4).

Friendship involves loyalty, sticking to the other person during times of difficulty. Jonathan's father Saul wanted to kill David, but "Jonathan spoke well of David" (1 Sm 19:4). True friends speak well of one another when they're not together. They focus on the positives and let the negatives slide.

Close friends encourage each other. When David was discouraged and hiding from those who wanted to hurt him, Jonathan came through. "And Saul's son Jonathan went to David at Horesh and helped him find strength in God" (1 Sm 23:16). This is a reflection of Proverbs 17:17, "A friend loves at all times and a brother is born for adversity."

Friendship involves mutuality, love, commitment, loyalty, and encouragement. Do you have a friend who reflects these qualities? Are you a friend who reflects them as well?[4]

"Let everything that has breath praise the Lord. Praise the Lord" (Psalms 150:6).

This is a test—yes, again. Take out a piece of paper and write your definition of the word *hallelujah*. Well, many of us would probably fail the test, even though we use the word again and again. It's a simple word. It means, "Praise the Lord." So whenever you say "Praise the Lord," you're saying "Hallelujah."

Did you know there are four groups of psalms that are actually called "Hallal Psalms"? That's because they have the word *hallelujah* in them. They are Psalms 104-6; 111-18; 135-36; and 146-50. Psalm 150 is the conclusion to the last group of these psalms. It's a wonderful psalm because it answers four questions about praising God: *Where? What? How?* and *Who?* Take a moment and reread Psalm 150 right now.

You've probably figured out the answers to these questions by now.

Where do we praise God? We praise him in his sanctuary and in his heavens. Praise him no matter where you are.

What do we praise him for? What *don't* we praise him for? Verse 2 says to praise him for his deeds, his greatness, who he is, and what he has done in the past.

How are we to praise him? Through a vast array of worship experiences. Perhaps you've been in a worship service where they have every instrument, from the soft melodious flute to the trumpets and drums, and creative worship dance as well. That's exactly what the psalm is talking about. It may be different from the way you worship, but it's okay.

Who is to praise God? Everything and everyone. No one is to be left out. And since we're talking about worship, it helps to remember who worship centers on. It's not the pastor, the choir, the special singers or dancers, or us. True worship centers on God. He's the object of our attention in worship.[5]

"Finally, brethren, whatever is true, whatever is honorable, whatever is just, whatever is pure, whatever is lovely, whatever is gracious, if there is any excellence, if there is anything worthy of praise, think about these things" (Philippians 4:8, RSV).

If you want a verse to keep you on track each day, here it is. Read it several times a day. Better yet, memorize it. Let's consider what it means.

The word *true* means just what it says. There are many concepts, New Age teachings, and assumptions that are deceptive.

Honorable is a difficult word to describe or translate. It actually refers to something that has the dignity of holiness about it. The idea in this verse is that we should set our minds upon things that are more serious, dignified, and have substance.

In the New Testament, the word *just* means a state of right being or right conduct. It is also used to describe people who are faithful in fulfilling their duty to God and to men. Our thoughts ought then to be on those things which would lead us to act in a way that reflects our relationship with Jesus Christ.

Pure describes that which is morally pure, free from defilement and contamination. It's easy for our thoughts to deteriorate when we dwell on negative ideas. Our thoughts need to be clean, especially in this society.

The word *lovely* means "pleasing, agreeable, or winsome"— thoughts of kindness, love, and acceptance as opposed to vengeful or bitter ones. How we think of others can determine how we act toward them.

Gracious means "of good report" or "fair-speaking." Perhaps it implies that the words that go though our own minds should reflect fairness. They should also be words we wouldn't be hesitant for God or men to hear.

The word *think* means "to consider or ponder or dwell on." Colossians 3:2 advises that we should set our minds and keep them set on what is above—the higher things—not on the things that are on the earth.

So there's the plan. Workable? Yes, but don't try it by yourself. Let the Holy Spirit work with you and you'll see a big difference in your thought life.

"When I call to remembrance the genuine faith that is in you, which dwelt first in your grandmother Lois and your mother Eunice, and I am persuaded is in you also" (2 Timothy 1:5, NKJV).

Dr. Lloyd Ogilvie tells this moving story about his own mother.

Some years ago I had an experience I will never forget. It was a gala occasion. I had just finished preaching in the church where I began my ministry. It was a time for memories and reflection.

Suddenly I was face to face with a gracious, radiant woman in her early seventies. She had tears of joy in her eyes, and somehow a handshake was not enough for us. She embraced me and drew me close. Then she kissed me and whispered in my ear, "Pay no attention to me. You belong to these people tonight." I kept an eye on her throughout the evening, catching a glimpse every so often through the crowd. She sat alone, greeted every so often by some of the people. She waited until most of the people had left. We looked long and hard at each other... and then laughed with joy. "Mother, how are you?" I said.

She had come to attend the service from a nearby community which had been my hometown, and to have a few hours together before I returned home. The memory of the visit has lingered pleasantly, but her words to me in the crowd have persisted for deep thought and reflection. She did not know all that she had said, but the true meaning of Christian motherhood was affirmed: "Pay no attention to me; tonight you belong to these people...."

In so speaking, she proclaimed the true essence of Jesus' message about the family and the special calling of mothers to prepare their children for service and then give them away to follow Him.[6]

"Honor your father and your mother, so that you may live long in the land the Lord your God is giving you" (Exodus 20:12).

The sound from the television is deafening as shouts and screams erupt from eighty-thousand people. Many are jumping up and down. A spirit of mayhem rules on the playing field. An electrifying play has just vaulted the home team to an overwhelming lead. One of the defensive backs intercepted a pass, cut through an army of opposing players, and sprinted across the goal line.

That was the easy part. Now he is fighting his way back to the sideline through an exuberant crowd of players and coaches who are hopelessly out of control.

Finally, the hero of the moment makes it to the bench and takes off his helmet, rivulets of sweat pouring down his face. He grabs an oxygen tank, takes a few whiffs to get his wind back, and grins broadly to acknowledge the congratulations of the other players.

Suddenly, he senses that the TV camera is focusing on him. He turns his six-foot five-inch muscular frame toward the camera, smiles, waves, and says, "Hi, Mom!" Soon his friends stick their heads in the camera and echo his words: "Hi, Mom! Hi, Mom!"

On the battlefields and in the hospitals of the Civil War, World Wars I and II, Korea, and Vietnam, wounded and dying soldiers cry out the same word in their native tongue: "Mother!" "Madre!" "Mom!" "Mama!"

Why is it that in times of both ecstasy and agony in a man's life he so often calls out a greeting or a plea to his mother? Why not call to his wife or father? Because mothers are still connected to their sons in some way. Perhaps it's because Mom was the first one to love and comfort us when we entered this life.

How was or how is your relationship with your mom? If she's alive, what might she need from you? It could be a note of appreciation for who she is. Do your own children hear from you more of the positives or the negatives about Mom? How does your relationship with your mother affect your responses to your wife?

Just a few questions for you to think about today.

"But to all who received him, he gave the right to become children of God. All they needed to do was to trust him to save them" (*John 1:12, TLB*).

D o you ever think of yourself as a son of God? Not too many of us go around thinking about this, but it's reality. You are. Not only did John say this but so did Paul.

> For now we are all children of God through faith in Jesus Christ."
>
> **Galatians 3:26**

That's kind of a frightening thought, isn't it? It's full of responsibility. How in the world did we get to be sons of God? It's quite simple, we were adopted. Consider this passage:

> Long ago, even before he made the world, God chose us to be his very own, through what Christ would do for us; he decided then to make us holy in his eyes, without a single fault—we who stand before him covered with his love.   **Ephesians 1:4**

If you know Jesus Christ as Savior, you were adopted into God's family. The apostle John wrote: "To all who received him, to those who believed in his name, he gave the right to become children of God" (Jn 1:12). Understanding the fullness of your spiritual adoption can redirect your thinking and responses to life. Your adoption is a gift of grace. This is how you have been chosen for blessing.

In Roman law during New Testament times it was common practice for a childless adult who wanted an heir to adopt an adult male as his son. We, too, have been adopted by God as his heirs. The apostle Paul wrote: "Now if we are children, then we are heirs—heirs of God and co-heirs with Christ" (Rom 8:17). "So you are no longer a slave, but a son; and since you are a son, God has made you also an heir" (Gal 4:7).

Do you remember the movie *Ben Hur*? Judah ben Hur was a Jewish slave until the Roman admiral, Arias, adopted him. Judah was given all rights and privileges of full sonship. He was accepted by Arias *as if* he had been born into the family. Similarly, when you received Jesus Christ as your Savior, you were adopted into God's family and received *all* the rights and privileges of a full heir. There are no limitations.

"For he has rescued us out of the darkness and gloom of Satan's kingdom and brought us into the kingdom of his dear Son." (*Colossians 1:13*).

How do you feel about being adopted by the King of the universe and being delivered from the kingdom of darkness? This is one of the greatest blessings the gospel offers you. You have been taken into God's family and fellowship, and you have been established as his heir. You may have come from a dysfunctional home, and perhaps experienced emotional or physical abuse in your natural family. But God is a Father who can fill the gaps in your life because you are part of his family. Closeness, affection, and generosity are the basis of your relationship with Father God. He loves and cares for you. Your relationship as an heir is the basis for your Christian life and the foundation for all the other blessings you receive in your day-to-day experience.

Our relationship as adopted children of God has a number of implications for the way we live our lives. Just as a child grows up imitating its father and mother, so we can become more and more like our Father God.

We see this, for example, in the Sermon on the Mount in which Christ calls us to *imitate* our Father: "Love your enemies and pray for those who persecute you....Be perfect, therefore, as your heavenly Father is perfect" (Mt 5:44, 48).

We are also called to *glorify* our Father: "Let your light shine before men, that they may see your good deeds and praise your Father in heaven" (Mt 5:16).

As we imitate, glorify, and please our Father, we begin to sense the thrill of participating in the destiny for which we were created. We not only enjoy the blessing of *being* God's children, we realize the personal benefits that come from *behaving* as God's children. Our knowledge of God grows, as does our awareness of his knowledge and love for us. As we live out our identity as God's adopted children day by day, we are personally transformed. We are blessed with the understanding that we are fulfilling our purpose in life.

In what way do you see yourself imitating, glorifying, and pleasing your Father?

"And whatever you do, whether in word or deed, do it all in the name of the Lord Jesus, giving thanks to God the Father through him" (Colossians 3:17).

Pastor Joe Brown, a former Navy officer, shared this story about giving our best effort to everything we do.

As a young man, President Jimmy Carter graduated from the Naval Academy and served as an officer on a nuclear-powered submarine. However, before he was able to assume that position, he had to have a personal interview with Admiral Hyman Rickover, the man considered to be the father of the nuclear navy. Carter was understandably nervous, knowing how much was at stake and that only the best, most disciplined officers were chosen to serve in this prestigious force.

When he stood before Rickover, it was soon obvious to the young officer that the wise admiral knew more about nearly every subject discussed than did he. Finally Rickover came to the last question on his seemingly never-ending list. "Where did you finish in your class, young man?"

Pleased with his accomplishments and thrilled to finally be presented a question he was sure of, Carter informed the Admiral that he had finished 59th out of a student body numbering 820. Then he waited for a commendation from the old sailor, but it never came.

Jimmy Carter later recounted the incident.

"Did you always do your best?" was the question that broke the uncomfortable silence between the two men.

Carter thought and then cleared his throat. "No, sir, I did not," was his hesitant reply.

Rickover turned his chair around, signaling the interview was over, and asked, "Why not?"

It's a good question—"Why not?"

How do you evaluate what you do? Poor, so-so, adequate, good, very good, outstanding? We are called to be people of excellence, to fulfill our potential. It's easy to coast along rather than make that extra effort. Some men are pretty good at that. But if you can do better, why not?[7]

"The lips of the wise spread knowledge; not so the hearts of fools" (Proverbs 15:7).

If you would like to be a man whom others respect, admire, look to for advice, and consult for solutions, then read on. There is a way for all that to happen. The principle that makes this happen is summed up in one word—*communication*. Communicate according to the Book of Proverbs, and other people will want to connect with you. But what does it mean to communicate this way?

First, be a man who is able to give good advice and wisdom. "Plans fail for lack of counsel, but with many advisers they succeed" (Prv 15:22). You'll be able to do this if you follow Proverbs.

Second, when you are on the receiving end of another person's exhortation or reproof, listen, accept, and evaluate. Don't react. "Wounds from a friend can be trusted, but an enemy multiplies kisses" (Prv 27:6).

And when someone else needs correction, don't run from it. Do it lovingly and sensitively. "He who rebukes a man will in the end gain more favor than he who has a flattering tongue" (Prv 28:23). But... timing is everything. This is where discernment, patience, and prayer on your part are needed. "A word aptly spoken is like apples of gold in settings of silver" (Prv 25:11).

Have a sense of humor. We need men who can be serious, but also laugh and help others to lighten up. "All the days of the oppressed are wretched, but the cheerful heart has a continual feast" (Prv 15:15). The words *continual feast* literally mean "to cause good healing." We don't laugh at the expense of others, but we need men to help us see the funny side of life.

One other guideline is essential. You need this, and so does your spouse, employee(s), children... everyone. Be an encourager. Be a cheerleader. Show your sincere appreciation and people will want to be around you. "A man finds joy in giving an apt reply—and how good is a timely word!" (Prv 15:23). "An anxious heart weights a man down, but a kind word cheers him up" (Prv 12:25).

Well, there's the plan. It's workable, and the best place to start putting it into practice is at home.

MAY 13

"But seek first his kingdom and his righteousness, and all these things will be given to you as well" (Matthew 6:33).

Jugglers look so smooth and cool. As the dishes fly through the air, the juggler's hands move in perfect rhythm and balance. It looks so effortless. We don't realize the endless hours of practice, the stacks of broken dishes, or the pursuit of missed balls that are part of the struggle to become proficient.

We probably identify more with the failures than we do with the achievements of the juggler.

We're all jugglers in one way or another. We try to juggle the demands of marriage, parenting, career, continuing education, church, community service, our own parents, and perhaps even a little time for ourselves now and then. And at times we feel like we're on the "rack" with ropes around each limb pulling in opposite directions.

Everybody wants a piece of us. Sometimes there is not enough to go around. So, what's a guy to do? Prioritize. Regroup. Cut and trim. Here are some suggestions to get you started.

First place in your life is for the Lord. Ask him, "What do you want from me?"

Second place in your life is for your wife. Ask her, "What do you want from me?"

Third place in your life is for your children. You and your wife determine what is needed for them.

Fourth place in your life is your career. What can you give to it?

Ask yourself, "Why am I doing all that I do? For what purpose? For whose glory is it?" Then make a list of every activity in your life. Evaluate them under the following formula: Anything important could either stay or go, and anything simply good goes! Think about it and then trim. You'll be glad you did.

"Better one handful with tranquillity than two handfuls with toil and chasing after the wind" (Ecclesiastes 4:6).

In the book *Becoming Soul Mates*, Les and Leslie Parrott have compiled over fifty stories of how couples have developed spiritual intimacy in their marriages. Here's a story to encourage you, if you're married, to nurture this dimension of your relationship.

A couple we knew gave us some advice several months before we married twenty-three years ago. That advice has served us well and upon reflection is one of the main ways we have cultivated spiritual intimacy in our relationship.

Our friends introduced us to the "principle of reintroduction." Simply put, this principle acknowledges that every day we change as individuals based on our experiences that day. In order to build a growing relationship as a couple, then, we must make time to "daily reintroduce" ourselves to each other. We share the mundane and the profound. We disclose what's going on in our lives and genuinely inquire about each other's life.

Frankly, this was fairly easy to do when we were first married and had few distractions. We had lots of time for meaningful dialogue, cups of coffee, and sharing activities together. But as children came and other adult responsibilities began to crowd our schedules, we were grateful we had established the habit early on and that it still prevails. For no amount of reading the Bible or praying together genuinely builds our relationship if we haven't bared our lives with each other on a regular basis and feel convinced that we are "naked and unashamed" with each other in the fullest sense of that biblical definition of intimacy.

Now our daily reintroduction habit usually takes the form of a long walk, an extended cup of coffee (decaf, now), or a long phone call if I'm out of town. But we keep very short accounts, and we can testify that we depend on this habit to keep us growing, both as individuals and as a couple.[8]

"Similarly, if anyone competes as an athlete, he does not receive the victor's crown unless he competes according to the rules" (2 Timothy 2:5).

The cry of the Olympic athlete is, "Go for the bronze!" No? Well, what about, "Go for the silver!" Not quite? How about, "Go for the gold!" Yes! That's what they're after—gold. We watch them on TV or perhaps we've even gone to the Olympic Games. What an experience!

What we see in competition is the result of years of sacrifice. To get there you've got to be disciplined. These athletes undertake a vigorous training schedule. They have to if they want a chance to even make it to the Olympics. Do you know what they go through in their attempt?

They begin training as young as possible. Their trainer knows the value of early training.

They develop all the muscles in their body, not just a few. Ice skaters take dance and gymnastics as well as skating lessons. Some of the men in pairs skating work at building their upper bodies in order to be able to lift their partners.

They master the fundamentals of their sport before hitting the competitions. Learning the basics prevents later disaster.

They know their equipment inside and out. They have to if they're going to use it.

They learn from the many mistakes they are going to make. They view their performances on videos again and again. They ask others for advice and learn from their experiences. They're teachable and get back on their feet after a fall. They build on their successes, as well.

They have learned how to focus. They concentrate and practice the same thing again and again, refining their technique.

As Christians, we have much to learn from these athletes. If we were to apply these principles to the Christian life, we'd quickly move from being Christians to being disciples. It's just a thought.[9]

"Then a man of the law came to him and said, 'Teacher, I will follow you wherever you go.' Jesus replied, 'Foxes have holes and birds of the air have nests, but the Son of Man has no place to lay his head'" (Matthew 8:19-20).

Have you ever felt like you didn't fit in? You know, sort of part of a group, but not really? It's an uncomfortable feeling, but it's normal if you're a Christian. When you follow Jesus, you won't really feel like you fit in... or at least you shouldn't. There's a good reason for that. You're an alien, a stranger just visiting this world for a while. Earth may be where you're living, but it's not really your home. Again and again God's Word says:

> If you belonged to the world, it would love you as its own. As it is, you do not belong to the world, but I have chosen you out of the world. That is why the world hates you. **John 15:19**

> Dear friends, I urge you, as aliens and strangers in the world, to abstain from sinful desires, which war against your soul. **1 Peter 2:11**

> But our citizenship is in heaven. And we eagerly await a Savior from there, the Lord Jesus Christ. **Philippians 3:20**

We are here on a visit and we have a purpose: to enjoy God as well as to love him forever, but also to help enlarge the kingdom of God. If you want an opportunity to introduce others to the kingdom, the next time someone asks you where you live, just tell them you're an alien on a visit and they wouldn't believe where your real home is. Go ahead, try it. And get set for some strange reactions. Once you've gotten their attention, share the Good News of Jesus with them!

"Therefore, I urge you, brothers, in view of God's mercy, to offer your bodies as living sacrifices, holy and pleasing to God—this is your spiritual act of worship" (Romans 12:1).

D_{ear} God,

I'm praying today for wisdom to know what I need to be doing in this world.

Help me to overcome my not wanting to face the truth, which I need to face.

Help me to overcome my laziness that keeps me from learning the truth.

Help me to overcome my prejudices that keep me from seeing what is truth.

Help me to overcome my stubbornness that keeps me from accepting the truth.

Help me to overcome my pride that keeps me from looking for the truth.

Keep my eyes and ears open so I can hear my conscience.

Take away my arrogance, which keeps me from accepting advice.

Open my locked-up mind, which resists even the Holy Spirit, the Spirit of truth.

Give me the grace and power to do what I know I ought to do.

Lord, keep me from the weakness of my will that gets off course now and then. Save me from my lack of resistance which gives into temptation all too easily.

Help me to overcome my procrastination of the things I need to do, but am hesitant to try.

Lift from my life the fears that have immobilized me in the past.

Give me the perseverance to complete the tasks that I now give up on.

Give me strength to tackle the hard things of life in place of settling for the easy.

Give me courage to let others know that I know and love you.

So now once again I ask for wisdom to know your will and do it.

In Jesus' name,

Amen.[10]

MAY 18

"But let him who boasts boast about this: that he understands and knows me, that I am the Lord, who exercises kindness, justice and righteousness on earth, for in these I delight,' declares the Lord" (Jeremiah 9:24).

Part of our American dream is enjoyment. Everyone wants a good time. Ads cry out to us to enjoy ourselves. From gun ads to tobacco ads to car ads, they appeal to our desire for enjoyment. There's nothing wrong with enjoyment... unless it becomes your god.

A document written in 1647 set out to instruct the readers in the dogmas of the church. It was called *The Westminster Shorter Catechism.* In it the question is asked, "What is man's chief end?" And the answer is, "To glorify God and enjoy him forever." That's a shocker for some. Worship him? Yes. Fear him? Yes. Pray to him? Yes. But enjoy him? How?

Enjoyment comes when we are more knowledgeable about something. The closer we get, the more familiar we are, the more we can enjoy whatever it is. Enjoyment means liking, relaxing in something's presence, and delighting. And when we enjoy God we're more apt to glorify him by serving him.

But there's one other thing: God *enjoys you!* How does that grab you? It's a foreign thought to some. They're more likely to think of all the reasons why God couldn't enjoy them. Remember there are things he doesn't enjoy about us like sin, failures, and drifting from him. But he delights in you as a person. His enjoyment and love for you is not conditional.

Think about these two ideas today: Your purpose is to enjoy God, and he enjoys you. That ought to do something for your outlook.[11]

MAY 19

"Where can I go from your Spirit? Where can I flee from your presence?" (Psalms 139:7).

Do your thoughts ever drift away when you're praying? Dr. Lloyd Ogilvie addresses this problem.

Meditation: "What do I do about wandering thoughts when I pray?" I've been asked that question repeatedly. A wandering attention simply tells us that our minds are on other things. Why not talk to God about what's really commanding our attention? Whatever our minds drift off to is an indication of what we really need to ask for help or solve or conquer.

But what about abhorrent thoughts or fantasies? They indicate a deeper need beneath the surface. Allow God to gently probe the cause. We are like a ball of yarn with one strand protruding. The Lord gets hold of that and begins to unravel us. Since He knows all about us, He's never surprised. Why do we think we can hide anything from Him? There is no place we can go, even into the depths of ourselves, where He's not there waiting for us.

How many times should I ask God for something in my prayers? Here is a formula that works for me: ask God once, and thank Him a thousand times. God is not hard of hearing, nor does He forget the requests we've made of Him. Thanks that He has heard is an effective method of recommitting the need to Him. The Lord knows what we need and will act when it is according to His plan and timing for us. Remember that prayer is not an argument with God to persuade Him to move things our way, but an exercise by which we are enabled by His Spirit to move ourselves His way.[12]

"Brothers, I do not consider myself yet to have taken hold of it. But one thing I do: Forgetting what is behind and straining toward what is ahead…" (Philippians 3:13).

Do you know what God wants to do with you today? Let me tell you. First of all, he wants to renew your mind. In 1 Corinthians 2:16 Paul states that "we have the mind of Christ." Romans 12:2 tells us that we can be "transformed by the renewing of your mind." In Philippians 2:5 we are challenged to "have this attitude in yourselves which was also in Christ Jesus." How will your life and your relationships be different when this happens?

After God renews your mind he wants to heal your emotions. In Romans 14:1 we are commanded to "pursue love." In Ephesians 4:26 we see that with God's help we can be angry and not sin. In Ephesians 5:1-2 we are told that we can be imitators of God as we "walk in love, just as Christ also loved you." How will your life and your relationships be different when this happens?

He also wants to direct any choices you make. Romans 13:12 instructs us to "lay aside the deeds of darkness and put on the armor of light." Ephesians 4:22-24 tells us that we can choose to "lay aside the old self" and "put on the new self, which in the likeness of God has been created in righteousness and holiness of the truth." In Philippians 3:13 we are encouraged not to dwell on the things of the past but to choose to reach forward to what lies ahead.

That's quite a plan for your life, isn't it? The good news is, it's workable. Have you had a better offer today? Probably not. And there won't be a better one tomorrow, either.[13]

MAY 21

"...keeps a promise even if it ruins him." (Psalms 15:4, TLB).

When your name is mentioned, what do you want people to think about you? Better yet, what do you want them to say about you? How about that you're honest? Honesty probably ought to be put on the endangered species list. It's harder and harder to find an honest man. Our society has learned to cut corners, shade the truth, leave out information (like on a tax report), and present the image that will get us what we want. It's not really profitable to be honest, especially if you're competing with others who aren't honest. Even Plato said, "Honesty is for the most part less profitable than dishonesty."

Fortunately, there are some honest people around. They are sincere, frank, and free from deceit or fraud. They are genuine. They are who and what they say they are. Others can trust and depend on them.

Our first president, George Washington, said, "I hope I shall possess firmness and virtue enough to maintain what I consider the most enviable of all titles, the character of an honest man."

Think about it. Can you give examples as to why others see you as an honest man? Are you thought of as someone who keeps his word? If you are married, does your wife see you as someone who listens, says yes to a request, and then follows through? When you tell the kids you'll be there, can they count on you? Honesty is a great way to say that you're a Christian. Who knows, someone may ask why you're the way you are... and they could be introduced to your Lord![14]

"When justice is done, it brings joy to the righteous but terror to evildoers" (Proverbs 21:15).

"There ain't no justice anywhere." Yeah, it's easy to think that way with some of the stuff that goes on today. Criminals caught in the act are released because of some technicality. Innocent people are sued and their lives ruined by those who lie on the witness stand.

In Washington it seems the special interest groups with the most money end up with laws going their way.

In the Old West there was a different form of justice that emerged every now and then. Vigilantes engaged in frontier justice. When they caught a horse thief or cattle rustler they found the nearest tree and hanged him on the spot. After all, who needed courts or judges when you had the thief with a branding iron in his hand!

We all want justice. Right should prevail and wrong should be punished. But justice is easily hindered and sometimes destroyed by powerful and angry people. Politicians, lynch mobs, business owners, and even those in the church have been known to prevent it.

God wants justice to prevail. He wants us to be just and fair.

To do what is right and just is more acceptable to the Lord than sacrifice.
Proverbs 21:3

The violence of the wicked will drag them away, for they refuse to do what is right.
Proverbs 21:7

When justice is done, it brings joy to the righteous but terror to evildoers.
Proverbs 21:15

By justice a king gives a country stability, but one who is greedy for bribes tears it down.
Proverbs 29:4

Many seek an audience with a ruler, but it is from the Lord that man gets justice.
Proverbs 29:26

We honor God when we act in a just and fair way. Yes, it's tough to do, but it's possible.

"Do not eat the food of a stingy man, do not crave his delicacies; as a man thinks in his heart so is he..." (Proverbs 23:6-7).

Your attitude can determine who and what you are. How you think about your problems can determine how you feel and behave.

There's an old story about two men confined to the same hospital room for an extended period of time. They were quite ill but unfortunately didn't have the typical diversions such as books or TV. They just had one another's presence, so they engaged in a lot of conversation. They talked about anything and everything, including their personal histories. Through this they became close friends.

Neither could leave his bed, but one man was next to the window. Each day for part of his treatment he would sit up for an hour. During this time he would bring the outside world to his friend by describing everything he saw. He talked in great detail about the people, the trees, the lake, the birds, the dogs, the color of the clouds and the sky. His friend saw life through his eyes.

In time, though, his friend began to think it wasn't fair for the other to have all the access to the world, while all he saw was the room. He didn't like thinking this, but with the abundance of time available to him he began to think this way more and more. Soon his thoughts of jealousy and envy dominated his thinking and his mood.

One night the man closest to the window woke up, coughing and choking. He tried to push the button to call the nurse but it dropped out of his hand. His bitter, jealous friend, who was awake, lay there listening to the other struggling for his life. He did nothing.

When the nurse arrived in the morning the man was dead. After a few days, the envious man asked to have that bed and was moved. As soon as the nurse left the room, he rose up on one elbow to look out. He discovered that the window through which his friend had filled his life with wonderful sights showed nothing except... a blank wall![15]

"Jesus replied, 'No one who puts his hand to the plow and looks back is fit for service in the kingdom of God'" (Luke 9:62).

W hen would you like to retire? It faces all of us, but what's the right time? Dr. Lloyd Ogilvie shares a new twist on this issue.

Some time ago, a full-page ad appeared in the *Wall Street Journal* entitled "How to Retire at 35."

I read the advertisement immediately. Though I had long passed 35, I wanted to know what I had missed. This is what it said:

It's so easy. Thousands of men do it every year. In all walks of life. And it sets our economy, our country, and the world back thousands of years in terms of wasted human resources. But worst of all, it is the personal tragedy that almost always results from "early retirement."

It usually begins with a tinge of boredom. Gradually a man's work begins to seem endlessly repetitious. The rat race hardly seems worth it any more.

It is at this point that many a 35-year-old boy wonder retires. There are no testimonial dinners or gold watches. He goes to work every day, puts in his forty hours, and even draws a paycheck. He's retired, but nobody knows it. Not at first, anyhow.

The lucky ones get fired in time to make a fresh start. Those less fortunate hang on for a while—even decades, waiting and wondering: waiting for a raise or promotion that never comes, and wondering why. With life expectancy approaching the century mark, 65 years is a long time to spend in a rocking chair.

I began to think of people I knew like that—not just in their work, but in their discipleship. Christ never allows us to take an early retirement. In fact, He recalls us today into active service.[16]

Still think it's a bit early to think about retirement? Perhaps not.

"A simple man believes anything, but a prudent man gives thoughts to his steps" (Proverbs 14:15).

Do you believe everything you hear? I mean, how do you respond to some of those TV commercials or infomercials? Do you believe the outrageous stories some people tell? Or how about all that rhetoric from politicians?

The verse above provides a warning that may help us stay out of difficulty. In another version, it says, "The naive believes everything, but the prudent man considers his steps" (NASB).

The Hebrew word for *simple* or *naive* presents the idea of "open-mindedness" or inexperience that leaves a person open to being conned. One writer describes the naive as "a person of undecided views and thus susceptible to either good or bad influences."[17] Do you know anyone like this?

Simple people are way too trusting. They are gullible and believe just about anything. They lack a discerning spirit. The Bible says they like the way they are. Proverbs asks the question, "How long, O simple ones and open [to evil], will you love being simple?" (1:22, AMP) Perhaps the reason is they rarely consider the consequences of what they do. They enjoy being openminded. They also lack good moral sense. They're lousy judges of character, and they often develop friendships with others like themselves. They can't seem to recognize evil. "A prudent man sees the evil and hides himself but the simple pass on and are punished (with suffering)" (Prv 22:3, AMP).

Is there hope for this person? How will they turn out? Well, wait until tomorrow for the rest of the story.

"Only a simpleton believes what he is told! A prudent man checks to see where he is going" (Proverbs 14:15, TLB).

If you've read yesterday's selection about the simple or naive person, you're probably wondering, "Is there any hope for this person?" And if the description sounded like one of your friends or family members, you may be really concerned!

Well, first look at what Proverbs says about the outcome of naiveté. "That is why you must eat the bitter fruit of having your own way, and experience the full terrors of the pathway you have chosen. For you turned away from me—to death; your own complacency will kill you. Fools! But all who listen to me shall live in peace and safety, unafraid" (Prv 1:31-33).

The naive may be satisfied with what they do but it comes back to haunt them. Proverbs 14:18 says: "The simpleton is crowned with folly; the wise man is crowned with knowledge."

He doesn't learn from what he does. He doesn't improve. He just gets worse. So, is there any hope? Only the Lord God can save them from themselves. "The Lord preserves (guards) the simple; I was brought low, and He saved me" (Ps 116:6, NASB).

The naive can change but not without some pain. "Strike a scoffer and the naive may become shrewd" (Prv 19:25, NASB); "When the scoffer is punished, the naive becomes wise" (Prv 21:11, NASB). Since the naive are so influenced by others, when they get into trouble they learn from their mistakes.

There is a second way the naive can learn and that is from the Word of God.

"The law of the Lord is perfect, restoring the soul; the testimony of the Lord is sure, making wise the simple [naive]" (Ps 19:7, NASB).

"The unfolding of thy words gives light; it gives understanding to the simple [naive]" (Ps 119:130, NASB).

That is the rest of the story.[18]

"No one can serve two masters. Either he will hate the one and love the other, or he will be devoted to the one and despise the other. You cannot serve both God and Money" (Matthew 6:24).

People die for it and lie for it. They curse it and save it. They can spend it or lend it. Money can be used by you or it can use you. You work all your life for it, but you can't take it with you. You can use it for the kingdom of God and save people from the wages of sin, or it can enslave you and lead you into a life of sin.

Our world revolves around who has money and how it's used. Poor people have the illusion that money will make them happy. Rich people soon discover that it can't.

God's Word has much to say about money. In fact, there are about five hundred verses in the Bible on prayer, but over 2,300 on how to handle money and possessions. Jesus summed up the problem of money in the verse for today. Patrick Morley gives us additional insight into this verse and why we need to take it seriously.

> The word *serve* translates "to be a slave to, literally or figuratively, voluntarily or involuntarily."
>
> It is not a question of *advisability*, "You *should* not serve both God and money." That would be a *priority* choice.
>
> It is not a question of *accountability*, "You *must* not serve both God and money." That would be a *moral* choice.
>
> Rather, it is a matter of *impossibility*, "You *cannot* serve both God and money." *There is no choice*; we each serve one, and only one, master. We are either a slave to God or a slave to money.[19]

What is your perspective on money? What were the messages you heard about it as you were growing up? How much time does money occupy in your thoughts and family discussions?

Money is not bad in itself. We all need it. It's useful. But we also need a financial guide for our lives. In fact, why don't you read the Book of Proverbs? Read one chapter a day for the next month. Write down what it says about money. It could change your financial future.

"Have nothing to do with godless myths and old wives' tales; rather, train yourself to be godly" (1 Timothy 4:7).

If you believe in something, really believe in it and want it, you'll persist no matter what. The obstacles may seem overwhelming or you may not feel fully equipped, but if you're convinced that this is for you, you go for it... like Christopher Columbus did. Columbus must have been so convinced of his dream that he became a super persuader! I mean, his idea of a transatlantic voyage in the 1400s was kind of far out! Centuries of superstition and traditions had to be overcome. Beside that, even though Columbus had been to sea several times, it had only been as a passenger, never as captain. To top it off, he was a foreigner (Italian) living in Portugal and then Spain. Then there was a minor problem: He didn't have the money to fund such a journey. And the only one who could legally fund an exploratory voyage was the head of a country like a king or queen. That certainly narrowed the possibilities!

But then... what he wanted personally from this voyage wasn't pennies. He wanted 10 percent commission on all new commerce between the mother country and the new land, the title of Admiral of the Ocean Sea, and the permanent position of governor of the newly discovered lands.

He asked again and again for what he wanted. For seven years he asked King John of Portugal for the funds. Nothing. No luck. Then he worked another seven years on Ferdinand and Isabella of Spain. Again and again he asked. One day the answer was yes! You know the rest of the story. Persistence pays.

Is there something you need to be persistent about in your life? What obstacles have to be overcome? Go for it as a team—you and your heavenly Father![20]

"Husbands, love your wives, just as Christ loved the church and gave himself up for her" (Ephesians 5:25).

"Who does a woman marry when she marries?" Sound like a dumb question? Perhaps the answer is obvious: She marries a man. Unfortunately, however, some don't. They find they have simply married a paycheck. Their husbands rationalize: "Hey! I'm working hard for us. I want to build a better life for you, to give you everything you want. Now, just be patient. This big deal at work will be over in three to six months and then we'll have some time together. In fact, I may even take you away for a weekend." The only thing that might be over in three to six months, however, is the marriage if this has been a pattern! I've seen it happen time and again. A wife wants a man, not things. She wants him to love her as Christ loved the church, sacrificially. And that doesn't mean working all the time.

Many men say all the work is to provide for their wives, but there are other reasons. It could be more comfortable at work, or he could be building his identity through work or avoiding conflict or intimacy at home. While men are off working and providing, their wives could be getting emotionally colder. If deep freeze is in process, it's because we (husbands) are not functioning too well as the thermostat. That's our role, you know. A wife needs our warmth, our time, our eyes and ears to listen, our emotions....

Sure, you could work and work and work like some men and have everything external but have nothing on the home front. Consider how Jesus loved the church. He gave *himself* for it. That's the key word for us too.

"The fruit of righteousness will be peace; the effect of righteousness will be quietness and confidence forever. My people will live in peaceful dwelling places, in secure homes, in undisturbed places of rest" (Isaiah 32:17-18).

We live in a polluted world. There are many kinds of pollution, but let's talk about one—noise pollution. You can't even go into a nice restaurant for dinner without having to contend with loud music. Noise—noise—noise—radios, TV, horns, airplanes, people talking and yelling, electric lawn mowers and blowers, freeways. Isn't there any place where there's no sound?

Chuck Swindoll has a few words to say about quietness.

That wonderful, much-needed presence has again come for a visit—*quietness*. Oh, how I love it… how I need it. The last time it was this quiet was a few weeks ago when I was walking with a friend along the sandy shore at Carmel. The silence of that early dawn was broken only by the rhythmic roar of the rolling surf and the cry of a few gulls floating overhead. The same thought I had then I have now: *I cannot be the man I should be without times of quietness.* Stillness is an essential part of our growing deeper as we grow older. Or—in the words of a man who helped shape my life perhaps more than any other:

We will not become men of God

without the presence of solitude.

Those words haunt me when I get caught in the treadmill of time schedules… when I make my turn toward the homestretch of the week and try to meet the deadline of demands, just like you.[21]

Can you handle the stillness of solitude? Is it unnerving to sit and listen to… nothing? Are you an activity addict? Are the noises in your head so loud you can't hear God talking to you? His still, small voice won't try to out-shout the noise. It will always be a still small voice. He's waiting for you to be quiet, to listen, to relax, so that you can be restored.

"Do you see anything? And he looked up and said, 'I see men for I am seeing them like trees, walking about'" (Mark 8:23-24).

I'm partially blind. So are you. We may have 20-20 or 20-40 vision, but in some ways we're blind. Our view of life is distorted.

Our ability to perceive life is similar to a camera. Photographers can alter the image of reality through the use of various lenses or filters. A wide-angle lens gives a much broader panorama, but the objects appear more distant and smaller. A telephoto lens has a narrower and more selective view of life. It can focus on a beautiful flower, but in so doing it shuts out the rest of the garden. Happy and smiling people seen through a fish-eye lens appear distorted and unreal. Filters can blur reality, bring darkness into a lighted scene, or even create a mist. Thus a photographic view of the world can be distorted.

It's easy to view life in a distorted way. Unfortunately, we sometimes distort how we see our spouse, our children, our coworkers, ourselves, and even God. Blindness can be selective, and there can be degrees of it in our lives. What we need is what the blind man received.

> And they came to Bethsaida. And they brought a blind man to Him, and entreated Him to touch him. And taking the blind man by the hand, He brought him out of the village; and after spitting on his eyes, and laying His hands upon him, He asked him, "Do you see anything?" And he looked up and said, "I see men, for I am seeing them like trees, walking about." Then again He laid His hands upon his eyes; and he looked intently and was restored, and began to see everything clearly.
>
> **Mark 8:22-25, NASB**

There is one who can open our eyes in many ways. But perhaps we need them opened spiritually more than any other way.

> I will lead the blind by a way they do not know, in paths they do not know I will guide them. I will make darkness into light before them and rugged places into plains. These are the things I will do, and I will not leave them undone. **Isaiah 42:16, NASB**

JUNE 1

"Live such good lives among the pagans that, though they accuse you of doing wrong, they may see your good deeds and glorify God on the day he visits us" (1 Peter 2:12).

When you're not around and other people bring up your name, what's the first thing that comes to their minds about you? Better yet, what do they say about you? Most of us will never know for sure. But it would be interesting to find out. What others are thinking and saying about us is based upon what we've let people know about us as well as how we've acted around them. We have a reputation. It follows us in the minds of others, even when we're not there. Webster's defines it as "estimation in which a person or thing is commonly held, whether favored or not; character in the view of the public."[1]

Sometimes people don't give you the time of day until you've established a good reputation. Artists have discovered this as have sports figures, writers, and ministers.

Everyone has a reputation, whether or not we want one. A good reputation is made—it's earned. It takes hard work, and consistency of word and deed.

How's your reputation? Why not check it out? If you're brave (or crazy, as some people would say) you could ask one of the following:

To your coworkers—"In your eyes, what is my reputation?"

To your wife—"In your eyes, what is my reputation?"

To your children—"In your eyes, what is my reputation?"

To the Lord—"In your eyes, what is my reputation?"

May you be well thought of!

JUNE 2

"Answer me, O Lord, answer me, so these people will know that you, O Lord, are God, and that you are turning their hearts back again" (1 Kings 18:37-39).

Can you imagine a guy who literally was on the top of the world with everyone in his country thinking he was the greatest man alive? And what does he do? He comes down with a good case of depression. It doesn't make much sense, does it? But it happened. Elijah actually got so depressed he wanted to die. (Read the account in 1 Kings 18 and 19.) Elijah is an example of a man who misinterpreted a situation and saw only certain elements of it. His misperceptions concerning himself, God, and other people were caused partly by the tremendous emotional and physical exhaustion he suffered. Have you ever felt that way?

Elijah had an intense emotional experience when he was used as an instrument to demonstrate the power of God on Mount Carmel. Perhaps he expected everyone to turn to the true God after that, but he was disappointed when Jezebel was still so hostile. He was physically exhausted because of the encounter on Mount Carmel and his twenty-mile race before the king's chariot. When Jezebel threatened his life he became frightened. He probably spent time dwelling on her threat, forgetting about God's power, which had just been demonstrated. Fearing for his life, Elijah left familiar surroundings and cut himself off from his friends. Have you ever done that?

All of these factors led to his depression. His distorted thinking is evident in his lament that he was the only one left, the only one still faithful to God. He was convinced that the whole world was against him. Evidently his self-pity caused him to lose further perspective. Sound familiar?

When you get down, discouraged, or even depressed (they're all normal responses), take a look at what you've been doing and thinking. It could be the Elijah Pattern. God straightened out Elijah's thinking and behavior. And he can do that for you too.

"But the fruit of the Spirit is love, joy, peace, patience, kindness, goodness, faithfulness, gentleness and self-control. Against such things there is no law" (Galatians 5:22).

Perspective can make a big difference in how you view what happens to you in life. For example, take the case of Fred, a landscape contractor. His first job was to remove a huge oak stump from a field. Fred had to use dynamite, but the only problem was, he had never used any before. He was kind of nervous about it, especially with the old farmer watching every move he made. So he tried to hide his jitters by carefully determining the size of the stump, the precise amount of dynamite, and where it should be placed to get the maximum effect. He didn't want to use too small an amount and have to do it over, nor did he want to use too much. He went about it scientifically.

When he was ready to detonate the charge, Fred and the farmer went behind the pickup truck where a wire was running to the detonator. He looked at the farmer, said a prayer, and plunged the detonator. It worked… all too well. The stump broke loose from the ground, rose through the air in a curving arc, and then plummeted down right on the cab of the truck. Fred's heart sank, and all he could think of was the ruined cab. Not the farmer. He was full of amazement and admiration. Slapping Fred on the back he said, "Not bad. With a little more practice you'll get it in the bed of the truck every time!"

Some of us are like Fred and some of us are like the farmer. We hit hard times and give in to discouragement, or we see how close we came to making it work and say, "Next time I'll get it right!"

The fruit of the Spirit is joy. It's a realistic optimism, not the absence of hardship. It's a choice we make to smile, when the tree stump lands on our truck, and say, "It could be worse. I'll learn how to make it better." Which perspective do you live by?[2]

"For if, when we were God's enemies, we were reconciled to him through the death of his Son, how much more, having been reconciled, shall we be saved through his life!" (Romans 5:10).

Most of us have done it at one time or another. We've made a mistake in the checkbook. All of a sudden we realize we're still writing checks but the well is dry. The money is used up. We rush to the bank with our savings book and immediately transfer funds into the checking account. Then we breathe a sigh of relief. We're saved. There's money to cover the checks. Of course we all wish the bank would be generous and just pour extra money into our account. Not quite! Someone has to pay, but not the bank.

Some people think of God as being generous. That's why he overlooks our sins and forgives us, right? Wrong. God is holy and can't overlook our sins. Exodus 34:7 talks about God: "...maintaining love to thousands, and forgiving wickedness, rebellion and sin. Yet he does not leave the guilty unpunished; he punishes the children and their children for the sin of the fathers to the third and fourth generation." God doesn't let a guilty person go unpunished. Sin has to be paid for.

So if you're guilty and I'm guilty, how can we get rid of the guilt and our responsibility for sin? Through the work of Jesus who was willing to die for our sins. Because he took our sins upon him we can live, because his righteousness was put upon us. It was similar to what happened at the bank. There was a transfer. This time, though, it wasn't money. This transfer is referred to as imputation. Our sins and sinful natures were imputed to Jesus, which makes us innocent. But in God's eyes we need to be seen as righteous. That's why it was necessary that Jesus' righteousness also be imputed to us.

Do we earn it? No. Do we deserve it? No. Praise God for this transfer![3]

"He picked up the cloak that had fallen from Elijah and went back and stood on the bank of the Jordan" (2 Kings 2:13).

I magine that you've been working with a man for years. He's had a highly responsible job. Known by many, he hasn't always been appreciated because of his brutal honesty. He never allowed any slack, and wouldn't let much slide by. He had standards, and held to them even when others didn't. He even spoke out against the majority, the *immoral majority* of his time.

But now, it's time for him to leave. He's going to die, to go into the presence of the Lord. The man who has been your mentor wants *you* to succeed *him*.

This man always wore a specific article of clothing that set him apart from others and designated who he was. When he dies, that cloak will be there for you to take up as you assume his position. It will designate who and what you are, but it will also bring some hostility from others. You won't always be liked, accepted, or popular. Picking up that cloak will bring you some grief. But you will know that you're doing the right thing.

So what do you do?

That's the dilemma Elisha faced with Elijah the prophet. You can read about it starting in 2 Kings 1. Elisha knew if he were going to follow Elijah he would need an abundance of God's strength, and that's what he asked for. When Elijah was taken up to heaven, he left his cloak behind. Elisha looked at it awhile. Then he picked it up.

We may not have a cloak to pick up and wear, but we do have the cross of Christ. If you think it's heavy, and that carrying it is kind of hard, remember what happened on it. It changed the world. It changed lives. It can change your life.

"These commandments that I give you today are to be upon your hearts. Impress them on your children. Talk about them when you sit at home and when you walk along the road, when you lie down and when you get up" (Deuteronomy 6:6-7).

D o you know...

What the calling is of a father? In what specific ways is a father to be involved with his children? Having a son is an opportunity to lead him to another father, our heavenly Father. A dad who is in a right relationship with God will have the greatest opportunity to be in a right relationship with his wife and his children.

I am a father of both a daughter and a son. I wish I had known thirty years ago what I know today. Part of the problem was due to the limited resources and information that were available. Today an abundance of information is available, but it still needs to be read, applied, and implemented. Perhaps the best way to start is with a strong, graphic statement of the father's importance:

> Fathers leave a lasting impression on the lives of their children. Picture fathers all around the world carving their initials into their family trees. Like a carving in the trunk of an oak, as time passes the impressions fathers make on their children grow deeper and wider. Depending upon how the tree grows, those impressions can either be ones of harmony or ones of distortion.
>
> Some fathers skillfully carve beautiful messages of love, support, solid discipline, and acceptance into the personality core of their children. Others use words and actions that cut deeply and leave emotional scars. Time may heal the wound and dull the image, but the impression can never be completely erased. The size, shape, and extent of your father's imprint on your life may be large or may be small but it is undeniably there.[4]

What kind of imprint are you leaving as a father?

"Moses' father-in-law replied, 'What you are doing is not good. You and these people who come to you will only wear yourselves out. The work is too heavy for you; you cannot handle it alone'" (Exodus 18:17-18).

Have you ever had an in-law make a suggestion to you? If so, how did you take it? Most of us don't want to take advice from our in-laws. Look at Moses. He was busy working for the Lord handling disputes, making decisions, giving out advice, listening to concerned complaints from dusk until dawn. Here he was doing his job all day long and half the night and do you think he was appreciated by his father-in-law, Jethro? It didn't seem so. It sounded like Jethro was critical: "Moses, what in the world are you doing?"

So Moses told him and ended with a statement that ought to put anyone in his place, "I was doing the Lord's work, Jethro." Maybe Moses thought, "That ought to get him off my back and put him in his place." But it didn't faze Jethro. He came back with the statement in the verse above. In essence he said, "Moses, lighten up. You're wearing yourself out. You need *help*! You can't do it all by yourself." Blunt! Direct! Confrontational! But necessary.

Has anyone ever told you that? It's not easy to hear, especially when you are conscientiously working to provide for your family and serve the Lord. But wait a minute. Can we really do it all?

Jethro simply suggested that Moses get other people to help him—that's all. Do you need help? Can you ask for it? Would you?

By the way, take a look at verse 24. Moses listened. He asked for help and his life changed for the better. Will you?

"I give them eternal life, and they shall never perish; no one can snatch them out of my hand" (John 10:28).

Pets can add a lot of enjoyment to our lives... as well as some additional work. Most families end up with at least a dog or a cat. Sometimes they teach us some valuable lessons. For instance, have you ever noticed how a mother cat carries her kittens? It's not like a kangaroo whose baby rides in a pouch or a baby monkey who grasps its mother with its little paws and holds on for all it's worth. A baby monkey's security depends on itself. That's risky. A kitten doesn't have to hang on—the mother grasps the baby by the neck with her teeth and carries it around. The kitten's security depends on the mother.

What does your sense of security depend upon? Work, ability, money, reputation, athletic ability? What about your spiritual security—your salvation? Does it depend on your ability to hang on like a baby monkey, or does it depend on who God is and what he does? What do you believe? Better yet, what does the Scripture teach? Sometimes we let our childhood and life experiences shape what we believe biblically and theologically rather than trust in what Scripture says.

Reread the passage for today and consider its truth. God gave you to his Son and your security is complete in him. Christ paid the price for your sins... in full. Nothing is owed (see Ephesians 1:7), and God is satisfied with the payment (see Romans 3:25). Jesus is continuing his work for you by constantly praying for you (see Colossians 2:13). How often do you think about that fact? When you accepted the Lord, at that moment you were sealed with the Holy Spirit—God owns you (see 2 Corinthians 1:22).

So, if there is a day when you feel insecure for any reason, remember that your other security in Christ is permanent.[5]

"Do not seek revenge or bear a grudge against one of your people, but love your neighbor as yourself..." (Leviticus 19:18a).

This is a message from one of America's pastors about relationships.

Relationships. America's most precious resource. Take our oil, take our weapons, but don't take what holds us together—relationships. A nation's strength is measured by the premium it puts on its own people. When people value people, an impenetrable web is drawn, a web of vitality and security.

A relationship. The delicate fusion of two human beings. The intricate weaving of two lives; two sets of moods, mentalities, and temperaments. Two intermingling hearts, both seeking solace and security.

A relationship. It has more power than any nuclear bomb and more potential than any promising seed. Nothing will drive a man to a greater courage than a relationship. Nothing will fire the heart of a patriot or purge the cynicism of a rebel like a relationship.

What matters most in life is not what ladders we climb or what ownings we accumulate. What matters most is a relationship.

What steps are you taking to protect your "possessions"? What measures are you using to ensure that your relationships are strong and healthy? What are you doing to solidify the bridges between you and those in your world?

Do you resolve conflict as soon as possible, or do you "let the sun go down when you are still angry"? Do you verbalize your love every day to your mate and children? Do you look for chances to forgive? Do you pray daily for those in your life?

Our Master knew the value of a relationship. It was through relationships that he changed the world. His movement thrived not on personality or power but on championing the value of a person. He built bridges and crossed them. Touching the leper... uniting the estranged... exalting the prostitute. And what was that he said about loving your neighbor as yourself?

It's a wise man who values people above possessions.[6]

"Each man should give what he has decided in his heart to give, not reluctantly or under compulsion, for God loves a cheerful giver" (2 Corinthians 9:7).

There is a rival god to the Almighty God in each of our lives. For some it's the god of money. This god propels us, drives us, dominates us, controls us, punishes us, and is never satisfied. Often there's never enough of it. And when there is, it still isn't enough. We want more.

The great reformer Martin Luther had an interesting observation about the term *conversion*. He said, "There are three conversions necessary: the conversion of the heart, the mind, and the purse." The latter is difficult for some because of their attitude.

Jesus confronted a group of people who used their giving as a cover-up for their selfishness. They tithed all right, but they were so picky and ritualistic about it that they missed the whole point of giving. Hear what Jesus said about them.

Woe to you, teachers of the law and Pharisees, you hypocrites! You give a tenth of your spices—mint, dill, and cumin. But you have neglected the more important matters of the law—justice, mercy, and faithfulness. You should have practiced the latter, without neglecting the former. You blind guides! You strain out a gnat but swallow a camel.   **Matthew 23:23-24**

One of the opportunities we all have is to give as much as we can. Les and Leslie Parrott, the authors of *Becoming Soul Mates*, say they changed their perspective from asking, "How much of our money should we give to God?" to, "How much of God's money should we spend on ourselves?"

By the way, do you know how you get rid of the god of money? Give it away. It works.[7]

JUNE 11

"Having eyes, do you not see? And having ears, do you not hear?"
(Mark 8:18, NASB).

"Y ou're not listening to me. What's wrong with you?" "Didn't you hear what I said to you? Where was your mind?" Most men have heard those confrontational words, or words like them, either as children or after they marry. Not too many men enjoy hearing them. One reason is because often they're true. We didn't really hear or, more accurately, we tuned out. We didn't listen. It's easy not to hear what we don't want to hear. We use our filters to act as a screening device, and then sometimes we fall back on the excuse, "I didn't hear you."

An Indian was in downtown New York, walking along with his friend, who lived in New York City. Suddenly he said, "I hear a cricket."

"Oh, you're crazy," his friend replied.

"No, I hear a cricket. I do! I'm sure of it."

"It's the noon hour. You know there are people bustling around, cars honking, taxis squealing, noises from the city. I'm sure you can't hear it."

"I'm sure I do." He listened attentively and then walked to the corner, across the street, and looked all around. Finally on the other corner he found a shrub in a large cement planter. He dug beneath the leaf and found a cricket.

His friend was duly astounded. But the Indian said, "No. My ears are no different than yours. It simply depends on what you are listening to. Here, let me show you."

He reached into his pocket and pulled out a handful of change—a few quarters, some dimes, nickels, and pennies. And he dropped it on the concrete.

Every head within a block turned.

"You see what I mean?" the Indian said, as he began picking up his coins. "It all depends on what you are listening for."[8]

What are you listening for? Who do you have difficulty hearing? It could be the Lord with a message that will make your life better than it is now. Not hearing someone may protect us or get us off the hook, but when we don't hear, we never really know what good thing we may have missed.

"If any of you lacks wisdom, he should ask God, who gives gener-ously to all without finding fault, and it will be given to him"
(James 1:5).

D o you like owls? Owls are fascinating creatures with their ability to see and fly at night as well as their heightened sense of hear-ing. But owls are mentioned in Scripture in a very unique way.

In the Bible, the owl is mentioned usually in connection with deso-lation foretold for nations and their proud cities. Zephaniah prophe-sied that Nineveh would be left "utterly desolate and dry as the desert" (2:13) and that the call of the desert owl and the screech owl would "echo through the windows" (2:14). Isaiah foretold of another doomed land, "The great owl and the raven will nest there" (34:11). Because owls lived in the ruins and caves of desolate, forsaken places, the psalmist said when he was feeling alone and distressed, "I am... like an owl among the ruins" (Ps 102:6). In the Bible (for example, Micah 1:3-8) the owl is associated with God's judgment on unbelief, because its haunting sound in the night can scare us.[9]

We tend to refer to the owl as wise. We're told to take this wisdom to heart. But there's a better place to get your wisdom. It's in God's Word. Proverbs 1:7-8 says, "The fear of the Lord is the beginning of knowledge, but fools despise wisdom and discipline."

We all need wisdom—the ability to accurately discern and make good decisions. All you have to do to get it is seek God, and you'll find him. Then ask him for wisdom, and you will receive.

JUNE 13

"The Lord is my shepherd, I shall not be in want. He makes me lie down in green pastures, he leads me beside quiet waters, he restores my soul. He guides me in paths of righteousness for his name's sake" (Psalms 23:1-3).

In the midst of the noise, and the hustle and bustle of everyday life, what would you like to see God doing in your life? Just think about it for a minute. Some have said, "I'd like to see that God cares. I'd like to see him do something good... for a change." Well, he's always doing good things for us.

One of the ways God does things for us is best explained by a hobby that many men enjoy—restoring old cars. They take that old wreck with the metal rusting, the tires flat, the spark plugs all chewed up, and the upholstery torn to shreds. But often after several months of painstaking effort, sanding, polishing, ripping out, and putting in, the car begins to look like it did the day it rolled off the assembly line. Instead of looking like a wreck, it is restored.

There will be times in all our lives when we want to be restored, when our goals are shattered and our dreams have turned into nightmares. Not only do we make mistakes and fail, but sometimes other people pull the rug out from underneath us.

Our God is a God who restores.

Our God is a God who heals.

Our God is a God who can reverse our fortunes from bad to good.

Just imagine that! The psalmist describes what God does so well.[10]

The Lord is close to the brokenhearted and saves those who are crushed in spirit. **Psalms 34:18**

He raises the poor from the dust and lifts the needy from the ash heap; he seats them with princes, the princes of their people. **Psalms 113:7-8**

"A father to the fatherless, a defender of widows, is God in his holy dwelling" (Psalms 68:5).

What were your parents like? Can you think back to being a preschooler? What did you think of your parents? When you were ten, what were your thoughts about your parents? When you became a teenager, your perception of your parents had probably changed radically.

Perhaps you haven't thought about your parents very much. When you were younger and defenseless you needed them to nourish and protect you. There were times when you went running to them because you were afraid or hurt. They probably came through for you... most of the time. But sometimes they were lacking. They weren't perfect. No parent is. You may have wanted them to listen to you more, love you more, or help you more.

Then you became an adult. If you think you outgrew your need for a parent, you didn't. We still need a parent, and we have one... God. Psalms 103:13 says that "as a father has compassion on his children, so the Lord has compassion on those who fear him."

The way he cares for you is far superior to anything you could ever imagine. He never makes mistakes. Time is not a problem for him. He is not limited by anything our parents were limited by.

If there is a cry inside of you for something your parents couldn't give you or do for you, that cry can be silenced. The needs of your life can be and have been met by your heavenly Father. You have been adopted by him with all—*not some*, but all—the benefits.

If you're in need of parenting, you've got it.

If you're in need of acceptance, you've got it.

If you're in need of love, you've got it.

"You then, my son, be strong in the grace that is in Christ Jesus. And the things you have heard me say in the presence of many witnesses entrust to reliable men who will also be qualified to teach others" (2 Timothy 2:1-2).

All fathers are different from one another. They respond differently to the challenges of fatherhood. But they all leave an imprint on our lives.

My own father did not talk very much. One day I asked him if he loved me, and he said of course he did. I knew it, but I just wanted to hear it from him.

I am an avid reader. I love to read Western and adventure novels. I grew up going to the library every week and reading practically every book in the children's section. Why? Because Dad, who only finished the eighth grade, read two books a week and was constantly at the library. I had a positive role model.

Dad did something else for me that totally influenced my life. As a child, I did not like going to church. I found every excuse possible to get out of going.

When I was twelve, my dad said he would like me to go with him to a new church. We would take the new members' class together, and then join the church together. That started my involvement at the First Presbyterian Church of Hollywood, where I practically lived throughout junior and senior high school. I was eventually influenced toward the ministry by Dr. Henrietta Mears in the college department.

Dad had his faults and his strengths, but who doesn't? Sons have a choice as to which of their fathers' characteristics they will focus on.

I appreciate my dad for who he was as a person and for the years we had together. I hope you appreciate your dad. If so, let him know, if he's still living.

And make sure you don't waste the time to do things with and for your children now so they will learn to appreciate you.

"Finally, brothers, whatever is true, whatever is noble, whatever is right, whatever is pure, whatever is lovely, whatever is admirable— if anything is excellent or praiseworthy—think about such things" (Philippians 4:8).

Lord Jesus, I come to you today asking for power, strength, and the grace that I need to overcome the temptations that are all around me and appeal to a man.

I need a pure heart that will slam the door of my heart to the wrong thoughts which seem to come in uninvited.

I need your strength for my willpower so I can be strong to fight against the temptations at work and on the television screen.

I ask for an abundance of love to replace all bitterness, to serve as you served and to forgive as you forgave.

May I be faithful so others, especially my family, can rely upon my word.

Help me to stick to my commitments and projects to see them through. When I tend to be lazy, please give me a shove in the right direction.

Give me clarity of mind to make the right decisions. When I don't know what to do give me the willingness to ask for help—and to listen to the advice.

I pray that I won't wallow in regrets over the past nor live in the dreams for the future—keep me in the real, present world so I don't overlook what you have for me or want me to do.

As your Word says, help me to fight the good fight as Paul did. May I be a race finisher and not just a starter. Help me to keep the faith and at the end receive the crown of righteousness you have promised.

Thank you for hearing me and for being faithful.

In your name,

Amen.[11]

"I made a covenant with my eyes not to look lustfully at a girl" (Job 31:1).

Let's talk about lust. God's Word talks about it. We all struggle with it at times. So... why not talk about it? Most men and women don't really know what God's Word says about it. For example, did you know there are four Hebrew and three Greek words translated into the English word "lust" or "to lust after"?

In Exodus 15 Moses and the people of Israel sing a song of praise to God after their deliverance from Egypt. In verse 9 they sing, "The enemy said, 'I will pursue, I will overtake, I will divide the spoil; My *desire* shall be gratified against them; I will draw out my sword, my hand will destroy them.'" The word *desire* in the *New American Standard Version* is translated "lust" in other versions.

Hedonism is an English word that comes from the Greek word *hedone,* translated "lust" in James 4:1 and 3 in the King James Version. In each instance in Scripture where the word *hedone* is used, whether translated "lust" or "pleasure," the emphasis is on gratification of natural or sinful desires.

You see, God designed sex to be part of a relationship. When whole persons interact with each other as objects, lust becomes a problem.

Without a relationship as a foundation for sexual intimacy, then, people treat each other as objects to gratify their lust rather than as whole persons.

The point is that within God's design, *desire,* even strong desire, is not wrong; it is good. The Greek word *epithumia* illustrates this. It denotes strong desire of any kind.

Since marriage is God's design, strong desire within marriage is not only natural, it is blessed. Even anticipative desire that precedes marriage is natural and blessed. This is where our desire belongs.

So what, then, is lust?

Lust is not noticing that a woman is sexually attractive. Lust is born when we turn a simple awareness into a preoccupied fantasy. When we invite sexual thoughts into our minds and nurture them, we have passed from simple awareness into lust. Luther put it this way: "We cannot help it if birds fly over our heads. It is another thing if we invite them to build nests in our hair."[12]

JUNE 18

"God said to Moses, 'I AM WHO I AM.' This is what you are to say to the Israelites: 'I AM has sent me to you'" (Exodus 3:14).

Who is the God you worship? Let's explore your beliefs to see if what you believe is really who God is or if you have created your own image of him. It happens, you know.

Remember when you were first born and an infant? Of course you don't. But when you were that young you were completely dependent. You couldn't do a thing. Your parents had to care for you. You were dependent on them for life and nourishment. Animals are dependent on other animals, vegetation, and water for survival. Trees and plants are dependent on sun, rain, and good soil for their survival. Everything in this world is dependent upon something else in order to survive.

All except God. God is the only one who is truly independent. As men, we might think we are, but we're not. God doesn't need to be dependent on anything else in order to survive because *he is God*. He has life in himself.

Perhaps you wonder what God meant when he said "I AM WHO I AM." It's a strange statement. He was saying to the people then and to you and me now that he is the one who has always existed. You and I are bound by time. *God isn't*. You and I have a beginning and we will have an end. *God doesn't*. He always exists. You and I have a past, present, and future. For God, everything is in the present. His name emphasizes his self-existence.

Well, that's a lot to comprehend. And think about this: Isn't it even more amazing that an independent, timeless God reaches down to love us?[13]

JUNE 19

"For I am the Lord, I do not change" (Malachi 3:6).

We live in a world full of rapid change. And it's occurring faster and faster all the time. There is one thing, though, that doesn't and won't change, and that is God. Change has a purpose. It's either for better or for worse. However, it's impossible for God to change. But what does that actually mean?

His *life* doesn't change. Created things have a beginning and ending, but God doesn't. He has always been. There wasn't a time he didn't exist. He doesn't grow older. He doesn't get wiser, stronger, or weaker. He can't change for the better. He's already there.

> They shall perish, but you go on forever. They will grow old, like worn-out clothing, and you will change them like a man putting on a new shirt and throwing away the old one! **Psalms 102:26, TLB**

> Listen to me, my people, my chosen ones! I alone am God. I am the First; I am the Last. **Isaiah 48:12, TLB**

God's *character* does not change. He doesn't become less or more truthful, or merciful, or good than he was or is. James talks about God's goodness, generosity to men, and holiness. He speaks about God as one "with whom there is no variation or shadow due to change" (1:17, RSV).

God's *truth* doesn't change. He doesn't have to take back anything he's ever said. God still keeps the promises of his Word.

God's *purposes* do not change. What God does in the context of time, he planned from eternity. All that he has committed himself to do in his Word will be done. Nothing takes God by surprise so that he has to revise his plan.

It's difficult to comprehend everything about God with our minds and thinking processes. But that just shows what a difference there is between us and God.[14]

JUNE 20

"It seems to be a fact of life that when I want to do what is right, I inevitably do what is wrong" (Romans 7:21, TLB).

Would you like to be successful? What man wouldn't? The problem lies in discovering the proper formula. But it's really no mystery; in fact, it's simple. All you have to do to succeed is fail. That's right, fail... and then learn from your failures. You may see failure as the enemy of success. But it's not. It's the first step toward success. Failure is a stern but helpful teacher.

Have you heard the story about the young executive who asked the company president how he became successful? The man replied, "By making good decisions." The young man then asked how he learned to make good decisions. The president answered, "By making bad ones." We can learn important lessons from bad decisions.

When you hear the name Babe Ruth, you probably think of his record 714 home runs. Few people know that he also set the record for striking out. So he failed a lot, but he also succeeded.

In 1978, after thirteen attempts over a period of 105 years, the first transatlantic balloon flight became a reality. What made the difference? One additional crew member and experience. One of the crew said, "I don't think you can fly the Atlantic without experience, and that's one reason it hasn't been flown before. Success in any venture is just the intelligent application of failure."[15]

We have a choice in how we will respond to failure, a choice that can make a big difference in our struggle toward success. Dr. Gary Oliver says,

> Failures can leave many different scars—hurt feelings, wounded relationships, wasted potential, broken marriages, shattered ministries—but they can also be used by God to sharpen the mind, deepen the spirit, and strengthen the soul. Those people who have learned to view failure through God's eyes emerge with a softer heart, stronger character, and a fresh awareness of God's grace.[16]

"Be strong and courageous, because you will lead these people to inherit the land I swore to their forefathers to give them" (Joshua 1:6).

We admire courage. Sometimes we say, "That took a lot of guts!" That means the same thing. It takes courage today to survive. It takes even more courage to live the Christian life. God wants men of courage. He gave us some great examples throughout his Word. Remember Joshua? It seemed as though everyone was telling him to be courageous. Twice Moses told him to be courageous, and four times God said the same thing to him. Even the leaders of the people said it!

If people kept telling you to be courageous, wouldn't it get to you after a while? After all, Joshua was no wimp! He had led the army for forty years! Why all the pushing to be courageous?

Perhaps it happened because of what was facing him, and it could be he knew he needed to hear those words again and again. Consider what he was going to be asked to do.

He would lead Israel—a huge group of people—on a military campaign to take over the land, and he had to provide moral leadership as well (see Joshua 1:6). What about you? If you're married, how are your leadership skills in your family? How are they expressed in the financial area? The spiritual?

Joshua was asked to be courageous because he had to obey God's law. "Be strong and courageous. Be careful to obey all the law my servant Moses gave you; do not turn from it to the right or to the left, that you may be successful wherever you go" (Jos 1:7). Not everyone followed it. Not very many follow God's law today. It will take courage on your part to follow it, especially at work.

God told Joshua one other thing about courage: He could be strong because God would support him. "Have I not commanded you? Be strong and courageous. Do not be terrified; do not be discouraged, for the Lord your God will be with you wherever you go" (Jos 1:9).

God is your source of courage, too. He's there, waiting to respond. Just ask![17]

"But I tell you the truth: It is for your good that I am going away. Unless I go away, the Counselor will not come to you; but if I go, I will send him to you" (John 16:7).

M ax Lucado, an insightful writer, helps us understand the Holy Spirit:

The Holy Spirit is not an "it." He is a person. He has knowledge (1 Cor 2:11). He has a will (1 Cor 12:11). He has a mind (Rom 8:27). He has affections (Rom 15:30). You can lie to him (Acts 5:3-4). You can insult him (Heb 10:29). You can grieve him (Eph 4:30).

The Holy Spirit is not an impersonal force. He is not Popeye's spinach or the surfer's wave. He is God within you to help you. In fact John calls him the Helper.

Envision a father helping his son learn to ride a bicycle, and you will have a partial picture of the Holy Spirit. The father stays at the son's side. He pushes the bike and steadies it if the boy starts to tumble. The Spirit does that for us; he stays our step and strengthens our stride. Unlike the father, however, he never leaves. He is with us to the end of the age.

What does the Spirit do?

He comforts the saved. "When I go away, I will send the Helper to you" (Jn 16:7).

He convicts the lost. "When the Helper comes, he will prove to the people of the world the truth about sin, about being right with God, and about judgment" (Jn 16:8).

He conveys the truth. "I have many more things to say to you, but they are too much for you now. When the Spirit of truth comes, he will lead you into all truth" (Jn 16:12).

Is John saying we don't need the book in order to dance? Of course not; he helped write it. Emotion without knowledge is as dangerous as knowledge without emotion. God seeks a balance. "God is spirit, and those who worship him must worship in spirit and truth" (Jn 4:24).[18]

JUNE 23

"Only be careful, and watch yourselves closely so that you do not forget the things your eyes have seen or let them slip from your heart as long as you live. Teach them to your children and to their children after them" (Deuteronomy 4:9).

Fathers, do not exasperate your children; instead, bring them up in the training and instruction of the Lord.   **Ephesians 6:4**

D r. Dave Stoop talks about the crucial role of a father's influence in his book *Making Peace with Your Father*. He suggests that a father's role includes that of a nurturer, lawgiver, protector, and a spiritual mentor. When a father nurtures his son, the son feels secure and valued and is able to bond with his dad. But he needs to see his dad approach life with competence and confidence as well. Lawgiving is not the same as being authoritarian. It means being involved in a son's life, as well as clarifying the rules and enforcing discipline. Stoop writes:

> When lawgiving is balanced with nurturing, a father helps his children learn to make decisions about right and wrong for themselves. It is not just a matter of "following orders." When it comes to rules and standards of behavior, children operate on a "show me, don't tell me" basis. They need to see morality modeled, struggled with, confronted, and dealt with realistically and honestly. A father who is comfortably balanced in his lawgiving role is able to *demonstrate* his sense of integrity and morality by the way he relates to his children, not just proclaim it to them.[19]

As a protector, a father especially needs to stand with his son during the adolescent years, when they are confronted by changes that can affect them both. This is a time to help a child prepare himself to battle effectively with life. Being a spiritual mentor means drawing the child into the future and helping him dream realistically. It means helping a son learn to live a life of faith.[20]

JUNE 24

"So I say to you: Ask and it will be given to you; seek and you will find; knock and the door will be opened to you. For everyone who asks receives; he who seeks finds; and to him who knocks, the door will be opened" (Luke 11:9-10).

P rayer has many elements. Too often, though, we focus our prayer on what we want, need, or expect. We focus on ourselves. But why not turn the focus upon the One we're praying to—God himself? Dr. Lloyd Ogilvie talks about the importance of the first essential element of prayer.

> *All great praying begins with adoration.* God does not need our praise as much as we need to give it. Praise is like a thermostat that opens the heart to flow in communion with God. Hallowing God's name is enumerating His attributes. When we think magnificently about God's nature we become open to experience afresh His glory in our lives. I once took a course in creative conversation. The key thing I discovered was that there can be no deep exchange with another person until we have established the value of that person to us. Just as profound conversation with another person results from our communicating that person's worth to us, so too, we become receptive to what God wants to do in our lives when we have taken time to tell Him what He means to us. Don't hurry through adoration. Everything else depends on it. Tell God what He means to you, pour out your heart in unhurried moments of exultation. Allow Him to remind you of aspects of His nature you need to claim in the subsequent steps in prayer. Don't forget He is the leader of the conversation. The more we praise the Lord, the more we will be able to think His thoughts after Him throughout our prayer. He loosens the tissues of our brains to become channels of His Spirit.
>
> Praise is the ultimate level of relinquishment. When we praise God for not only all He is but what He is doing in our lives, we reach a liberating stage of surrender.[21]

These are words of wisdom that could change your relationship with God. Adore him today.

"Let him kiss me with the kisses of his mouth—for your love is more delightful than wine" (Song of Solomon 1:2).

Have you ever considered the sexual benefits of being a Christian? That's a far-out question. But think about it.

Are there any benefits sexually to being a Christian? Many have viewed Christianity as being restrictive rather than freeing, negative rather than positive, anti-sex rather than pro-sex. God is for sex. It was His idea. He created not only the pleasurable drive but the best and proper context for its total expression.

For many Christians, their faith and their sexuality have existed like a double set of train tracks, paralleling one another as far as one can see going off into the distance. But they never come together. What *are* the benefits? Consider these:

1. Negative attitudes toward our body and sex can be overcome by accepting what God has said about our body and sex.

   When we come to the realization that God and Christ are aware of our love-making as a married couple and are saying, "That is as was intended!" We can relax and rest in His approval. God approves that it is pleasurable. Pleasure is God's bonus. It's His gift of ecstasy and joy.

2. The presence of Christ in a person's life can give him the ability to love another with agape love. Because of His unconditional love, we can move toward that love which brings a greater sexual life.

3. The potential for greater commitment to one another is available because of the presence of Christ in our life.

4. Jesus also assists a person to communicate in an open and honest manner. Vulnerability can occur and hidden hurts and concerns can come to the forefront. These barriers once eliminated help to create a closer relationship.

5. Forgiveness is another benefit. Having been forgiven by God, an individual has the capability of forgiving himself for past events and the total forgiveness of others.

   Romans 8:1 states there is "no condemnation for those who are in Christ Jesus." For many, this has meant no condemnation *except* in sexual matters. Not so.[22]

Sex is God's idea. It has a purpose and a place. Thank him for it and... enjoy.

"God ...in these last days has spoken to us in His Son..." (Hebrews 1:1-2, NASB).

Has God ever spoken to you directly? I don't mean necessarily an audible voice, but in some other way? This passage tells about the fact that God has revealed himself to people in a variety of ways.

One of the interesting means God used to reveal himself in the Old Testament was through theophanies. Have you ever heard of this before? A theophany is when God shows himself in and through some created thing. When God revealed himself to Moses, how did he do it? It was through a bush burning with divine glory.

But God also revealed himself through dreams, and quite frequently, too. Have you ever experienced this? Remember some of them in the Bible? There were Jacob, Joseph, Nebuchadnezzar, and Zacharias. In the New Testament, God also spoke to Joseph and to Pilate's wife through dreams.

Others saw visions. Ezekiel, Isaiah, and Peter were awake when they experienced God speaking to them in this way.

Did you ever wonder how the people responded to those who saw a theophany or had a dream or vision? We know how people would view us today—skeptically!

How does God speak to us today? I've experienced God's direction through a sermon or message that I felt was just for me. His Word speaks to us. And he speaks to us through prayers.

"Follow me" *(Luke 9:49).*

We often ask, "What's it going to cost me?" It's a good question. You need to know what something costs before you commit to it. The Christian life is the same way. Dr. Lloyd Ogilvie addresses this question:

> Today's Scripture shows us several responses to the cost of commitment. Jesus' mood is determined and decisive: He is on the way to Jerusalem, and He wants followers who can count the cost. The three different levels of commitment represented in people He met along the way expose the ways Christians relate to their discipleship today.
>
> The first man made a grand, pious commitment that went no deeper than words. He promised to follow the Master wherever He went. Jesus challenged the man to count the cost. So often we come to Christ to receive what we want to solve problems or gain inspiration for our challenges. He gives both with abundance, but then calls us into ministry of concern and caring. We are to do for others what He has done for us. Loving and forgiving are not always easy.
>
> The second man had unfinished business from the past. He wanted to follow Christ, but a secondary loyalty kept him tied to the past. In substance, Christ said, "Forget the past; follow Me!" We dare not misinterpret His words to suggest a lack of concern for life's obligations, but rather a call to be concerned about His call to live rather than worry about what is dead and past.
>
> The third person wanted to say goodbye to his family. Jesus' response to him stresses the urgency of our commitment. He was concerned about competing loyalties in the man. Our commitment must be unreserved to seek *first* His kingdom. We are left with a question about ways that we have one hand on the plow of discipleship and the other reaching back to the past or to lesser commitments. In what ways are you looking back?[23]

JUNE 28

"And my God will meet all your needs according to his glorious riches in Christ Jesus" (Philippians 4:19).

There is an old legend about three men and their sacks. Each man had two sacks, one tied in front of his neck and the other tied around his back. When the first man was asked, "Hey, what's in the sacks?" he said, "Well, in the sack on my back are all the good things my friends and family have done. That way they're out of sight and hidden from view. In the front sack are all the bad things that have happened to me. Every now and then, I stop, open the sack, take the things out, examine them, and think about them."

Because he stopped so much to concentrate on all the bad stuff, he really didn't make much progress in life.

The second man was asked, "What have you got in those two sacks?" He replied, "In the front sack are all the good things I've done. I like them, I like to see them. So quite often I take them out to show them off to everyone around me. The sack in the back? Huh, I keep all my mistakes in there and carry them with me all the time. Sure, they're heavy. It's true that they slow me down. But you know, for some reason I can't put them down."

When the third man was asked about his two sacks, his answer was, "The sack in front is great. In this one I keep all the positive thoughts I have about people, all the blessings I've experienced, and all the great things other people have done for me. The weight isn't a problem. It's like the sails of a ship. It keeps me going forward.

"The sack on my back is empty. There's nothing in it. I cut a big hole in the bottom of it. So I put all the bad things in there that I think about myself or hear about others. They go in one end and out the other so I'm not carrying around any extra weight at all."

What are you carrying around in your sacks?

Who are you carrying around in your sacks?

Which sack is full, the one full of blessings or the one in back?[24]

"In Him you have been made complete" *(Colossians 2:10, NASB).*

Remember the TV miniseries *Roots?* Perhaps you read the book by Alex Haley. It was the fascinating story of an African-American man searching for his roots and heritage, whose journey took him back to Africa.

Many of us are interested in our genealogy. Doing a historical search of your family and heritage can help you understand yourself in a new way. But as Christians we enjoy an additional heritage. Our roots are found in the fact that we were created in the image of God. And God wants his work to be complete in us. Enjoy the following description of your heritage in Christ:

> This, then, is the wonder of the Christian message: that God is this kind of God; that He loves me with a love that is not turned off by my sins, my failures, my inadequacies, my insignificance. I am not an anomalous disease crawling on the face of an insignificant speck in the vast emptiness of space. I am not a nameless insect waiting to be crushed by an impersonal boot. I am not a miserable offender cowering under the glare of an angry deity. I am a man beloved by God Himself. I have touched the very heart of the universe, and have found His name to be love. And that love has reached me, not because I have merited God's favor, not because I have anything to boast about, but because of what He is, and because of what Christ has done for me in the Father's name. And I can believe this about God (and therefore about myself) because Christ has come from the Father and has revealed by His teaching, by His life, by His death, by His very person that this is what God is like: He is "full of grace."[25]

"For as a man thinks in his heart so is he" (Proverbs 23:7, NKJV).
"Let not your heart be troubled..." (John 14:27, NASB).

Did you know that most stress comes from ourselves—our thought life and our attitudes? That's right, our inner responses are the culprit. What we put into our minds and what we think about affects our bodies. Consider one way in which your thought life is affected daily: what you listen to on the radio or what you watch on TV, especially if it's the news.

What is the first thing you listen to on the radio in the morning? What is the last TV program you watch at night before you try to go to sleep? There may be a correlation to the stress you feel.

What you think about when you're driving can stress you out, too. If you are stuck on the freeway and have an appointment in twenty minutes, for which you will now be late, what do you say to yourself? Do you sit there and fuss and say things like, "I can't be late! Who's holding us up? Those clowns! I've got to get out of this lane"? Do you lean on the horn and glare at other drivers? That's why you are getting upset—it's caused by your thoughts and the way you are responding to a situation over which you have no control. You're butting up against a brick wall.

In a situation over which you have no control and there is nothing you can do, quit fighting it. Go with it! Give yourself permission to be stuck in traffic. **Give yourself permission** to be late. Tell yourself, "All right. I would rather not be stuck here and would rather not be late. But I can handle it. I give myself permission to be here, and I can make use of the time." Instead of fussing you could pray, read a book, put on a tape, smile at the other drivers, or sit back and relax. By doing this, you take control of the situation—and your inner responses—and your stress drains away. You may not be able to take this attitude in every situation, but in many you can. Why not try it today? It may keep your heart from being troubled.

"Call to me and I will answer you and tell you great and unsearchable things you do not know" (Jeremiah 33:3).

There's an important choice all of us must make. We can plod along in our Christian life, using our own ideas, plans, and strength. Or we can really get with the program and let God amaze us by what he will do. With God's help you may surprise yourself by what you're able to do, just like a certain woodpecker I heard about in a book called *Battle Fatigue*.

> It seems he went through life much as the other woodpeckers, bouncing from tree to tree, drilling holes, searching for grubs, occasionally running from a hungry cat. He was comfortable.
>
> Then it happened! One afternoon, as he was going about his business of boring into tree trunks—suddenly, unexpectedly, without announcement or warning—a bolt of lightning zapped that tree, splitting it right down the middle. The poor woodpecker was thrown several feet into the air and out over the forest. When he landed, he was belly up on the forest floor. He slowly opened his eyes. Dazed, feathers smoking, beak tingling, he shook himself. As he surveyed the demise of the mighty oak, he rubbed his smoldering beak and raised a skeptical eyebrow. Then, he stood straight up, thrust out his charred chest feathers, and strutted off through the woods saying, "My, I didn't I know I had that in me!"
>
> How many Christians are like that woodpecker? We spend our appointed days in the doldrums of the ordinary, frightened by the unscheduled, content to walk in the familiar, well-worn ruts of life. Then suddenly, God intervenes in our lives, moves us out of the mundane, changes our routine, lifts us above the forest floor for a brief moment—by doing something which takes us totally by surprise—and we look at our smoking beaks, dust ourselves off, and say, "Did I do that? I didn't know I had that in me."[1]

What would you like to be doing in your Christian life? If you don't know, ask God for instructions. If you do know, ask him to take you by surprise so you can say, "I didn't know I had that in me!"

"Now Moses was a very humble man, more humble than anyone else on the face of the earth" (Numbers 12:3).

I s there a meek man in your life? Perhaps there's one at work, in the family, or at church. What do you think of him? Is he a man you'd like to be like or would rather stay away from? Are there any meek men on the Dallas Cowboys football team or the L.A. Kings hockey team?

We tend to equate meekness with being a wimp! Not so. Moses wasn't passive. He took on an Egyptian overseer, stood up to Pharaoh, and hiked the desert for forty years. It's kind of hard to see him as a wimp.

Meek doesn't mean what we think. Bottom line, it's being humble before God. It's a choice. It's deliberately harnessing your strength and tempering it to use in a controlled way. Meek isn't weak. It's believing and obeying God... even when you don't particularly want to.

Moses wasn't always enthusiastic about what God wanted. Nor did he feel capable. Sort of like us at times. When God called him to lead the people out of bondage he didn't exactly say, "Right on!" It was more like, "Me! You've got to be kidding. Try someone else" (see Exodus 4:10-13).

God's response..."I will be with you."

When you're debating whether to teach that Sunday school class, feeling hesitant and inferior, God says, "I will be with you."

When you wonder whether you can make it another day with the stress of your job, he says, "I will be with you."

When you're faced with a tough decision and wondering what to do, he says, "I will be with you."

You may be a bit reluctant. So was Moses. But he obeyed God. Moses believed him, did what he said, and said what he was told.

So can you... and that's being meek.[2]

"What profit is there if you gain the world—and lose eternal life? What can be compared with the value of eternal life?" (Matthew 16:26, TLB).

We all want to be successful in some way. But there are so many conflicting ideas on what success is. How do you balance the demands of the family, the job, and the teachings of Scripture to arrive at success?

Perhaps it comes back to a basic question, "What is important to you?" After all, that's usually what determines why we do what we do. Perhaps the best way to decide is by asking *and* answering these questions.

- In what way am I putting God first in my life? "But seek first his kingdom and his righteousness, and all these things will be given to you as well" (Mt 6:33).

- In what way am I in the center of God's will? "For it is God who works in you to will and to act according to his good purpose" (Phil 2:13).

- In what way am I constantly seeking after the will of God? "Do not conform any longer to the pattern of this world, but be transformed by the renewing of your mind. Then you will be able to test and approve what God's will is—his good, pleasing, and perfect will" (Rom 12:2).

- In what way should I be the husband, father, and provider? "If anyone does not provide for his relatives, and especially for his immediate family, he has denied the faith and is worse than an unbeliever" (1 Tm 5:8).

- In what way am I seeking to be financially responsible? "Whoever can be trusted with very little can also be trusted with much, and whoever is dishonest with very little will also be dishonest with much. So if you have not been trustworthy in handling worldly wealth, who will trust you with true riches? And if you have not been trustworthy with someone else's property, who will give you property of your own?" (Lk 16:10-12).[3]

Well, what did you learn? And what will you do about what you have learned?

JULY 4

"If the Lord is pleased with us, he will lead us into that land, a land flowing with milk and honey, and will give it to us. Only do not rebel against the Lord. And do not be afraid of the people of the land, because we will swallow them up. Their protection is gone, but the Lord is with us. Do not be afraid of them" (Numbers 14:8-9).

Sometimes kids look for ways to avoid doing their chores, especially if the chores are difficult. Some carry this pattern with them into adulthood. If it's difficult, risky, or a challenge they think of many creative ways to avoid the task.

Fortunately, only a few men are like that. Most are like Caleb. Remember good old Caleb? He and Joshua were the only two men who survived the forty years of wandering in the wilderness and were allowed to enter the Promised Land. In Joshua 14:6-12, Caleb made an unusual request of Joshua. Here is the last portion of what he said:

> So here I am today, eighty-five years old! I am still as strong today as the day Moses sent me out; I'm just as vigorous to go out to battle now as I was then. Now give me this hill country that the Lord promised me that day. You yourself heard then that the Anakites were there and their cities were large and fortified, but, the Lord helping me, I will drive them out just as He said.   **Joshua 14:10b-12**

This man was ready to take on the Anakites, who were giants!

Caleb still believed that God wanted his people to possess the land.

Caleb still had confidence in God. He didn't give excuses. He wanted the challenge. And he rose to it.

Do you have friends who see life in this way? Do you see life this way? Full of challenges and opportunities? You may have giants facing you, but it's amazing, when you face them they seem to shrink. There may be a giant you have to face today. Do it with the Lord![4]

JULY 5

"Do not withhold good from those who deserve it, when it is in your power to act" (Proverbs 3:27-28).

Often at funerals and memorial services one or more family members or friends deliver a eulogy. They share the positive qualities, characteristics, and accomplishments of the deceased. They extol the person's virtues and go into detail as to why the person will be missed. Everyone there hears the kind and affirming words except one—the person they are talking about. Sometimes you wonder if they knew while they were alive that this is how others felt about them. You wonder how much of what was shared at the memorial service was ever told to them directly. In most cases, it probably wasn't.

The passage in Proverbs certainly gives us clear directions. There are some families who have taken this to heart in a dramatic way. They have conducted living eulogy services with a family member who is terminally ill. The family members and friends come together with the person in their hospital room or home and each one shares face-to-face with this individual what they would say if they were giving the eulogy. Of course, this is better than waiting until someone is gone before acknowledging his or her importance. But what a difference it might have made had such statements been made throughout that person's life!

So many parents and children end up saying, "If only I had told them how much I loved them, what I appreciated, how much they meant to me...." "IF only"...words of regret and sadness over missed opportunities. The presence of positive words can motivate, encourage, and lift up. The absence, well, perhaps they would never know what they missed. Or they could have been living with the longing for a few well-chosen words. We can't change the times we've missed, but we can fill our family members' lives now and in the future. Who needs words of love and encouragement from you? And who do you need to hear from? What others hear from you may help them do likewise.[5]

"A man of many companions may come to ruin, but there is a friend who sticks closer than a brother" (Proverbs 18:24).

"You just can't depend on anyone. They let you down when you need them the most." Have you ever felt that way? Whether it happens to you in business or with a friend, it's disappointing. You look for predictability in other people, yet when they let you down, it's irritating. The best description of this dilemma is found in Proverbs: "Trust in a faithless man in time of trouble is like a bad tooth or a foot that slips" (25:19, RSV).

When you encounter unfaithfulness in a friend, you feel like the rug has been pulled out from under you. And it often happens when you're the most vulnerable. The Scriptures are filled with examples of this problem. One example was David. He was more wounded emotionally by his friends than by his enemies. He shared this hurt in one of the psalms. "If an enemy were insulting me, I could endure it; if a foe were raising himself against me, I could hide from him. But it is you, a man like myself, my companion, my close friend, with whom I once enjoyed sweet fellowship as we walked with the throng at the house of God" (55:12-14).

You expect friends to keep their word as well as your confidences. Faithful friends do that. When this trust is violated, the relationship is often severed. Proverbs states: "A perverse man stirs up dissension, and a gossip separates close friends" (16:28).

So, is it worth it to have close male friendships? Oh, you bet it is. Any relationship involves a risk. We can let a bad experience poison us against other involvements. We can concentrate on what others have done, become gun-shy with people, and isolate ourselves. Or we can see what we can learn from the experience.

Regardless of what someone has done to you, be a faithful friend yourself. Other people need your friendship, your faithfulness. Everyone will benefit. It's worth the risk.[6]

JULY 7

"Then the Lord said, 'Rise and anoint him, he is the one'"
(1 Samuel 16:12b).

How do you handle it when you see one of those guys? You know, the kind who has everything—looks, muscles, brains, voice, ability, smarts? It almost seems immoral for anyone to have so much. Sometimes you wonder why everything was poured into one person. Couldn't God have spread it around a bit? Where's the fairness in this!?!

Well, perhaps there were people in David's time who felt the same way. He was a man, as the Scripture says, who was good-looking and without a fault physically (see 1 Samuel 16:12). To be a shepherd took a tremendous amount of intelligence and skill. And then, well, how would you like to take on a bear and a lion, not with a 30.06, a 270, or a double-barrel shotgun with slugs, but with a spear! Talk about giving the animals an edge! David did it, though. He was also one of the most gifted musicians of his time, and a prolific poet as well.

He was brilliant as a politician, military leader, and guerilla fighter. He was also able to unite the tribes of Israel into a nation. It wasn't easy. They had as many differences culturally and politically then as the PLO and Israel do today.

Sure, David was gifted. So are you. Maybe not in the same way, but you have abilities. Have you discovered them? Better yet, are you using them for his glory? That's why you have them.

By the way, if you're tempted to compare yourself with some outstanding guy like David, keep in mind we've all got our failings. David did. After all, he murdered a man and committed adultery. That's a bit sobering. We're all a mixture of strengths and weaknesses. The good news is, God uses us, regardless.

"And take the helmet of salvation, and the sword of the Spirit ..."
(Ephesians 6:17, NASB).

For hundreds of years, battles were won or lost by the use of a sword. Even when guns were introduced, swords still had their place. And they still do today in the life of a Christian. Paul describes the armament we need in this life, and he states that the Scriptures are our sword. He was actually referring to a short dagger used in hand-to-hand combat.

When you and I come into an encounter with Satan, we have the Holy Spirit who will bring to mind the right passage of Scripture to confront the problem. For example:

- When you're exhausted and need strength: "But those who hope in the Lord will renew their strength. They will soar on wings like eagles; they will run and not grow weary, they will walk and not be faint" (Is 40:31).

- When you're struggling with fear: "But now, this is what the Lord says—he who created you, O Jacob, he who formed you, O Israel: 'Fear not, for I have redeemed you; I have summoned you by name; you are mine. When you pass through the waters, I will be with you; and when you pass through the rivers, they will not sweep over you. When you walk through the fire, you will not be burned; the flames will not set you ablaze'" (Is 43:1-2).

- When you feel like you're dealing with life all by yourself: "Keep your lives free from the love of money and be content with what you have, because God has said, 'Never will I leave you; never will I forsake you'" (Heb 13:5), or "...and teaching them to obey everything I have commanded you. And surely I am with you always, to the very end of the age" (Mt 28:20).

- When you feel boxed in with all sorts of impossibilities: "Call to me and I will answer you and tell you great and unsearchable things you do not know" (Jer 33:3).

Why not commit these verses to memory? You'll soon see the difference they make in your struggles with the problems of life.[7]

JULY 9

"Do not be anxious about anything, but in everything, by prayer and petition, with thanksgiving, present your requests to God" (Philippians 4:6).

Have you ever felt wound up like a rubber band, like you're being twisted tighter and tighter? If so, you're under a lot of stress.

Stress is a common, catch-all word to describe the tension and pressure we often feel. But do you know what stress is?

Stress is the irritation you feel in any bothersome life situation. The word for stress in Latin is *strictus*. It means "to be drawn tight." In Old French the word is *estresse*, which means "narrowness" or "tightness." Stress is anything that places conflicting or heavy demands upon you.

What do these stressful demands do to you? They cause your equilibrium to be upset. Your body contains a highly sophisticated defense system that helps you cope with threatening situations and challenging events. When you feel pressure, your body quickly mobilizes its defenses for fight or flight. In the case of stress, we are flooded with an abundance of adrenaline, which disrupts normal functioning and creates a heightened sense of arousal.

A stressed person is like a rubber band that is being stretched. When the pressure is released, the rubber band returns to normal. But if stretched too much or too long, the rubber begins to lose its elastic qualities, becomes brittle, develops some cracks, and eventually breaks. That's what happens to us if there is too much stress in our lives.

What is stressful to one individual may not be stressful to another. Some get stressed about future events that cannot be avoided or events after they have occurred. For others stress means simply the wear and tear of life. They're like pieces of stone that have been hammered for so long they begin to crumble.

How are you feeling right now? Are you relaxed? Uptight? As you think about what's facing you today, what does your body say? If you're feeling stressed, take out your Bible and turn to Philippians 4:6-9. Read it, practice it, and experience your stress getting an eviction notice.

JULY 10

"Let the word of Christ richly dwell in you, with all wisdom teaching and admonishing one another with psalms and hymns and spiritual songs, singing with thankfulness in your hearts to God" (Colossians 3:16).

What are your relationships like with other people? Are they deep relationships, or just, well, you know... so-so? There are four levels of relationships. Let's consider them.

Minimal relationships. Minimal relationships involve simple, surface-level verbal interaction, which is generally pleasant instead of hostile. People in relationships at this level usually do not give or receive help, emotional support, or love from each other. They just speak and listen to each other when it is necessary.

Moderate relationships. A moderate relationship contains all the characteristics of a minimal relationship but includes one more: an emotional attachment. In moderate relationships, you want emotional support and you are willing to give it. There is an openness that enables both parties to listen to each other's hurts, concerns, joys, and needs. Ideally, this openness is a two-way street. But even when it is not, we believers are called to respond with openness regardless of the other person's response. Moderate relationships occur by taking the initial steps of emotional openness and support. The other person may follow suit or be threatened by our openness.

Strong relationships. The difference between a moderate relationship and a strong one is found in the word *help*. Strong relationships develop when you really become involved with people by reaching out to minister to them in tangible ways. You're ready to provide help when they need it, and you accept help from them when you need it.

Quality relationships. All the elements of the previous levels lead to the deepest level of all: quality relationships. Quality relationships include the added element of loving trust. You feel safe with these people when you reveal to them your inner needs, thoughts, and feelings. You also feel free to invite them to share their inner needs, thoughts, and feelings, and they feel safe in doing so.

Who are the people in your life today that fit each classification? What are your feelings about them? How often do you pray for them and *how* do you pray for them?

"If I rise on the wings of the dawn, if I settle on the far side of the sea, even there your hand will guide me, your right hand will hold me fast" (Psalms 139:9-10).

Nobody likes to face a crisis! We'd rather walk on water than face the flood. In fact, we reason that godly men should be so on top of things that they just don't have the same problems as others. The truth is, all people face the water, the fire, and the flood. There are, however, some special conditions in which God's children face these. The beginning passage of Isaiah 43 reads: "Do not fear, for I have redeemed you; I have called you by name; you are mine!" (Is 43:1). That's a promise that helps you face your trials.

And don't forget, my friend, God loves you. And he may well have allowed the experience that has you backed up to the wall, or lying flat on a hospital bed. He wants to do something in your life or make-up that just wouldn't and couldn't happen apart from the circumstances facing you. God explained that he allowed the circumstances to happen because his children are "precious in his sight" (see Isaiah 43:4).

He then begins to describe what he's going to do because of the deep waters he's allowed his people to pass through. More than ten times the phrase "I will" appears in the passage immediately following. God says that he will give other people in exchange for your life. He will bring your offspring from the east and the west—something that was fulfilled in the establishment of the modern state of Israel. He will not remember your sins, which is a New Testament picture of God's forgiveness. He says he will pour out water on thirsty land, and his spirit on their offspring. He promises to go before them and make rough places smooth, and more.

Can you take these promises personally? Without a doubt! God is no respecter of persons. He will meet you at the point of deepest trial, and, as Isaiah whispered long ago, you will hear him say, "I will be with you!" (Is 43:2). How much more important to know this, than to be exempt from trials and wonder if the bridge over which we must cross is strong enough to hold us.[8]

"So then, as occasion and opportunity open to us, let us do good [morally] to all people [not only being useful or profitable to them, but also doing what is for their spiritual good and advantage]. Be mindful to be a blessing, especially to those of the household of faith [those who belong to God's family with you, the believers]" (Galatians 6:10, AMP).

Everyday life is full of choices, and there are just as many opportunities to do good as to do evil. Dr. Neil Anderson shares some of these opportunities from an unknown author.

People are unreasonable, illogical and self-centered.
Love them anyway.
If you do good, people will accuse you of selfish, ulterior motives.
Do good anyway.
If you are successful, you will win false friends and true enemies.
Succeed anyway.
The good you do today will be forgotten tomorrow.
Do good anyway.
Honesty and frankness make you vulnerable.
Be honest and frank anyway.
The biggest people with the biggest ideas can be shot down by the smallest people with the smallest minds.
Think big anyway.
People favor underdogs but follow only top dogs.
Fight for the underdog anyway.
What you spend years building may be destroyed overnight.
Build anyway.
People really need help, but may attack you if you help them.
Help people anyway.
Give the world the best you've got and you'll get kicked in the teeth.
Give the world the best you've got anyway.[9]

That's not a bad game plan, is it?

"Be joyful always; pray continually; give thanks in all circumstances, for this is God's will for you in Christ Jesus. Do not put out the Spirit's fire; do not treat prophecies with contempt. Test everything. Hold on to the good. Avoid every kind of evil. May God himself, the God of peace, sanctify you through and through. May your whole spirit, soul and body be kept blameless at the coming of our Lord Jesus Christ" (1 Thessalonians 5:16-23).

Remember when you were a kid? Perhaps you were in the Boy Scouts or you camped out with your parents. Campfires were part of those times, and when the evening came to a close there was one important task that had to take place. Someone had to douse that fire and make sure it was out. You had to *quench* the fire....

But there are times when quenching something is not the best step to take. That's what Paul is talking about here. Sometimes we can stifle the fire that God builds in our hearts or the hearts of others.

We can stagnate our life by what we think. Look at the "Seven Steps to Stagnation" below. Have you ever thought or voiced any of these statements?

1. We've never done it that way before.
2. We're not ready for that.
3. We're doing all right without it.
4. We've tried that once before.
5. It costs too much.
6. That's not our responsibility.
7. It just won't work.[10]

Resistance statements inhibit, limit, and stagnate! Paul's words will expand your life. Go back and reread the passage for today. Then open your life to opportunities.[11]

JULY 14

"I can do everything through him who gives me strength"
(Philippians 4:13).

Sometimes we let what others say about us limit us. Sometimes we let setbacks limit us, too. We can give up or we can press on. Consider where we would be today if these people had given in and given up!

"As a composer, he's hopeless." That's what Beethoven's music teacher said about him.

When Isaac Newton was in elementary school, his work was evaluated as poor.

One of Thomas Edison's teachers told him he was unable to learn.

Caruso's music teacher told him he didn't have any voice.

Einstein didn't speak until he was four, and couldn't read until seven. He struggled with dyslexia.

Walt Disney was fired by a newspaper editor, because he didn't have any good ideas.

Louisa May Alcott's editor told her that her writings would never appeal to anyone.

Someone once evaluated Henry Ford as having "no promise."

Admiral Richard Byrd had been evaluated as "unfit for service."

Guess who failed the sixth grade? Winston Churchill.

The Royal College gave Louis Pasteur an evaluation of "mediocre" in chemistry.

Fortunately, these people pressed on. So did those in the Bible who faced obstacles that included other people who didn't believe in them. God can take our failures and mistakes and make them learning experiences.[12]

JULY 15

"The Son is the radiance of God's glory and the exact representation of his being, sustaining all things by his powerful word. After he had provided purification for sins, he sat down at the right hand of the Majesty in heaven" (Hebrews 1:3).

Dear God,

You have shown your love for us by sending your Son Jesus Christ and because of this our lives have been changed. Thank you for this wonderful gift.

I thank you for the years that Jesus spent living amongst us.

I thank you for every act of love that he did.

I thank you for the words and teaching that he left for all mankind.

I thank you for his obedience unto death and then his triumph over death.

I thank you for the presence of his Spirit with me now.

Help me to remember

His eagerness to help others rather than to be helped himself,

His sympathy to those suffering,

His willingness to suffer on my behalf,

His meekness to turn the other cheek, which is so difficult for me to do,

His simple lifestyle and willingness to mix with those who were different from his own people,

His complete reliance upon you. I want this for my own life and ask for wisdom and discernment in order to do this.

I ask for grace so that in each of these ways I would be able to follow Jesus.

May today be a day of patient understanding of those around me, a day of doing what you want, and a day when your Word is seen in what I do.

In Jesus' name,
Amen.

JULY 16

"How long, O Lord? Will you forget me forever? How long will you hide your face from me? How long must I wrestle with my thoughts and every day have sorrow in my heart? How long will my enemy triumph over me?" (Psalms 13:1-2).

You think you've had a hard day? David was probably in even worse shape when he wrote this psalm. He was the king-elect, but he was living and hiding like an animal in the desert and forest, because Saul was trying to kill him. That's when he wrote this psalm. It's a prayer, but the first two verses reflect the fact that he's overwhelmed by life.

Have you ever been there? You probably haven't had the king's hit-men tracking you down, but it could be the crying kids, a broken water heater, unpaid bills, the IRS, bill collectors, and guess who's coming for a two-week visit! You feel like David when he says, "God has forgotten me—forever!" When you don't have any relief, you tend to lose hope. You wonder if you haven't been abandoned by God himself.

And when you feel abandoned you end up feeling that God doesn't even care about you. "How long will you hide your face from me?" We call this self-pity.

Later in the psalm David says he's going to have to take matters into his own hands and find solutions himself if God won't help. The Hebrew term *take counsel* means "to plan." Perhaps the result of trying to do it his way is the reason for the phrase "having sorrow in my heart all the day." Proverbs 3:5 offers a better choice: "Trust in the Lord with all your heart and lean not on your own understanding."

Did David stay in this condition? Fortunately, no—emphatically no. He found an answer, and so can you. Why not read about it in verses 3-6? If it worked for David, it will work for you.[13]

JULY 17

"And God spoke all these words: 'I am the Lord your God, who brought you out of Egypt, out of the land of slavery'" *(Exodus 20:1-2).*

Laws! We are a country filled with laws. We have no idea how many laws are on the books. There are even laws to help in formulating new laws. Some laws are good, while others need to be dropped from the system. There are probably some you'd like to get rid of. Our lives are regulated by laws. But it doesn't mean we always keep them, especially traffic laws! (Sorry if I'm meddling now.)

Laws come from God. He is the originator. He gave them so that we would get the most out of life. Consider the Ten Commandments, for example. Do you remember them? Can you list them? Take a minute and think about them. They were applicable when they were given and they still are today.

It's true that as Christians we live under the grace of God and we're saved by grace. But we still need the laws of God. There are benefits to the law. Law and grace are not at odds with each other. The law actually reveals God's grace. The law was founded on God's grace. The passage from Exodus reveals this. Because of his grace the children of Israel were to follow the Ten Commandments, not for the purpose of gaining salvation but out of thanksgiving for what the Lord had done for them! It was God's grace that brought them out of slavery.

That's why you and I are to follow the teachings in the New Testament. Following them won't save you but it will reflect the fact that you are a follower of Jesus. Jesus fulfilled the law, and when we come to know him we have an opportunity to reflect him by following the law. Even the Ten Commandments.[14]

"Do not think that I have come to abolish the Law or the Prophets; I have not come to abolish them but to fulfill them. I tell you the truth, until heaven and earth disappear, not the smallest letter, not the least stroke of a pen, will by any means disappear from the Law until everything is accomplished" (Matthew 5:17-18).

We live in a world of law breakers. Some believe that laws were made to be broken. Some rules are fair. Some rules are unfair. They restrict, they confine, they regulate, but they also provide structure and order.

There are laws that you would like to see changed. But what about the laws that God has given us? How do you feel about them? Do you see them as restrictive or beneficial? Hampering you or making your life better? Difficult to keep or easy? Or have you even thought about God's laws?

God's laws will bless you if you follow them. David gave us a thorough description of the benefits of the law.

The law of the Lord is perfect, reviving the soul. The statutes of the Lord are trustworthy, making wise the simple. The precepts of the Lord are right, giving joy to the heart. The commands of the Lord are radiant, giving light to the eyes. The fear of the Lord is pure, enduring forever. The ordinances of the Lord are sure and altogether righteous. They are more precious than gold, than much pure gold; they are sweeter than honey, than honey from the comb. By them is your servant warned; in keeping them there is great reward. Who can discern his errors? Forgive my hidden faults. Keep your servant also from willful sins; may they not rule over me. Then will I be blameless, innocent of great transgression. May the words of my mouth and the meditation of my heart be pleasing in your sight, O Lord, my Rock and my Redeemer. **Psalms 19:7-14**

What does the law do? It reveals God's holiness. It invites you to be holy. Its purpose is to help you know the lawgiver better and to make your life full.

By the way, if we didn't have laws we would have what happened in the Book of Judges, when "every man did what was right in his own eyes" (Jgs 17:6). Perhaps we already do!

"I am the Lord your God, who brought you out of Egypt, out of the land of slavery" (Exodus 20:2).

Have you ever wondered what it would have been like to have been there when God gave the Ten Commandments? Read what happened. Try to picture it in your mind. See it. Hear it. Smell it. Feel it. The children of Israel did. Have you been in a thunderstorm that was so intense that the sounds rolled and roared? Have you seen the lightning flash from peak to peak and then flash with continued displays of sheet lightning? Have you felt the rumble and shake of an earthquake? Put all these together and you have the scene.

> On the morning of the third day there was thunder and lightning, with a thick cloud over the mountain, and a very loud trumpet blast. Everyone in the camp trembled. Then Moses led the people out of the camp to meet with God, and they stood at the foot of the mountain. Mount Sinai was covered with smoke, because the Lord descended on it in fire. The smoke billowed up from it like smoke from a furnace, the whole mountain trembled violently, and the sound of the trumpet grew louder and louder. Then Moses spoke and the voice of God answered him.   **Exodus 19:16-19**

The giving of the law is a description of God's gracious nature. He did not have to do what He did. He chose to. What God did then is what He has always done for us. It is an act of grace. When the Law was given the second time, Moses reminded the people of this.

> The Lord did not set his affection on you and choose you because you were more numerous than other peoples, for you were the fewest of all peoples. But it was because the Lord loved you and kept the oath he swore to your fore-fathers that he brought you out with a mighty hand and redeemed you from the land of slavery, from the power of Pharaoh king of Egypt.   **Deuteronomy 7:7-8**

That's what he does today because the Lord loves you. The children of Israel couldn't earn God's love. Neither can you. Neither can any of us. He paid the way for his people then. He pays it now.

JULY 20

"You shall have no other gods before me" (Exodus 20:3).

Nothing, absolutely nothing is to come before God. The first commandment is plain and simple... and easy to break. Today gods have multiplied. Some worship the earth. Many worship Elvis and his memory. Everyone today has a god, whether they call it God or not. A famous preacher from years ago, G. Campbell Morgan, said:

> It is as impossible for a man to live without having an object of worship as it is for a bird to fly if it is taken out of the air. The very composition of human life, the mystery of man's being, demands a center of worship as a necessity of existence. All life is worship.... The question is whether the life and powers of man are devoted to the worship of the true God or to that of a false one.[15]

What you place first in your life may be your God. It could be your job, wife, golf, an accumulation of the things that make up the good life, or sex. Anything that takes priority over God has removed him from the throne. When God said you shall have no other gods before me, he was saying you shall have *ME!*

Do you understand what it means to have God, to love him? Everything we do is to be done to honor and glorify him. It's our life's calling. It's expressed best by David:

> O God, my God! How I search for you! How I thirst for you in this parched and weary land where there is no water. How I long to find you! How I wish I could go into your sanctuary to see your strength and glory, for your love and kindness are better to me than life itself. How I praise you! **Psalms 63:1-3, TLB**

How can you fulfill this commandment today?[16]

"You shall not make for yourself an idol in the form of anything in heaven above or on the earth beneath or in the waters below" *(Exodus 20:4).*

This commandment is not the same as the first one. The first one forbids the *existence* of other gods. But this commandment forbids the *making* of other gods. In other words, we are not to purposely create other gods. Verse 5 takes this commandment even further.

> You shall not bow down to them or worship them; for I, the Lord your God, am a jealous God, punishing the children for the sin of the fathers to the third and fourth generation of those who hate me.   **Exodus 20:5**

This commandment may disturb you because we have pictures and statues in our churches. It's all right to use them as visual reminders created by man's perception. But the commandment does forbid the use of objects such as pictures and statues of Jesus and of God in *private* and *public worship*.[17]

Images limit God, yet he is limitless. Images obscure God's glory. They are made to reveal God but they actually do the opposite! They hide the real God. Did you know that it's possible to buy a machine-washable Jesus doll? There are also plans to bring out a God doll that is a white-haired, white-bearded, white man in a rainbow colored robe with all the animals of creation flowing from him. When you create an idol it is supposed to give you something. Not only does it not do that, it actually takes away from what we have.

The God who created the universe, the God who created us, cannot be confined in a manmade image. When we try to create something to represent him, we detract from the worship of who God really is. We cannot see him. He is above being seen. That adds to his holiness and majesty. What about it? Are there images of any kind in your life? What about in your church? Think about it.

"You shall not misuse the name of the Lord your God, for the Lord will not hold anyone guiltless who misuses his name" (Exodus 20:7).

This commandment is a joke... by the way it is ignored, and mistreated, and violated today. You can hardly find a movie or TV show that doesn't violate this commandment. In some films you'll find it violated two to three hundred times. And who bothers to think about it anymore? Times have changed.

The children of Israel had such respect and reverence for some of the names of God that they wouldn't even use those names. The name Jehovah was so sacred that it was said only once a year by the priest when he gave the blessing on the Day of Atonement (see Leviticus 23:27).

There are many ways we violate this commandment. We may use God's name in an insincere or empty way. We may take an oath in God's name and break it. When we do these things a violation of this commandment has occurred.

> Do not swear falsely by my name and so profane the name of your God. I am the Lord. **Leviticus 19:12**

Scripture is very clear that when we use God's name irreverently, we violate the commandment. What do you say when you hit your thumb with a hammer? "Ouch!" Or ...? Some men have a highly developed skill of swearing, using God's name. Lord Byron said, "He knew not what to say, so he swore." Someone has said that "swearing is a substitute for the inarticulate." Another violation is using God's name to curse others. When you damn someone using God's name, this commandment is violated. There are consequences for this violation. Read Exodus 20:7 again and then look at this verse.

> But I tell you that men will have to give account on the day of judgment for every careless word they have spoken. For by your words you will be acquitted, and by your words you will be condemned. **Matthew 12:36-37**

That's sobering, isn't it?

"Remember the Sabbath day by keeping it holy. Six days you shall labor and do all your work, but the seventh day is a Sabbath to the Lord your God. On it you shall not do any work, neither you nor your son or daughter, nor your manservant or maidservant, nor your animals, nor the alien within your gates" (Exodus 20:8-10).

*R*est. God is saying that once a week we need to take a break. He is saying there is more to life than work. He is also urging us to follow his pattern: "For in six days the Lord made the heavens and the earth, the sea, and all that is in them, but he rested on the seventh day. Therefore the Lord blessed the Sabbath day and made it holy" (Ex 20:11). Since God is God, he didn't need to rest as we know it. He certainly wasn't worn out. He just decided to. And he wants us to.

We need rest physically. There is a rhythm to the seventh day of rest that is the best balance of work and rest, even though people have tried other plans and failed.

Spiritually we need this time to refocus our lives. For the children of Israel this was a day to celebrate their redemption and liberation. God wanted the people to spend one day looking to him and thanking him for being liberated. Listen to what the Lord said to Isaiah:

> If you keep your feet from breaking the Sabbath and from doing as you please on my holy day, if you call the Sabbath a delight and the Lord's holy day honorable, and if you honor it by not going your own way and not doing as you please or speaking idle words, then you will find your joy in the Lord. **Isaiah 58:13-14**

So, what do you do on the Sabbath? Some of us work; some of us spend the entire day playing. But it's a day that belongs to God. How are you using it? Who comes first on that day? It's a day to serve, worship, rejoice, and rest. Take a look at how you use the Sabbath.

"Then God issued this edict: 'I am Jehovah your God who liberated you from your slavery in Egypt'" (Exodus 20:1-2).

Kent Hughes has written an exceptional book on the Ten Commandments titled *Disciplines of Grace*. In fact it's the basis for much of our study of this passage in Exodus. He gives a provocative summary of the first four commandments. He calls each one a Word of Grace.

What a remarkable enabling bouquet we have in the first four words—to help us live out the Shema—loving God with all we have. Each of the words is magisterial and foundational, and each is uniquely powerful. But like a floral bouquet, their maximum effect comes when they are held together, for then comes the sweet power to love God. Consider the bouquet:

The First Word of Grace—the primacy of God: "You shall have no other gods before me." That is, "You shall have Me! I must be in first place." If God is first, if there is nothing before Him, you will love Him more and more! Is He truly first in your life?

The Second Word of Grace—the person of God: "You shall not make for yourself an idol in the form of anything..." That is, you shall not make a material image or dream up a mental image of God according to your own design. God wants you to see Himself in His Word and in His Son, because if you do, you will love Him more. The clearer your vision, the greater your love. How is your vision?

The Third Word of Grace—reverence for God: "You shall not misuse the name of the Lord your God." That is, "You shall reverence God's name." Reverently loving Him in your mind and with your mouth will elevate and substantiate your love. Honestly, do you misuse or reverence His name?

The Fourth Word of Grace—the time for God: "Remember the Sabbath day by keeping it holy." This tells us to keep holy the Lord's Day. Are you week by week offering it up in love to Him?[18]

"Honor your father and your mother, so that you may live long in the land the Lord your God is giving you" (Exodus 20:12).

The emphasis of the fifth commandment is on loving others. The first four are on loving God, which makes it possible to fulfill the next six. If you have a right relationship with God you can have a right relationship with others. And it begins with your parents.

Honor—it's not a word we use much today nor practice. The Hebrew word comes from a verb which means "to be heavy." In a sense you give weight to a person you honor or hold in high esteem. You elevate them. You see them as important.

When children honor their parents they're to obey them. Ephesians 6:1 says, "Children, obey your parents in the Lord, for this is right." But you're an adult, not a child. How can you honor your parents?

When you're an adult you reverence your parents. There are four ways you can do this.

You can respect them. "Each of you must respect his mother and father, and you must observe my Sabbaths. I am the Lord your God" (Lv 19:3). How? Quite simple. *Respect* means you speak kindly to them and about them.

You can provide for them. Don't neglect your parents when they are older. Give them time, attention, love, your listening ear, as well as help with their physical needs.

You can treat them with consideration. Make their remaining years easier. Encourage them to spend your inheritance on themselves!

You can honor them by the way you live your life. Give them something to be proud of. "The father of a righteous man has great joy; he who has a wise son delights in him. May your father and mother be glad; may she who gave you birth rejoice!" (Prv 23:24-25).[19]

"You shall not murder" (Exodus 20:13).

Don't kill! That sums up this commandment. Life is precious. Man was made in the image of God. "So God made man like his Maker. Like God did God make man; man and maid did he make them" (Gn 1:27).

If you live in America you live in a country where the future is excellent—for murder. The American culture kills. Look at the statistics. Violence of all types, murder, and terrorist attacks are on the rise. The atrocity and mayhem of the Oklahoma City bombing as well as the rise of the killing of one's family members stare us in the face.

Life is sacred. We have been called to cherish, honor, and protect our own life and the lives of others. "And the second is like it: 'Love your neighbor as yourself'" (Mt 22:39).

The Scripture says no to *homicide*.

The Scripture says no to *suicide*, which is not only violence toward oneself but against any remaining family members and friends. Even medically assisted suicides for the ill and elderly are wrong, regardless of what society says.

The Scripture says no to *feticide*—abortion. It's a direct sin against God. Sometime and somewhere we will all have to take a stand on this issue. God's Word comes first.

But you may be thinking, "This is great—for someone else. I'm no murderer." True. But consider these words from Jesus, which apply to all of us.

> You have heard it said to the people long ago, "Do not murder, and anyone who murders will be subject to judgment." But I tell you that anyone who is angry with his brother will be subject to judgment. Again, anyone who says to his brother, "Raca," is answerable to the Sanhedrin. But anyone who says, "You fool!" will be in danger of the fire of hell.
>
> **Matthew 5:21-22**

Haven't we all had anger and contempt in our hearts for others? Haven't we all had thoughts of murder in our hearts for others? That's where it all begins—and thoughts do lead to actions.[20]

"You shall not commit adultery" (Exodus 20:14).

This commandment is laughed at even by many Christians. They don't take it seriously. But God does. Otherwise it wouldn't have been mentioned so much in his word. The frequency of its mention in the Old Testament is second only to idolatry. In the New Testament its frequency is second to none.

Adultery—it violates the sacredness of marriage, which is something God created. It breaks the marriage covenant.

It's also a sin against one's own body. "Flee from sexual immorality. All other sins a man commits are outside his body, but he who sins sexually sins against his own body" (1 Cor 6:18).

Paul says that a Christian's body is a member of Christ. "Do you not know that your bodies are members of Christ himself? Shall I then take the members of Christ and unite them with a prostitute? Never! Do you not know that he who unites himself with a prostitute is one with her in body? For it is said, 'The two will become one flesh.' But he who unites himself with the Lord is one with him in spirit" (1 Cor 6:15-17).

Adultery is a sin against Christ himself, and it's definitely a sin against God.

But, like other sins, it is forgivable. Repentance, which means "to change and commit, to never repeat the offense," makes it so. What I recommend next will not be popular. If a man has committed adultery, it's a sin that needs to be confessed to God, to his wife, and to the church. For his wife, since he has violated her, he should take a blood test for AIDS, and for the church, if he is in any position of service in the church, he should resign and go through a time of healing and restoration until he can serve once again. Harsh? No. Necessary. You could be one of many men who have never fallen. Praise God. But just one other gentle nudge. Jesus said something else that cuts to the heart of the matter.

"You have heard that it was said, 'Do not commit adultery.' But I tell you that anyone who looks at a woman lustfully has already committed adultery with her in his heart" (Mt 5:27-28).

How's your heart and your thought life?

"You shall not steal..." (Exodus 20:15).

What would happen if a group of people were walking along and someone came up behind them and yelled, "Stop! Thief!" Most would probably stop, and rightly so. Haven't all of us stolen something at one time or another?

If the IRS had all the money it's been cheated out of, and every company had all the money stolen by employees, we'd be in great shape financially. "Don't steal" covers all kinds of thefts.

If you stole anything in Old Testament times, you were in for a rough time. If you took and disposed of a sheep or ox, you were required to give back four sheep or five oxen! And if the original animal was found, the restitution was double! (see Exodus 22:1-4).

Today theft is common... and subtle. In the book *The Day America Told the Truth*, the authors conclude this about workers in our country:

> The so-called Protestant ethic is long gone from today's American workplace.
>
> Workers around America frankly admit that they spend more than 20 percent of their time at work totally goofing off. That amounts to a four-day work week across the nation.
>
> Almost half of us admit to chronic malingering, calling in sick when we are not sick, and doing it regularly.
>
> Only one in four give work their best effort; only one in four work to realize their human potential rather than merely to keep the wolf from the door.[21]

Stealing is not limited to shoplifting or taking all the cash out of a cash register. It's much easier to steal time—long breaks and lunch hours, late to work and early to leave. Not working up to our full capacity is theft. What about misuse of the fax machine, photocopier, phone, or supplies for personal use? It happens all the time.

We can steal away another person's reputation and plagiarize their work or cheat on an exam or our income tax return. Have we covered enough? No. There's one more. God's Word says it clearly.[22]

> Will a man rob God? Yet you rob me. But you ask, "How do we rob you?"
> In tithes and offerings.   **Malachi 3:8**

"You shall not give false testimony against your neighbor"
(Exodus 20:16).

We are a country of proficient liars. We cultivate and practice telling lies. We're good at it no matter how young or how old we are. Unfortunately, research tells us that men do it more than women. And two out of three people in our country see nothing wrong with lying.[23]

We can destroy another's reputation and cripple the ministry of a person or a church by our lies. But worst of all we destroy ourselves before God. "The Lord detests lying lips, but he delights in men who are truthful" (Prv 12:22). "There are six things the Lord hates, seven that are detestable to him... a false witness who pours out lies and a man who stirs up dissension among brothers" (Prv 6:16, 19).

We lie by adding to and embellishing stories we tell. We lie by leaving out portions to create another impression. We can speak the truth in such a way that it destroys. But God's Word says to speak the truth in such a way that it better cements your relationship. "Instead, speaking the truth in love, we will in all things grow up into him who is the Head, that is Christ" (Eph 4:15).

We can make insinuations about others or situations and then back out of it by saying we didn't mean it. "Like a madman shooting firebrands or deadly arrows is a man who deceives his neighbor and says, 'I was only joking!'" (Prv 26:18-19).

We lie by spreading gossip. You know, information that may be true—or may not be. Sometimes we're walking supermarket tabloids. God's Word says: "The words of a gossip are like choice morsels" (Prv 18:8).

Pray that God will help you to be a man of truth. And remember this: "An honest answer is like a kiss on the lips" (Prv 24:26). "Set a guard over my mouth, O Lord; keep watch over the door of my lips" (Ps 141:3).

"You shall not covet your neighbor's house. You shall not covet your neighbor's wife, or his manservant or maidservant, his ox or donkey, or anything that belongs to your neighbor" (Exodus 20:17).

We always want more. We think we're satisfied and then we see something we think is better, bigger, flashier, or more beautiful. Then we covet, which means we desire it. But coveting also means "lust" or "passionate longing." To top it off, we live in a culture that promotes dissatisfaction and coveting. The violation of this commandment to not covet leads to the violation of other commandments. The writer of Proverbs warned about this: "All day long he craves for more, but the righteous give without sparing" (Prv 21:26). Jesus warned us about it: "Watch out! Be on your guard against all kinds of greed; a man's life does not consist in the abundance of his possessions" (Lk 12:15).

We live under the misbelief that more is better and things make you happy. We find it hard to rejoice in what others have. We want it ourselves. We envy the rich who have it all. But the problem is, they don't have it all. Most are missing that special something called peace and satisfaction.

Have you ever coveted? Probably. We all have. Often it's the big three that we covet: Possessions, Position, and People.

We can covet and we can possess, but there's a better way. Jesus said, "But seek first his kingdom and his righteousness, and all these things will be given to you as well. Therefore do not worry about tomorrow, for tomorrow will worry about itself. Each day has enough trouble of its own" (Mt 6:33-34).

When you're content, you won't covet. It's possible; Paul says so. "I am not saying this because I am in need, for I have learned to be content whatever the circumstances.... And my God will meet all your needs according to his glorious riches in Christ Jesus" (Phil 4:11-19).

If you want to do some good coveting, you could covet the best for someone else, such as your wife or a friend.[24]

"I am the Lord your God, who brought you out of Egypt, out of the land of slavery" (Exodus 20:2).

Is it really possible to follow the Ten Commandments? Paul talked about the law again and again. Take a minute and read Romans 7:7-11. Then consider these words from Kent Hughes.

> However, if one knows Christ, it is possible, through discipline, to live within the spiritual parameters, the borders, of the Law. How so? Because Jesus Christ fulfilled the Law (Matthew 5:17).
>
> - Jesus never put any god or, indeed, anything before his Father.
> - Jesus never constructed materially or mentally an idol in the form of anything; He worshiped God, as He taught others, "in spirit and in truth."
> - Jesus never misused the Father's name but instead "hallowed" it.
> - Jesus kept the Sabbath day holy.
> - Jesus unfailingly honored his earthly father and mother.
> - Jesus never indulged in a murderous, hateful thought.
> - Jesus never engaged in mental adultery, much less physical adultery.
> - Jesus never stole or even had a larcenous thought.
> - Jesus never once bore false testimony—no slander or gossip or flattery or untrue words—only perpetual truth.
> - Jesus never coveted anything except another's spiritual well-being.
>
> Therefore, because Jesus Christ fulfilled the Law, and because we are in Christ and He is in us (cf. 2 Corinthians 5:21; Colossians 1:27), we can live within the blessed borders of the Law. Jesus' indwelling puts our souls in spiritual sympathy with the Law. We resonate with it—and we want to live it out. The indwelling Christ also sends the Holy Spirit as "another Counselor," one like Himself, to empower us to live out His life (see John 14:16). Admittedly, no Christian ever perfectly lives out the Law, but hosts of believers live within its borders.
>
> To so live is to live in grace, because it is to live by the divine pattern. To so live is to "Love the Lord your God with all your heart and with all your soul and with all your mind." To so live is to "Love your neighbor as yourself." To so live is to live with passionate upward love for God and a passionate outward love for humanity. To so live is to live as we were created to live. This is a great grace![25]

"Blessed is he whose transgressions are forgiven, whose sins are covered. Blessed is the man whose iniquity the Lord does not count against him, and in whose spirit is no deceit" (Psalms 32:1-2).

Have you ever had the experience of finally overcoming some habit or problem that plagued you for years? When that problem has been laid to rest (with no resurrection), that's an occasion to celebrate. And that's what David is doing in the above verses. He's overjoyed about the removal of problems he once had. Read the verse again and look at the four specific words or terms that are used for wrongdoing.

The first is *transgression*. It is a Hebrew word which means "to rebel or revolt." It's when you know the rule, you know what's right, and you deliberately violate it.

You've heard about the second term, *sin*. It means "to miss the mark." You deviate from the way God wants you to go.

The third term is *iniquity*. It's the feeling of guilt. We know we did something wrong and now guilt is the payoff.

The word used for the fourth term, *deceit*, means "treachery, deception, and self-deception"! Self-deception sets in like it did in David's life when you override those guilt feelings and refuse to face and overcome the sin in your life. David is saying, "When these four things are gone from your life, what a relief it is!"

If you had a friend come to you and say, "I've been transgressing and sinning. I feel full of guilt and I'm deceiving myself," what would you suggest he do? Look at these verses for a clear answer to share.

"Then I acknowledged my sin to you and did not cover up my iniquity. I said, 'I will confess my transgressions to the Lord'—and you forgave the guilt of my sin" (Ps 32:5).

"He who conceals his sins does not prosper, but whoever confesses and renounces them finds mercy" (Prv 28:13).

"If we confess our sins, he is faithful and just and will forgive us our sins and purify us from all unrighteousness" (1 Jn 1:9).

The answer is clear. It's simple. It works. It's God's way.[1]

"He who covers his transgressions will not prosper, but whoever confesses and forsakes his sins shall obtain mercy" (Proverbs 28:13, AMP).

Blame and excuses. Have you ever come to the place where you're fed up hearing other people trying to get off the hook by giving a lame excuse? It happens constantly. No one wants to take responsibility for the problem. Even in marriage it happens: "Yeah, my marriage would be a lot better if 'you know who' would get with the program." Perhaps you've heard some of these excuses or even... Naw, you wouldn't have used these.

- Some men blame their health:
    I have migraine headaches and...
    I'm just tired all the time.
    My metabolism is just different from yours.

- Some men blame their feelings:
    My nerves are so shaky, and you don't help them at all.
    I've been depressed.
    The kids make me so upset.

- Some men blame their nature:
    I'm just this way, that's all. I always have been.
    I can't change.
    I'm a phlegmatic—you know what they're like.

- Some men blame others:
    Her mother is always...
    Her friends are really...
    It's the darn kids. They just never go to sleep at the right time.
    My boss just gets to me. And then...

- Some men blame the past:
    She has always been that way.
    My other marriage was lousy, too.
    My mother always used to put me down.

- Some men blame their partners:

  If only she'd shut up and listen to me.
  If she'd ever clean the house I'd faint.

- Some men blame "Why":

  If only I could understand why she does...
  But why can't she stay home on Saturdays and not shop so much?

There's a better way. It's in the verse for today. Take responsibility ... 'fess up. Admit you could do better. Then, do so. You'll like the results. So will the other people in your life.

"You made all the delicate, inner parts of my body, and knit them together in my mother's womb. Thank you for making me so wonderfully complex! It is amazing to think about. Your workmanship is marvelous—and how well I know it. You were there while I was being formed in utter seclusion! You saw me before I was born and scheduled each day of my life before I began to breathe. Every day was recorded in your Book!" (Psalms 139:13-16, TLB).

Do you ever feel like you don't exactly fit in—you know, your image or the way you act or dress is a bit different from the people at work or at church? In many ways we're continually fighting an "image syndrome." We feel the pressure to wear the right suits, tennis shoes, underwear; or we need to act a certain way to fit in with everyone else. *Conformity* is the word, and clones are the result. If you try to do things a different way at church or in a work presentation you get flack because you didn't match up to "the image."

People say there's a right way and a wrong way to be. But is that really true? Have you ever wondered how some of the prophets or John the Baptist fit in with the rest of society? Probably not too well at times.

The truth is, you are you! You are who God created you to be. Have you discovered who that is? Have you discovered your unique characteristics and talents? Probably not if you're trying to fit in.

Keep in mind that you were created by God and then that mold was broken. No one else is like you. You're unique. You're special. It's all right to be you. Don't let others shape you—what you do, say, or think. That's God's task. He started with you and he will finish with you. And he really does want you to be you.[2]

"Therefore everyone who hears these words of mine and puts them into practice is like a wise man who built his house on the rock. The rain came down, the streams rose, and the winds blew and beat against that house; yet it did not fall, because it had its foundation on the rock. But everyone who hears these words of mine and does not put them into practice is like a foolish man who built his house on sand. The rain came down, the streams rose, and the winds blew and beat against that house, and it fell with a great crash" *(Matthew 7:24-27).*

"Is this the real thing? How do you know it's authentic?" These are questions we're all asking today. What you see isn't always what you get. Labels can even be misleading. You buy an expensive piece of clothing, shoes, or even furniture, and then, as you more closely examine it, discover it wasn't what you thought at all. You feel ripped off!

Sometimes Christians aren't what they seem either. They say one thing but act another way. They behave one way at church and another way at work. They're not real. They're not authentic. They're bluffers! They try to bluff their way through life. You've seen them at work. They have no depth.

There's an area in our life that needs to be authentic. It's called *faith.*

Do you know what authentic faith is?

It's a mixture of joy as well as conviction. It's not afraid to ask questions, hard questions, that will actually expand your faith. Have you asked any recently?

Authentic faith is honest and is expressed so others can understand you. How have you expressed your faith recently? It doesn't use clichés, platitudes, or terminology that confuses. Who have you shared your faith with recently?

Authentic faith is not centered on yourself, but upon Jesus Christ.

Authentic faith admits you struggle, but finds its solution in Jesus.

Who have you asked to pray for you recently? Your faith may help someone else in discovering faith. Let's keep that in mind.[3]

"If you really knew me, you would know my Father as well. From now on, you do know him and have seen him" (John 14:7).

How you and your father connected as you were growing up impacts how you respond as a man in your adulthood. How *was* your relationship? Did you really know your dad? What he thought? What he believed? What he felt? Many men say, "Yes, I knew my father," until they are faced with those questions.

Many men have a father hunger in their life. It's often activated when they have a son of their own, when they hit mid-life, or when they experience a loss. Look at the themes of fathers and sons in films. Do you remember the shock Luke Skywalker experiences meeting his father Darth Vader in *The Empire Strikes Back*? Or the newfound strength that Indiana Jones discovers as he talks with his aging father in *The Last Crusade*? In *Backdraft* a firefighter's sons follow in his footsteps; and in *Field of Dreams* a man plays baseball with his father in the spirit realm, which frees him emotionally.

There are popular songs like Paul Overstreet's *Seein' My Father in Me*, Chet Atkins' *My Father's Hat,* and *A Boy Named Sue* by Johnny Cash. All of these have the same message of portraying a man's boyhood and his longings as an adult to be connected to his father.

Is your father living? If so, what is your relationship with him? If he's deceased, you may still be longing for something from him.

Sometimes our dads can't give us what we wanted or still want. But there is a Father who can fill all your needs. Have you met him? He's the one who is always available and accessible. And he wants a relationship with us more than we do with him… or it may seem that way.

Your Father is waiting. Talk to him today.[4]

"I have brought you glory on earth by completing the work you gave me to do" (John 17:4).

W hy was Jesus so effective in dealing with people?

Jesus' ministry involved helping people achieve fullness of life, assisting them in developing their ability to deal with the problems, conflicts, and burdens of life. We too have been called to minister in this way.

Jesus was obedient to God. Foremost in Jesus' personal life was obedience to God. There was a definite relationship between him and his Father. "For I did not speak on my own initiative, but the Father himself who sent me has given me commandment, what to say, and what to speak" (Jn 12:49).

Jesus lived a life of faith. Because of this he was able to put things in proper perspective. He saw life through God's eyes. In what way does your faith need to be strengthened?

Jesus lived a life of prayer. "But the news about him was spreading even farther, and great multitudes were gathering to hear him and to be healed of their sicknesses. But he himself would often slip away to the wilderness and pray" (Lk 5:15-16). Is prayer a daily event for you?

Jesus spoke with authority. "For he was teaching them as one having authority, and not as their scribes" (Mt 7:29). When we realize the authority that we have in Jesus, we can become more effective in talking about Him.

Jesus was personally involved. He wasn't aloof; he was personal, sensitive, and caring. Are these qualities seen in our lives?

Jesus had the power of the Holy Spirit. This power enabled Jesus to be effective. We see how his ministry began when Jesus received the power of the Holy Spirit in Luke 3:21-22: "Now it came about when all of the people were baptized that Jesus also was baptized, and while he was praying, heaven was opened, and the Holy Spirit descended upon him in bodily form like a dove, and a voice came out of heaven, 'Thou art my beloved Son, in thee I am well-pleased.'"

"So then, each of us will give an account of himself to God"
(Romans 14:12).

We're all accountable to someone. It could be our employers or company CEOs. We're definitely accountable for our money through the wonderful and kind auspices of the IRS. And we're accountable to God, especially in the future.

But what about the kind of accountability you can choose to have in your life or not? I'm talking about accountability to other Christian men. I don't mean simply friendship and fellowship with them. I mean accountability—a relationship in which they can ask you and you can ask them hard personal questions so you all stay on track. We all need to answer to someone so we can reflect the presence of God in our lives in a genuine way.

Why is accountability necessary? When you don't have someone to answer to, you're more likely to blow it. It's that clear and simple. We all like to be in charge of our own lives, to be our own bosses, but we are all blind and deaf to some of our greatest areas of need. Other people can challenge us, support us, confront us, encourage us.

As believers we are called to be accountable in many ways.

> Brothers, if someone is caught in a sin, you who are spiritual should restore him gently. But watch yourself, or you also may be tempted. Carry each other's burdens, and in this way you will fulfill the law of Christ.
>
> **Galatians 6:1-2**

> Two are better than one, because they have a good return for their work: If one falls down, his friend can help him up. But pity the man who falls and has no one to help him up! **Ecclesiastes 4:9-10**

> Wounds from a friend can be trusted, but an enemy multiplies kisses.... As iron sharpens iron, so one man sharpens another. **Proverbs 27:6, 17**

What about it? If you don't have an accountability group of men in your life, think about it and pray about it. Reach out to others and your life will never be the same.

AUGUST 8

"The poor will eat and be satisfied; they who seek the Lord will praise him—may your hearts live forever!" (Psalms 22:26).

"Man, am I filled up." You've said it and so have I. Usually following the Thanksgiving or Christmas feast. Sometimes it's a good, satisfying feeling. Other times our skin is so tight we think we're going to explode.

The phrase "filled up" is used in many settings. We drive into a gas station and say, "Fill 'er up." There's nothing worse than driving around and having that "E" light come on the dash. Driving on empty is no fun. Eventually you stop.

Going hungry isn't very pleasant either. It begins to hurt after a while. But perhaps it isn't all that bad to feel the pangs of hunger. It helps us anticipate the best that is to come in the future. Our hunger pangs can cause us to think about the One who one day will have us sit with Him at a final banquet. We won't be hungry again. Listen to the promise of God's Word as the psalmist talks about God filling our needs.[5]

For he satisfies the thirsty and fills the hungry with good things.

Psalms 107:9

He upholds the cause of the oppressed and gives food to the hungry. The Lord sets prisoners free, the Lord gives sight to the blind, the Lord lifts up those who are bowed down, the Lord loves the righteous. The Lord watches over the alien and sustains the fatherless and the widow, but he frustrates the ways of the wicked. **Psalms 146:7-9**

"In your anger do not sin. Do not let the sun go down while you are still angry" (Ephesians 4:26, AMP).

L et's think for a moment about the positive side of anger. You need to be angry. That's right, it's okay. Ephesians 4:24 tells us to "be angry and sin not." The word *angry* in this verse means an anger which is an abiding, settled habit of the mind and is aroused under certain conditions. The person is aware and in control of it. There is a just occasion for the anger here. Reason is involved, and when reason is present, anger such as this is right. The Scriptures not only permit it but on some occasions *demand it!* Perhaps this sounds strange to some who have thought for years that anger is all wrong. But the Word of God states that we *are to be angry!*

Christians do and should get angry at the right things, such as injustice and many of the problems we see in the world around us. Righteous anger is not sinful when it is properly directed.

There are several characteristics of righteous anger. First of all, it must be controlled; it must not be a heated or unrestrained passion. Even if the cause is legitimate and is directed at an injustice, uncontrolled anger can cause great error in judgment and increase the difficulty. *Be angry and sin not.*

Second, there must be no hatred, malice, or resentment. Anger that harbors a counterattack only complicates the problem. Jesus' reaction to the injustices delivered against him is a good example of a man in control of his anger.

> When he was reviled *and* insulted, He did not revile *or* offer insult in return; when He was abused *and* suffered, He made no threats (of vengeance); but He trusted (Himself and everything) to Him Who judges fairly. **1 Peter 2:23**

A third characteristic of righteous anger is that its motivation is unselfish. When the motivation is selfish, usually pride and resentment are involved. Anger should be directed not at the wrong done to oneself but at injustice done to others.

So... how can you use your anger constructively today?

Knowing their thoughts, Jesus said, "Why do you entertain evil thoughts in your hearts?" (Matthew 9:4).

My wife and I have come to see life more and more as a war. Ultimately, our battle is with the forces of evil, but on a daily level war involves a struggle with time, money, priorities, health, and unplanned crisis. If we are to fight as allies, then we must grow in greater intimacy. To this growth we devote our time before dinner. This time is sacred and rarely crowded out by other activities. It is our R and R to return to fighting well.

This has required repeated instructions to our children not to interrupt us. It requires us to let the phone ring, to let guests wait for their hosts to return, and to offend countless others who see that as a selfish venture. In fact, it is a refueling time that allows us to engage with our world with a clearer loyalty to one another, a deepened passion for what is good, and a sense of rest that can come from no other place.

The time is seldom less than a half-hour and occasionally may stretch for an hour. We usually begin by catching up on the events of the day. Soon, the events become the springboard for conversation about what was provoked in us that caused distress or delight. Often my wife will have read or thought about things that she recorded in her journal, and she will read to me. Other times I will want her to listen to something I have written. We find it crucial to read out loud together: It not only crystallizes our vague struggles, but it also records our progress together through life.

Our time is unstructured, but it is not uncommon for us to move from events to feelings, from a struggle to joy, or from reading to prayer. In conclusion and consummation we call on God to deepen our heart for him. We return to our family and world refreshed in our sense of being intimate allies.[6]

"God made him who had no sin to be sin for us, so that in him we might become the righteousness of God" (2 Corinthians 5:21).

Many men make some choices in life that are questionable. No, let's be honest. We all make some questionable choices at times. One of the most questionable is the decision to live with guilt rather than without it. Why would anyone choose to live with guilt? I mean, when there's a choice to opt for forgiveness, why not? Let me give you the basics about forgiveness.

First, you can be forgiven regardless of what you've done or thought. Moses the murderer was forgiven. David the adulterer was. Saul who had Christians killed was forgiven. We can all be forgiven in the same way.

Second, forgiveness comes through Jesus Christ alone and not through self-punishment. You can't do it yourself nor can another person. Only the Son of God. He faced our problem (sin) and paid the penalty for it.

Third, forgiveness can't be purchased or bargained for. It's a gift. And it can eliminate your guilt forever. "If we confess our sins, he is faithful and just and will forgive us our sins and purify us from all unrighteousness" (1 Jn 1:9).

Fourth, forgiveness is not limited. It's forever. It lasts. It's hard to conceive of what *forever* means, but it's a long time.

"As far as the east is from the west, so far has he removed our transgressions from us" (Ps 103:12).

If we choose to live with guilt, we've made a choice that God says doesn't have to exist. Guilt drives people to insanity, drinking, drugs, addictions, abuse, and abandonment. If those are the results, why choose it? God is in the business of creating solutions, not problems. Forgiveness can set us free. Who in their right mind wants to live life as a captive?[7]

"Do not eat the food of a stingy man, do not crave his delicacies; As a man thinks in his heart so is he" (Proverbs 23:6-7).

It is interesting how Scripture talks so much about our heart. Perhaps it's because it can determine who we are and what we do in life. Norman Vincent Peale told the story of his experience on the streets of Kowloon in Hong Kong. He walked by a tattoo studio and stopped to notice the samples displayed in the window. Among the typical ones was an unusual expression: "Born To Lose." He went into the shop and, pointing to the words, asked the tattoo artist if anyone actually had that tattooed on his body. The man said "Yes, sometimes." Dr. Peale said he couldn't believe that anyone in their right mind would do such a thing. The Chinese man tapped his forehead and said in broken English, "Before tattoo on body, it on mind."[8]

Arnold Palmer is well known for being one of the greatest golfers of all time. He's won hundreds of trophies and awards. But in his office you will find two items—the cup for his first professional win in 1955 and a plaque on the wall that says:

If you think you are beaten, you are.
If you think you dare not, you don't.
If you'd like to win but think you can't,
It's almost certain you won't.
Life's battles don't always go
to the stronger or faster man,
But sooner or later, the man who wins
Is the man who thinks he can.[9]

"But one thing I do: Forgetting what is behind and straining toward what is ahead, I press on toward the goal to win the prize for which God has called me heavenward in Christ Jesus" (Philippians 3:13b-14a).

Pay attention! Those words echo in my mind from childhood. Teachers, piano teachers, and parents gave me that message time and time again. Perhaps you heard it, too. Sometimes we get distracted trying to listen, when we're praying, or trying to accomplish some goal. Some distractions can be fatal. Sometimes we paralyze our progress by trying to accomplish several things at the same time or else we put our energy into doing a task that isn't very important and neglect something that's vital.

A number of years ago an Eastern Airlines jumbo jet crashed in the Florida Everglades. You may remember the story of flight 401. It carried a full load of passengers and had taken off from New York bound for Miami. As the plane came closer to the Miami airport and began its approach to land, the pilots noticed that the light which indicates the landing gear is down failed to come on. The pilots flew in a large looping circle over the Everglade swamps while they worked on the problem. It could have been that the landing gear wasn't properly deployed, or it could have been a defective light bulb.

The flight engineer tried to remove the light bulb but it was stuck. The other members in the cockpit tried to help him loosen the bulb. While they were distracted with trying to get the bulb out, they all failed to notice that the plane was losing altitude, and it flew right into the swamp. Dozens of passengers were killed. The cockpit crew had a job to do, but they were distracted by a stuck seventy-five cent light bulb. This was a fatal distraction.

What distracts you from doing your job? And what distracts you from your relationship with God? That's the major question![10]

"Do not worry about what to say or how to say it. At that time you will be given what to say, for it will not be you speaking, but the Spirit of your Father speaking through you" (Matthew 10:19-20).

What in the world will I say?

At some time in life we're all confronted with this challenge. We all struggle for the appropriate words to share a thought or concern with someone at some time. And when pressure situations occur, sometimes our minds tend to shut down and we don't know what to say.

In today's passage Jesus is talking about our concern over what to say when we are faced with giving testimony about him in a setting hostile to the Christian faith. He assures us that the Holy Spirit will give us the thoughts, the words, and the courage we so often lack. When you are concerned about sharing your faith in Christ with someone or when you are challenged in your faith by other people, rely upon the fact that God is the source of your thoughts and words at those times. Dr. Lloyd Ogilvie says:

> Our only task is to open our minds in calm expectation of wisdom beyond our own capacity. We were never meant to be adequate on our own. It is when we think we are adequate that we get into trouble. A Christian is not one who works for the Lord but one in whom and through whom the Lord works. We are not to speak for God but to yield our tongues to express the thoughts the Lord has implanted.[11]

What can we draw from these words? Listen to the Lord before you speak, and after you have heard him, speak with confidence and concern. Perhaps today you can identify an area of concern in your life regarding something you need to say to someone. Pray for this situation and then ask God for the words and the confidence you need.[12]

"May your fountain be blessed, and may you rejoice in the wife of your youth" (Proverbs 5:18).

Doug Rosenau has some words of wisdom about sex. Consider his thoughts:

The Bible says you are to love your neighbor or your mate just as you love yourself. Fun sex depends on a husband and wife who have learned to love themselves. This means you take care of your health and exercise your body to keep it in shape. You should also enjoy and accept the body God gave you. Self-acceptance, self-esteem, and a good body image are healthy parts of sexiness and Christian self-love. Think of how difficult it is to sexually focus on your mate when you are embarrassed, inhibited, or self-conscious.

Psychological research has shown us that the people and things we are more familiar with, we tend to like more. People who live in the same apartment complex or go to church together seem to grow to like one another just by being in proximity with one another and sharing common things. As you get more comfortable with seeing your body and allowing it to be in your thoughts without negative criticism, you will start to like it more.

An important part of love is respecting and unconditionally accepting your mate. If you want to find and focus on flaws, you will put a damper on your partner's sexiness and the whole lovemaking process. First Corinthians tells us that true love protects, forgets, and doesn't keep a record of wrong (13:4-7). Allowing your mind to become preoccupied with the size of body parts or age is very destructive.

You reap the benefit (or the destructiveness if you stay obsessive) of nurturing and helping your love revel in sexual appeal. Every time you affirm some particular aspect of masculinity or femininity that you admire and enjoy, you lovingly increase your mate's sex appeal. It is such a growth-producing process when you are unconditionally committed to accepting your own sexiness and affirming the sexiness of your partner. It creates the environment for a comfortable, safe, sexual greenhouse in which playfulness and risk-taking blossom. Unconditional love and acceptance and affirmation set the temperature for some fantastic sex.[13]

AUGUST 16

"Hear my prayer, O Lord!" (Psalms 102:1a).

God, you have made everything. It was your creative power that created this earth. When you first created light you looked on the first morning and saw it was good. It is still good and I thank you for it. I praise you for another day to experience you.

I praise you for the life within me.

I praise you for the world around me. Help me to discover the unseen good that I overlook.

I praise you for the clouds and sky which I tend to overlook by walking through life so fast with my head down.

I praise you for the work you've given me and for being able to work.

I praise you for my friends.

I praise you for the things I enjoy. Help me to keep them in perspective and to never compete with you.

But there are others who have difficulty praising you or even believing in you, because of the pain and turmoil of their life.

Make me sensitive to those in whom the pulse of life is weakening; to those who have to lie in bed all day; to those who cannot see the light of day because of blindness; to those who are overworked and cannot experience the pleasure of play; to those who have no job and are discouraged; to those who are deep in grief. Empower me to help as best I can.

Lord, don't let anything that I do darken my life and keep me from experiencing you. May the Holy Spirit rule my heart and life.

In Jesus' name,

Amen.[14]

"So overflowing is his kindness towards us that he took away all our sins through the blood of his Son, by whom we are saved" *(Ephesians 1:7, TLB).*

"His presence within us is God's guarantee that he really will give us all that he promised; and the Spirit's seal upon us means that God has already purchased us and that he guarantees to bring us to himself. This is just one more reason for us to praise our glorious God" *(Ephesians 1:14, TLB).*

Do you feel like a forgiven person? Do you act like one? Are you experiencing the benefits of being forgiven? Remember the death of Jesus was the complete payment for everything you've done wrong. And it was a payment!

The penalty for our sins had to be paid. God spared nothing to secure for you an eternal identity in Christ. He willingly gave his cherished Son in order to give you the right to be with him forever. Not only that, you are safe in his care forever.

Perhaps the best way to explain the security we enjoy is to describe how I feel when I go to my bank and ask to see my safety deposit box. I have to sign in to prove my ownership, have my signature evaluated, and produce the proper key. Only then will the attendant take out the bank's key and use both keys to let me see my box.

When I leave, my box is locked up and the outer doors of the safe are locked as well. I go away feeling comfortable and confident that my valuables are well protected.

Of course, my sense of security is based on human standards and structures. Unfortunately, human measures of security have their limitations. Even the most securely guarded banks and locked vaults can be robbed.

But you and I have been *sealed* by the Holy Spirit, and we are totally secure in Jesus Christ. We have been purchased by the blood of Christ. God owns me. And if you have surrendered your life to Jesus Christ, then God owns you. You don't have to be concerned about being tossed out, kicked out, rejected, or dropped. You have been permanently sealed as God's possession.

"Only be careful, and watch yourselves closely so that you do not for-get the things your eyes have seen or let them slip from your heart as long as you live" (Deuteronomy 4:9a).

"**D**on't forget." Remember the words? You probably heard them time and time again as a child. Parents love to remind us. But sometimes as adults the words continue. Now they come from our spouses, children, or employers. Is it easy for you to remember? It should be. As a man you are called "the remembering one." Genesis 1:27 says we were made in God's image. The Hebrew word for "man" is *zakar* which means "the remembering one."

Perhaps it means that we were created to recall the past, to benefit from what we have experienced and then pass it on so other people can benefit from it as well. Are there events in your life that are signifi-cant, and yet very few people, if any, know about them? Perhaps by sharing them, your family members and others will have a more com-plete picture of who you are as a man.

Have you ever stopped to recall the spiritual events or milestones in your life that have shaped you? Or is the memory dim or faded?

When you're having a difficult time, it helps to remember how God has worked in the past so you can anticipate how he will work with you in the future. Take some time and reflect upon your memories. What memory can help you today? What passages from God's Word were you more familiar with than you are now? You can't recreate the past or its experiences. But you can benefit from it and move to a new and fresh relationship with the Lord. Jesus wants you to remember who he is, what he has done for you, and what he will do for you! These remembrances make the present livable.[15]

AUGUST 19

"For you must worship no other gods, but only Jehovah, for he is a God who claims absolute loyalty and exclusive devotion" (Exodus 34:14).

We all experience jealousy at times. That we can accept. But how can God be jealous? That's a human malady, isn't it?

It sounds contradictory for God to be jealous. We see it as something negative because envy is part of it. But there can be a positive jealousy. The Hebrew word for jealousy can also be translated as "zealous." This means "a strong emotion expressing desire or possession of an object."

But why is God jealous? How could he be jealous? Well, he's jealous for his name. He wants to be the one we worship, not anyone or anything else. He deserves it. The Israelites got into deep trouble because they made idols and worshiped them.

> They angered him with their high places; they aroused his jealousy with their idols. **Psalms 78:58**

It wasn't a real bright move on their part! They ended up going to Babylon as guests of the Babylonians.

> Then at last my fury against you will die away; my jealousy against you will end, and I will be quiet and not be angry with you anymore.
> **Ezekiel 16:42**

God is jealous for his people. He wants our complete, not our half-hearted, devotion.

> What? Are you tempting the Lord to be angry with you? Are you stronger than he is? **1 Corinthians 10:22**

Basically, he's jealous when we are not giving him what is his to begin with. Our complete attention, devotion, and worship. It belongs to him. But let's turn this around. Are you jealous for him? When you hear his name taken in vain and misused, how do you respond? When you see his teachings violated, how do you feel? Perhaps you've never considered this before. This may be a good time to do so.[16]

"O Lord, you have examined my heart and know everything about me" (Psalms 139:1).

What comes into your mind when you think of God? Can you describe or list the qualities or characteristics of God? Can you describe him for someone else? Hard questions? Perhaps, but important ones. What comes into your mind when you think about God could be the most important thing about you. It will affect both your worship and your daily living. That's why we need to take a close look biblically at who God is.

If you would like to amaze some people at work, church, or anywhere else for that matter, walk into a room and announce the following: "Let me tell you something about God that you may already know or perhaps you don't know. God doesn't ever learn a thing. He knows all things. He doesn't have to go around spying on people to discover what's going on, he knows. Remember when you were in school and struggled in some class trying to learn something? Well, God cannot learn and has never learned. He doesn't need to. He knows everything instantly. He knows everything equally well. He never wonders about anything, never discovers anything, and is never amazed by anything. He also knows all the possibilities that can happen."[17]

I can't guarantee or predict how others would respond to your statement. But it's a summation of the fact that God is all-knowing, or omniscient. What's the significance of it to you and me? It's a comfort. He knows all of our troubles and struggles. And he knows everyone's heart, everyone's thoughts. He knows everything about you... and still loves you, and me, and the whole world. That too is amazing.[18]

"I can never be lost to your Spirit! I can never get away from my God!" (Psalms 139:7).

"Can anyone hide from me? Am I not everywhere in all of heaven and earth?" (Jeremiah 23:24).

We attend church for the purpose of worshiping God. Why? Is that where he is? You've probably been in a service or a meeting and the person praying says, "Oh, God, as we come into your presence..." Is that right? Not really. God is everywhere, not just in a building or outside that building. He is everywhere. He is at the same time near as well as far off. There isn't any place that you can get away from him.[19]

We live in a world where people disappear from one another. Spouses leave a marriage never to be seen again. Children are kidnapped and disappear forever. Some people change their name and start a new life. Our government provides a witness protection program and gives those who testify against powerful crime figures a new life and identity. It's as though the earth just swallowed them up. But no one disappears from God.

David talked about this in Psalms 139:7-12. He knew he couldn't hide from God. He could go to heaven or Sheol or he could take wings and fly or go to the depth of the sea, but God "would be" there.

It's hard to grasp some of these thoughts about God. But it's only our thoughts that are limited, not God. Perhaps it's good that it's a bit overwhelming. It may help us to have more respect, more reverence, and more awe.[20]

The knowledge that God is everywhere is a comfort. Jesus taught this to bring encouragement to his disciples.

... and teaching them to obey everything I have commanded you. And surely I am with you always, to the very end of the age.   **Matthew 28:20**

So when you're at work or at home or playing golf, serving him and living for him, remember that he is always with you. He's there to support and love you.

"Ah, Sovereign Lord, you have made the heavens and the earth by your great power and outstretched arm. Nothing is too hard for you" (Jeremiah 32:17).

Power. We're all enthralled by it. We like to feel powerful. We enjoy sitting in the cab of a truck with hundreds of horsepower revving up under that hood just waiting to be unleashed. Some have tied into a four- or five-hundred-pound tuna while deep-sea fishing, and they can tell you about power.

There's someone who is so all-powerful that we cannot even imagine it—God. The word *almighty* helps us understand his power. Did you realize that when you begin a prayer with "Almighty God," in a sense you're saying, "All-Powerful God"? God can do whatever he pleases, as it says in Psalms 115:3. Nothing, but nothing can hinder him. What he is going to do, he will do.

Remember what he has done. He made a ninety-nine-year-old man a father (Gn 17:1). Jesus said that he could appeal to the Father to send seventy-two thousand angels to rescue him. He didn't do that, you know, but that's something he could have done. Perhaps the greatest display of his power was the resurrection of his Son Jesus. That has implications for you.

But do you realize there *are* some things God cannot do? There are. Do you know what it is he can't do? Think about it.

God can't associate with sin. That's clear (see Hebrews 1:13).

God can't go back on his Word (see 2 Timothy 2:13).

God can't die (see Hebrews 6:18).

Remember, there's nothing, absolutely *nothing* too difficult for your God![21]

"God 'will give to each person according to what he has done'"
(Romans 2:6).

Do you ever get disgusted with our justice system? There are times when the innocent seem to get punished and the guilty are set free. Open-and-shut cases against the criminal element are tossed out of court by some minor technicality, and the guy is free to prey on society again. Sometimes a first-time offender for a minor crime gets a longer sentence than a hard-case repeat criminal. Is there any justice anymore? Probably not in this world. At least it's not consistent. It's enough to discourage a guy.

But, wait. There is still some justice out there; it's with God. He is the only one who is just in everything he does. God is correct, consistent, and fair in all he does. When he punishes, it's not too much nor too little.

There are times, though, when we don't see the justice of God. We wonder where he is and why he's silent. We think he ought to be intervening. Perhaps we need to remember that his timing is not ours, nor do we see the whole picture. Some ask, "How is God just?" Well, God rewards those who love him over the generations. They do what he's asked. Paul talked about looking to the "righteous judge" to reward him for having fought the good fight (see 2 Timothy 4:8). But God does punish those who break his laws (see Romans 2:9), and in Revelation it states he will judge this world at the end of the age (see Revelation 16).

He's just, but he's also good. He can look at that lawbreaker and see his sin, but when that man confesses his sin and acknowledges Jesus as Lord and Savior, that man experiences God's forgiveness. There is no more payment for what he did. Someone else already paid—Jesus. This puts a new word alongside justice. It's called *grace*.

"But he said to me, 'My grace is sufficient for you, for my power is made perfect in weakness.' Therefore I will boast all the more gladly about my weaknesses, so that Christ's power may rest on me" (2 Corinthians 12:9).

What's your handicap? All of us have some kind of a handicap to deal with. If you're a golfer you know what I mean. In some sports a handicap means a weight or impediment put on an athlete who is outstanding. It's used to balance out the odds. Winning horses are actually weighted down to even the other horses' chances of winning. In golf a high-scoring player has a high handicap while the low-scoring player has a low handicap.

So, back to the question. What's your handicap? "I'm not a golfer," you say, "and I don't play the horses, so I'm off the hook." Not so.

Every one of us is handicapped. There's something in our lives or background that limits us in some way or another. With some people it's visible and obvious. In others it's hidden. If you do not see yourself as handicapped in any way right now, consider the words of pastor R. Scott Sullender:

> There is a handicapped person in your future: you! Handicapped persons are dealing in the present moment with what you and I will have to deal with later. Sooner or later each of us will become handicapped in one way or another. Sooner or later each of us will have to deal with one or several major losses in our health. Then we will travel down the same path that the handicapped person currently walks. Then we will know their pain, frustration and sufferings. Perhaps if we could learn from them now, whatever our age, we would be better prepared for our own future.[22]

That puts a different light on your life, doesn't it? Some day we will all be crippled and broken. Perhaps it reminds you of something someone did for you many years ago. Christ's body was broken, bruised, and battered for us. Our brokenness will come from age. His was a choice, and it was made out of love. Keep that in mind as you grow old.

"As for you, you were dead in your transgressions and sins, in which you used to live when you followed the ways of this world and of the ruler of the kingdom of the air, the spirit who is now at work in those who are disobedient. All of us also lived among them at one time, gratifying the cravings of our sinful nature and following its desires and thoughts. Like the rest, we were by nature objects of wrath" (Ephesians 2:1-3).

Paul is talking about the living dead. A contradiction? Not at all. Many people are spiritually dead, even though they're walking around breathing. You've heard the expression, "Man, that's living!" But when do we use that phrase? Usually when we see a pretentious home, a couple lounging on a yacht, or someone having Maine lobster and caviar each night for dinner.

The extreme of this style of living is told in a story about two gravediggers who had to dig a grave fifteen feet long and eight feet wide. They didn't know why they were doing this and naturally complained constantly. When it was done a crane rolled up, while just behind it was a trailer truck. On this trailer was a beautiful, classy gold-plated Rolls Royce. The funeral director arrived in the hearse, took out the casket, and placed it by the Rolls Royce. Opening the lid of the casket and the door of the car, he lifted the body out, propped it behind the steering wheel, put the hands on the wheel, molded the face into a smile, and finally opened the corpse's eyes. The crane swung around, hooked the cable to the top of the car, lifted and carried it over to the grave. Slowly the car was lowered into the grave. The gravediggers were watching all this and one turned to the other and said, "Man, that's living!"

Isn't it interesting what we think the good life is all about? There is a better life, a life that is really living. It's found in Ephesians: "But because of his great love for us, God, who is rich in mercy, made us alive with Christ even when we were dead in transgressions—it is by grace that you have been saved" (Ephesians 2:4-5).[23]

AUGUST 26

"How good and pleasant it is when brothers live together in unity!" (Psalms 133:1).

I magine that you are college-age and not yet married. You're with a group of college students at a meeting and everyone is very involved. But why not! It's on the subject of marriage and how to find the right mate. The speaker asks each person to take several minutes to write down all of the qualities and characteristics of the person they would like to marry. They do so, and a number are asked to share their list with the group.

After a while the speaker makes a simple comment and asks a question. "You've all had the opportunity to describe the person you would like to marry. My question is this. Let's say you met this person. What would there be about *you* that would cause this person to fall in love with you?" That's a thought-stopper! Most people are looking for the right one instead of working on becoming the right person.

It's a question that carries over into marriage as well. What is there about you that is keeping your wife in love with you? We just assume that our partners are going to stay in love with us, so we coast along. Keep in mind it's in the process of being a certain person and doing things for your partner that she fell in love with you. It's in the very process of being a certain person and doing things for your partner that she'll stay in love with you! Once you marry you *don't* stop being who you were or let up on the attentive responses to your wife. Continue to develop your character qualities and your loving behaviors toward her. That is, if you want her to stay in love with you.

"Brothers, I do not consider myself yet to have taken hold of it. But one thing I do: Forgetting what is behind and straining toward what is ahead" (Philippians 3:13).

Some men are content with a few things in life. Some want it all. Everything! Some have a hard time removing the clutter from their lives, even though it hurts them. They can't seem to eliminate what they don't need. They're like the Englishman who was with a group of climbers preparing to tackle Mont Blanc in the French Alps. The night before the climb the guide met with the group and gave them some simple instructions. He told them it would be a hard climb; if they wanted to get to the top, they should bring only what was necessary.

In the morning the Englishman showed up with the necessary gear, plus much more. It included a heavy blanket, cheese, a bottle of wine, several bars of chocolate, and two cameras with multiple lenses. The guide took one look and said, "You'll never make it with all that stuff."

The Englishman was a bit stubborn and went ahead of the group to prove it could be done. The rest of the group followed the guide's instructions. As they climbed they saw articles scattered along the way—a blanket, bottle of wine, cheese, etc. Eventually, when they reached the top, they found the Englishman, tired but wiser. He shook his head and said, "It would have been easier if..."

Your life might be easier if you cleaned house. Consider this poem by William H. Hinson:

He who seeks one thing, and but one,
May hope to achieve it before life is done.
But he who seeks all things wherever he goes,
Must reap around him in whatever he sows,
A harvest of barren regret.[24]

"We do not want you to be uninformed, brothers, about the hardships we suffered in the province of Asia. We were under great pressure, far beyond our ability to endure, so that we despaired even of life. Indeed, in our hearts we felt the sentence of death. But this hap-pened that we might not rely on ourselves but on God, who raises the dead" (2 Corinthians 1:8-9).

There are days when you feel like throwing in the towel. You're wiped out, exhausted, crushed, and devastated. Even Paul felt this way. He said there was a time when there was so much opposition that he was worn out. Not just worn out, he was so tired of what had gone on that he wished he were dead.

Perhaps you've felt that kind of weariness. It could be the opposition is coming from other people at work, at church, or even in your own family. When you have to face opposition from others over a period of time, your defenses and resolve slowly erode until nothing is left to face the onslaught.

Paul wasn't the only one to face this. David had his time, too. His son Absalom literally "stole the heart of the men of Israel" (2 Sm 15:6, RSV) and created conditions that were so bad that David had to leave Jerusalem. He had to evacuate his home, his throne, and the city he built. Then a distant relative of Saul came by and proceeded to attack, curse, and stone David. That was like rubbing salt in the wound. It was not a fun trip. He was bone weary when they arrived at their destination. "The king and all his men were worn out when they reached the Jordan and they rested" (2 Sm 16:14, TLB).

Opposition exhausts. What do you do at a time like this? May I suggest that you put into practice the three Rs.

Remember. You're not alone; and there is One who is with you.

Rest. There is no substitute for allowing your body and mind to heal. Look to the One who gives you rest.

Resolve. When your strength is back, as much as possible try to resolve the differences between you and those opposing you. Your adversaries may not change, but at least you went the second mile.

"Be strong and very courageous. Be careful to obey all the law my servant Moses gave you; do not turn from it to the right or to the left, that you may be successful wherever you go" (Joshua 1:7).

Forty years of dreaming. That's probably how long Joshua dreamed about going into the Promised Land. Then one day God said, "It's time to stop dreaming and start doing." God was very specific in what he said:

> "Moses my servant is dead. Get ready to cross the Jordan River into the land I am about to give to them—to the Israelites. I will give you every place you set your foot, as I promised Moses. No one will be able to stand up against you all the days of your life…. As I was with Moses, so I will be with you; I will never leave you nor forsake you. Be strong and courageous, because you will lead these people to inherit the land I swore to their forefathers to give them. Be strong and very courageous." **Joshua 1:2-7a**

And move into the land he did. But there were obstacles. Joshua was older, the report of the spies was negative, the land was filled with giants. They had to work the land and fight the enemies, as well.

Some days you may feel like Joshua. You hit one obstacle after another again and again. But that's a part of life.

Who ever said that life would be easy? Probably no one. But we all hope for it. The problem is the more you believe that it should be easy, the more likely you are to give up and retreat. Turning back from difficulty wasn't in Joshua's vocabulary. It doesn't have to be in ours either. Sure, you may have to back up and re-group a bit, but that's all right. And there is something you can do to help you press on. It's in the instructions given to Joshua.

> Do not let this Book of the Law depart from your mouth; meditate on it day and night, so that you may be careful to do everything written in it. Then you will be prosperous and successful **Joshua 1:8, NIV**

"God is our refuge and strength, an ever-present help in trouble. Therefore we will not fear, though the earth give way and the mountains fall into the heart of the sea.... The Lord Almighty is with us; the God of Jacob is our fortress" (Psalms 46:1-2, 7).

Scripture itself gives us numerous guidelines for prayer. Let's consider some of these as we look at three important questions. First of all, *when* should we pray? "Pray continually" (1 Thes 5:17).

We are invited to talk to God all the time, in all places, and in every situation. He is available all the time. It means that in every decision, whether large or small, we include Him. Every move we make is to be with his guidance. You can pray during a meeting, while you're driving, and when you wake up in the middle of the night. "I have set the Lord always before me. Because he is at my right hand I shall not be shaken" (Ps 16:8).

Where should we pray? "I want men everywhere to lift up holy hands in prayer, without anger or disputing" (1 Tm 2:8). Every experience you and I are involved in is an invitation to pray. Psalm 139 describes David's experience of everywhere: "Where can I go from your Spirit? Where can I flee from your presence? If I go up to the heavens, you are there; if I make my bed in the depths, you are there" (Ps 139:7-8). God is inescapable. Don't limit him. It can't be done. Take the initiative: pray all the time and everywhere!

What should we pray about? "Rejoice in the Lord always, I will say it again: Rejoice! Let your gentleness be evident to all. The Lord is near. Do not be anxious about anything, but in everything, by prayer and petition, with thanksgiving, present your requests to God. And the peace of God, which transcends all understanding, will guard your hearts and your minds in Christ Jesus" (Phil 4:4-7).

You may find some things difficult to pray about. Perhaps that's even more reason to pray.

Why not make a note to remind yourself how to pray, using the When? Where? and What? questions. The answer? All the time, everywhere, and for everything. It could change your life![25]

"Do not be anxious about anything, but in everything, by prayer and petition, with thanksgiving, present your requests to God" (Philippians 4:6).

Worry is one of the results of the fall of man. It distorts the usage of one of God's gifts to us—our minds. Scripture has much to say about the results of worry and the benefits of a calm mind.

"I heard, and my [whole inner self] trembled, my lips quivered at the sound. Rottenness enters into my bones and under me—down *to my feet*—I tremble" (Hb 3:16, AMP).

"Anxiety in a man's heart weighs it down" (Prv 12:25, AMP).

"A tranquil mind gives life to the flesh" (Prv 14:30, RSV).

"All the days of the desponding afflicted are made evil [by anxious thoughts and foreboding], but he who has a glad heart has a continual feast [regardless of circumstances]" (Prv 15:15, AMP).

"A happy heart makes a cheerful countenance, but by sorrow of heart the spirit is broken" (Prv 15:13, AMP).

Worrying intensely about the possibility of some event happening not only *does not prevent it* from happening but can actually help to bring it about!

People who worry about having an accident when they are driving on the freeway are very accident-prone. They are actually more likely to have accidents than others because they constantly visualize the event.

Worrying about a problem or potentially dangerous situation usually exaggerates the chances of its actually occurring. Why? Because the energy used in worry is not directed toward solving the problem. The classic example is the person who worries about getting an ulcer and in a few months is rewarded for his efforts.

The problem here is that if you spend time seeing yourself as a failure or as failing, you will more than likely follow that example in your performance. You actually condition yourself for that kind of performance because of your negative thinking. However, if you spend that same amount of time and energy planning how to overcome those anticipated mistakes and visualize yourself being successful, your performance will be far better.

Our thinking patterns affect how we perform. Proverbs says that *"as a man thinketh in his heart, so is he."* It doesn't pay to worry.

"Do not conform any longer to the pattern of this world, but be transformed by the renewing of your mind. Then you will be able to test and approve what God's will is—his good, pleasing and perfect will" (Romans 12:2).

Do you want to be your own man? Sure you do. We all do. But sometimes, instead of creating who we want to be we allow ourselves to be shaped and conformed by society. It's a lot of pressure.

Society has said we are:

- to *be* something
- to *do* something
- to *own* something
- to *achieve* something
- to *prove* something.

All of these pressures say we have to be successful to be acceptable. All right, but who sets the criteria for success? We have a choice—we can follow society's standards or we can follow God's. Society says take more, make more, spend more, and above all, get more!

Sometimes we equate God's blessings with affluence. Is driving a BMW a sign of blessing or of caving in to society's standard of success? It's something to consider.

It's easy to get caught up in the wants and shoulds. And sometimes it's the pressure of another family member that pushes you. Go back to those five statements society has defined as success and ask yourself these questions.

What do you want to be?
What do you want to do?
What do you want to own?
What do you want to achieve?
What do you want to prove?

You don't have to *do* anything, *prove* anything, *own* anything, or *achieve* anything. Jesus Christ has done all of this for you. So relax. Jesus asks you to follow him and let him live life for you. Didn't he say, "Seek first his kingdom and his righteousness, and all these things will be given to you as well" (Mt 6:33)?[1]

SEPTEMBER 2

"The Lord is compassionate and gracious, slow to anger, abounding in love.... He does not treat us as our sins deserve or repay us accord-ing to our iniquities" (Psalms 103:8, 10).

How does God see our failures? They don't ever surprise him. He knows we will fail and he loves us anyway. That's good news in this competitive world!

When we fail, we may be tempted to blame someone or something, but let's leave God out of the loop. He doesn't cause our failures. He simply allows them to occur.

Some failures involve sin. Some do not. No matter what, God has promised to never leave us, forsake us, or turn his back on us.

"The Lord is close to the brokenhearted and saves those who are crushed in spirit" (Ps 34:18).

"The Lord upholds all those who fall and lifts up all who are bowed down" (Ps 145:14).

Did he dump Adam and Eve after their disobedience that affected the entire human race? No. Did he turn his back on Moses after he murdered the Egyptian? No. Did he reject David after his adultery and scheme to kill his lover's husband? No. Our God is the God of the second chance... and the third and the fourth....

God fully understands what we can learn from our failures. He wants us to know that in each failure lies a seed of growth.

Perhaps the best news of all is that he sees *beyond* our failure.[2] He's not stopped by what is. We may say, "Look how I've blown it. I can never be used again." God says, "Look how you've blown it. Let's discover what you can learn through this and put it to use for my kingdom." We look at our lives through a microscope. God looks at our lives with binoculars and says, "I wish you could see what I see for you in the future. I wish you could know what I know about your future." Now if that doesn't give you hope, nothing will!

"But the fruit of the Spirit is love, joy, peace, patience, kindness, goodness, faithfulness, gentleness and self-control. Against such things there is no law" (Galatians 5:22-23).

Most skills are built on proper technique. Take baseball for example: the players spend hours trying to master their technique in hitting the ball. They work on getting the bat off their shoulder at the proper time, keeping their head down, stepping into the ball, using the strength of their legs, keeping their swing level. Hours go into mastering the proper form. But it won't make any difference in the score of the game or the amount of the player's salary unless he does one thing—hit the ball consistently. Technique is one thing, results are another.

Theology is the same way. You may know some guy whose theology is exacting and correct. He can quote chapter and verse for his belief as well as the doctrines of John Calvin and Martin Luther. But unless this theology is translated into something else, it's not worth much. What you and I believe is important, but not as much as who we are as a person and the way we behave.

You can have correct theology, but no joy.

You can have correct theology, but no peace.

You can have correct theology, but have no self-control.

If that's the case, what good is your theology? It's not what's in your head that counts, it's what's in your heart and what you do.

Correct theology by itself won't draw others to the Lord, but the fruit of the Spirit will. What others see in you has more impact than what you tell them you believe.

In baseball it's easy to have a good technique and still strike out.

It's the same with our faith. If you're striking out, it's time for a change, isn't it?[3]

"One day the angels came to present themselves before the Lord, and Satan also came with them" (Job 1:6).

S atan. What do you think of when this name is mentioned? Is it just a name? Is Satan real? Do you have an image of him in your mind? Do you believe in Satan? I hope so. He would just love for you *not* to believe in him. That just gives him more access to your life.

We need to be aware of his reality and what he does. He was created as one of the angelic beings. He was one of God's angels, but there was a problem. He fell with others into a state of rebellion. Now, keep in mind he is just that, a fallen angel. He is not equal with God. He doesn't have the power or presence of God. And he doesn't live in hell. That's an idea people have created. At the last judgment *he* and *all* the wicked will be sent there. Where does he live now? Right here... on earth. In the Book of Job, when God asks Satan where he has been, Satan says he was roaming the earth. He still is. He's got work to do. He's got a job to do... and it's against us.

Do you know what the word *Satan* literally means? It means "slanderer" or "accuser." His job is to accuse us against God. He tempts us to sin, but his main job is to accuse us. Take a look at Job 1 and 2. Satan is hard at work slandering Job. He loves to give us as believers a bad name, and not just before God, but before others here on earth as well. Then he goes a step further. He tries to get you to accuse yourself. He throws doubt in your mind and may even sow some doubts about your salvation. Watch out for him! What can you do about it? Fill your life with the presence of God. Saturate your mind with the teachings of Scripture. Memorize his Word. When you have doubts, don't feed on them. Ask some questions and get some answers... from the Source.

"Love bears up under anything and everything that comes, is ever ready to believe the best of every person, its hopes are fadeless under all circumstances" (1 Corinthians 13:7, AMP).

I f you're married, have you ever thought that "nothing can change or improve our relationship"? If so, don't believe it. If you do it will become a self-fulfilling prophecy. If you or anyone else believes that nothing can improve your marriage, test this belief. Challenge it. Look at, define, and clarify some of the problems, then select one that appears to be the easiest to change.

One husband just wanted to be able to have discussions with his wife without defensive arguments that seemed to erupt constantly. He learned some ways he could stay out of the argument and eliminate his defensiveness. This is what he did.

1. He chose to believe that his wife wasn't out to get him or simply to argue with him out of spite. She might have some good ideas.
2. He committed himself not to interrupt her, not to argue or debate, and not to walk out on her.
3. He would respond to what she said by making such statements as: "Really," "That's interesting," "I hadn't considered that," "Tell me more," and "I'd like to think about that."
4. He chose to think the following: *Even if this doesn't work the first time, I'll try it at least five times.*
5. He determined to thank her for each discussion, and when her response was even 5 percent less defensive, to compliment her for the way she responded.

Five weeks later, he said, "The fourth discussion was totally different. It's starting to work. My belief that nothing can improve our relationship is destroyed. There's a bit of hope now."

To counter your negative and hopeless beliefs, focus upon passages from God's Word that are future-oriented and filled with hope. For example, in Jeremiah we read, "'For I know the plans that I have for you,' declares the Lord, 'plans for welfare and not for calamity to give you a future and a hope'" (29:11, NASB).

What about you? What would you like to change? The first step may be to change your beliefs.[4]

"For this very reason, make every effort to add to your faith goodness; and to goodness, knowledge; and to knowledge, self-control; and to self-control, perseverance; and to perseverance, godliness; and to godliness, brotherly kindness; and to brotherly kindness, love" (2 Peter 1:5-7).

You don't have much time left. In fact, it has to happen immediately. If you don't act now, the opportunity is lost... gone forever. And you could end up with a feeling of regret because you missed it.

What are we talking about? The opportunity on a split second's notice to be kind to someone. When you see an opportunity unfold before you, there may be no time to debate what to do. You need to act or the window of opportunity is shut forever.

Consider the TV filmmaker who has to shoot a scene set up by his producer. It's a forty-story building he found that was going to be demolished. What a chance! The explosion expert has planted the material so the building will implode (instead of explode, hopefully). It will take perhaps ten seconds. But the filmmaker takes hours to set up several cameras and consider the lighting. Why? He's got one chance to capture the collapse. After that, it's gone. There's no second chance. Only regrets. Just like acts of kindness.[5]

A woman drops her groceries coming out of the store and they scatter. It's a chance to show kindness. The homeless vet is asking for a meal. Sure, you could take the position that he shouldn't be smoking, or he could get a job if he tried, or you'll encourage his begging behavior if you help. Do you feed him? I think Jesus would have. He'd listen to people, give them a word of encouragement, even write someone a thank-you note. Kindness counts.

SEPTEMBER 7

"I looked for a man among them who would build up the wall and stand before me in the gap on behalf of the land so I would not have to destroy it, but I found none" (Ezekiel 22:30).

The book *Real Men Don't Eat Quiche* sold almost a million copies within a few days of its release. It was a spoof rather than a serious book. But the title raises a unique question. What is a real man?

What would God see as a real man? Looking at us (me included) the word *macho* wouldn't be used. Physical strength, boasting, domination, strutting, chasing, and conquering one woman after another are not on God's list of qualities for a man. God is looking for men who are authentic and genuine. They have the inner strength to stand alone when they need to. They know who they are. Their security doesn't come from conquests or whiskey, but from inner qualities. They are secure because they know who they belong to and who they reflect—God. They're strong enough to control or dominate others but their strength is displayed in choosing not to. They don't try to prove themselves to the world. They're capable of doing things contrary to the way our culture and society dictate.

Real men are willing to learn. They can admit, "I'm wrong" or "I don't know how but I'm willing to learn." They know what humility is too. There are a lot of these men around. We don't hear about them in the press or on TV, but they are noticed by those who know them and especially by God![6]

SEPTEMBER 8

"The Lord God said, 'It is not good for the man to be alone. I will make a helper suitable for him'" (Genesis 2:18).

David, an honest man, shared it like it was. In Psalm 142 he really cut loose. He says to God, "I cry," "I complain," "My spirit grows faint," "No one cares about me" (vv. 1-4). Cries of pain, cries of loneliness. Sometimes when a man feels lonely, he feels ashamed. We take our loneliness as a sign of failure and inadequacy. *Webster's Ninth Collegiate Dictionary* defines it as "a sadness from being alone... producing a feeling of bleakness or desolation."[7] When you're lonely you feel like no one is there for you and no one cares. But God did not create us to live in isolation. He created us for relationships and fellowship.

Sometimes when we feel lonely we expect other people to know this and reach out to us. They ought to be able to read our minds and know our situation.

"But," you say, "what's so bad about being lonely? I like my solitude!" Loneliness and solitude are not the same. Solitude can give us rest, strength, and provide a sense of renewal. It builds and refreshes. Loneliness leads to stagnation and alienation.

Have there been times in your life when you've been lonely? Who knew about it at the time? Some people just resign themselves to being lonely. That won't work. Some people wait for others to rescue them. That won't work, either. Some people face their loneliness and say, "I don't have to be lonely. I'm going to reach out to God and other people." That works.

God can use your loneliness to draw you into a deeper relationship with him and other people. Use it as a motivational tool to do something new with your life. If loneliness hurts, why stay in pain? There's a better way to live.

"And now all glory to him who alone is God, who saves us through Jesus Christ our Lord" (Jude 24).

Have you ever seen a person walking along a congested sidewalk with their gaze glued to the ground? Well, look around. You'll find them. And if you observe them long enough you begin to wonder about them. Their behavior is kind of odd. Most of us look ahead when we walk. But not this group. Do you wonder why?

Some people are so insecure that they just can't face others. Some are afraid of tripping or stumbling so they concentrate on looking at the ground for any obstacles. They want to make sure they place their feet in the right place. It seems strange but these are the people who end up tripping or stumbling more than anyone else. They concentrate so much on what they don't want to do that they actually end up doing it.

Karl Wallenda, one of the greatest high-wire tightrope artists of all time, involved his own family in his acts. They performed all over the world. In 1978 he was walking a seventy-five-foot wire between two structures when for some reason he lost his balance and fell to his death. Later on his wife said that for the previous three months Karl had done something he had never done before. He constantly thought about falling. It's as though his entire focus was on falling rather than on walking across the wire successfully.

Have you ever found yourself concentrating on what you want to avoid rather than on what you want to accomplish? If so, watch out. The very thing you want to avoid may become a reality. There's a better direction to look and focus on. It's Jesus Christ. Eyes focused on him keep us from stumbling, no matter what situation we're concerned about.

"May God Himself, the God of peace, sanctify you through and through. May your whole spirit, soul and body be kept blameless at the coming of our Lord Jesus Christ. The one who calls you is faithful and he will do it" (1 Thessalonians 5:23-24).

It's a nightmare. Or you hope it is. A rope is tied around each arm and each leg—four ropes all pulling in different directions. You feel like your body is being torn apart. But it's no dream. You've got so much coming at you, so much to decide, and so much to do that you feel fragmented, wrenched apart and torn in all directions.

Paul knew the struggle we have. He describes our situation graphically: "When I want to do good, I don't; and when I try not to do wrong, I do it anyway. Now if I am doing what I don't want to, it is plain where the trouble is: sin still has me in its evil grasp. It seems to be a fact of life that when I want to do what is right, I inevitably do what is wrong. I love to do God's will so far as my new nature is concerned; but there is something else deep within me, in my lower nature, that is at war with my mind and wins the fight and makes me a slave to the sin that is still within me. In my mind I want to be God's willing servant but instead I find myself still enslaved to sin. So you see how it is: my new life tells me to do right, but the old nature that is still inside me loves to sin. Oh, what a terrible predicament I'm in! Who will free me from my slavery to this deadly lower nature? Thank God! It has been done by Jesus Christ our Lord. He has set me free" (Rom 7:19-25).

You can be free from this frantic state. Rest in the promise of Scripture to give you clarity of thought, vision, and direction. Jesus is at work in you. He can make you whole and complete. The power is yours through Jesus Christ. There is wholeness in him, as well as peace.[8]

> *"Again, it will be like a man going on a journey, who called his servants and entrusted his property to them. To one he gave five talents of money, to another two talents, and to another one talent, each according to his ability. Then he went on his journey. The man who had received the five talents went at once and put the money to work and gained five more. So also the one with the two talents gained two more.... His master replied, 'Well done, good and faithful servant! You have been faithful with a few things: I will put you in charge of many things. Come and share your master's happiness"* (Matthew 25:14-17, 21).

Would others call you an ambitious person? *Ambition* is an interesting word. It comes from a Latin word and means to "go around." It's a movement around the opportunities to reach a goal.

The two men described above were ambitious for their master. They made a good investment. You need ambition in order to be successful, to get ahead, to make a mark in this world. An ambitious person is someone who's on the move. They're not standing still.

Which direction are you moving? Is it toward God or the opposite way? Sometimes our ambition takes us the wrong direction. Remember Paul? He very ambitiously persecuted the Christians. God didn't put a damper on his ambition. Paul was just going the wrong way so God changed his direction.

What about you? Are you making good investments for the Lord? Do you see your walk with him and your faith growing? Are you ambitious in your work, your family, and for the kingdom of God?

You may be a mover and a shaker. If so, God can use you. He can direct you. He wants you to be ambitious for him and make an investment for him. Think about this today: What's a new way you can be ambitious for the Lord? If you want adventure in life, this is the way to get it.[9]

SEPTEMBER 12

"Where there is no revelation, the people cast off restraint; but blessed is he who keeps the law" *(Proverbs 29:18).*

Every now and then a swimmer steps off the shore of England and sets out for France. Can you imagine even trying to swim the English Channel? It's difficult enough trying to complete a few laps in a calm, heated pool, let alone fight the waves, treacherous currents, and icy water of the Channel. But many swimmers have. Some of them failed and some of them made it.

One swimmer started out and immediately ran into rough seas. But since he had trained in the ocean, he was in peak physical condition. The next problem was the temperature—icy cold and each mile it seemed to get colder. But both the rigorous training and the oil used to grease his body became a form of insulation. The swimmer's trainers were in a boat alongside and every now and then handed over some hot soup.

Hour after hour, arm over arm, the swimmer put mile after mile behind him. Then a fog bank descended, cutting off visibility and filling the air with a chilling mist. The swimmer continued to push ahead, but for some reason, the waves seemed larger and now cramps were beginning in his arms and legs. The swimmer's muscles were in agonizing pain, and with less than two miles to go he asked to be pulled from the water.

Later on the swimmer was asked, "Didn't you know that you were almost there?" He replied, "No, I didn't. I didn't have it clearly in mind. I lost sight of my goal. I guess I just lost sight of that other shoreline on the horizon. I didn't have a vision for it anymore."

What's the vision that keeps you going in life? Is it clear or has a fog drifted in?

What are you keeping in your mind's eye? Don't let the waves of life blot out your vision or throw you off course.

"His mouth is his undoing! His words endanger him" (Proverbs 18:7).

"You fool!" How many times have we said this about someone or even to his face? We use the word, but do we know what a fool really is? They were in school with you; did you recognize them? You may work with them; can you identify them? You may even have some in your family!

They must be a problem. Why else would the word *fool* be mentioned about seventy times in the Book of Proverbs? There are three different Hebrew words that are translated "fool." One of them is used almost fifty times. It means a person who is dull and obstinate, and it's a choice he has made. He is not really willing to search patiently for wisdom. He just feels it should be handed to him. He shares his opinions with you quite freely, but they're not worth much. "A wise man thinks ahead; a fool doesn't, and even brags about it!" (Prv 13:16) And what he says falls flat or comes back to haunt him.

The problem is, the fool doesn't learn from his mistakes! "In the mouth of a fool, a proverb becomes as useless as a paralyzed leg. A rebel will misapply an illustration so that its point will no more be felt than a thorn in the hand of a drunkard. A rebuke to a man of common sense is more effective than a hundred lashes on the back of a rebel" (Prv 26:7, 9; 17:10). He likes the way he is. He wants to stay as he is, and he returns again and again to his folly. "As a dog returns to his vomit, so a fool repeats his folly" (Prv 26:11).

It's actually best to avoid this guy. Don't spend time with him. "Be with wise men and become wise. Be with evil men and become evil" (Prv 13:20). To be blunt, he's a menace. He's like a loose cannon. If you want your time wasted, spend it with a fool. "If you are looking for advice, stay away from fools" (Prv 14:7).

It's kind of sobering, isn't it? But we're not finished with the fool. There's more to come tomorrow.

SEPTEMBER 14

"Even a fool is thought to be wise when he is silent. It pays him to keep his mouth shut" (Proverbs 17:28, TLB).

Yesterday you learned about one of the words in Scripture that is translated "fool." There are two more. You'll see why we're considering these in a day or so.

The second Hebrew word is used nineteen times. It suggests stupidity and stubbornness. But this word is darker or more serious than the first. How do you identify a fool? It's easy. As the verse above suggests, as soon as he opens his mouth, he gives himself away. He quarrels. Boy, does he quarrel. He doesn't have any restraint or self-discipline. He just goes for it, regardless. "It is an honor for a man to stay out of a fight. Only fools insist on quarreling" (Prv 20:3). You're in real difficulty if you're stuck with such a person at work or anywhere else, for that matter.

The last Hebrew word occurs just three times. It's similar to the others, except for adding the quality (if you can call it that) of being a bore. The fool is a person whose mind is closed to God as well as to reason. That doesn't leave him with much, does it?[10]

There is one characteristic to keep in mind about the fool. He hates learning, clear and simple. It's not for him. "You simpletons! she cries. How long will you go on being fools? How long will you scoff at wisdom and fight the facts?" (Prv 1:22). Give him a warning sign and it doesn't register. He won't learn from what you say or do for him. "Wisdom is a fountain of life to those possessing it, but a fool's burden is his folly" (Prv 16:22). He knows it all. He's right. Don't confuse him with the facts! "A fool thinks he needs no advice, but a wise man listens to others" (Prv 12:15). He just won't respond. It makes you shudder a bit, doesn't it? But wait until tomorrow. It gets worse. The problem is his mouth!

"Wisdom is the main pursuit of sensible men, but a fool's goals are at the ends of the earth!" (Proverbs 17:24, TLB).

For any family or organization to run smoothly you've got to have good healthy communication. That involves controlling two things: your tongue and your temper. James talks about the problem graphically: "But no human being can tame the tongue. It is always ready to pour out its deadly poison. Sometimes it praises our heavenly Father, and sometimes it breaks out into curses against men who are made like God. And so blessing and cursing come pouring out of the same mouth" (Jas 3:8-10).

The fool knows no limits. He violates boundaries. Self-control is a dirty word to him. "A rebel shouts in anger; a wise man holds his temper in and cools it" (Prv 29:11). What he says weighs heavy on those around him. "A rebel's frustrations are heavier than sand and rocks" (Prv 27:3).

This person is an out-and-out troublemaker. He loves to quarrel. "It is an honor for a man to stay out of a fight. Only fools insist on quarreling" (Prv 20:3). He expresses everything without regard to the impact it may have on others.

Some people know when to speak and when to shut up. The fool? Forget it. It never crosses his mind to be quiet and gain from it. "Even a fool is thought to be wise when he is silent. It pays him to keep his mouth shut" (Prv 17:28).

This fool is your classic gossip. He loves to talk about others, whether the information is true or not. He's got an opinion for everything, a self-proclaimed expert! "To hate is to be a liar; to slander is to be a fool! The wise man is glad to be instructed, but a self-sufficient fool falls flat on his face" (Prv 10:8, 18).

But what he says will bring him down. It will ruin him. "His mouth is his undoing! His words endanger him" (Prv 18:7).

There he is in all his splendor. What do you do with a fool? What can you do? Tomorrow, it all comes together.

"God doesn't listen to the prayers of men who flout the law"
(Proverbs 28:9).

What can you do with someone who's a fool? Proverbs has some guidelines.

- *If you talk with a fool, be careful.* And be firm. "When arguing with a rebel, don't use foolish arguments as he does, or you will become as foolish as he is! Prick his conceit with silly replies!" (Prv 26:4-5, TLB).

- *Don't bother giving a fool responsibilities.* It won't work. "To trust a rebel to convey a message is as foolish as cutting off your feet and drinking poison!" (Prv 26:6, TLB).

- *It's useless to try to spend your time educating a fool.* It won't register. "In the mouth of a fool a proverb becomes as useless as a paralyzed leg" (Prv 26:7, TLB). He doesn't want to learn.

- *Don't honor the fool.* I don't know why anyone would want to, but unfortunately it does happen. We've seen it in business, government, and politics. "Honoring a rebel will backfire like a stone tied to a slingshot!" (Prv 26:8, TLB).

- *Do not give work to a fool.* He'll blow it, and the more skilled it is the worse the result. "A rebel will misapply an illustration so that its point will no more be felt than a thorn in the hand of a drunkard. The master may get better work from an untrained apprentice than from a skilled rebel" (Prv 26:9-10, TLB).

The last two guidelines may seem harsh and unforgiving, but they are necessary.

- *Don't expect a fool to change.* His character is set.

- *Stay away from such a fool.* You'll be influenced by him. "As a dog returns to his vomit, so a fool repeats his folly. There is one thing worse than a fool, and that is a man who is conceited" (Prv 26:11-12, TLB). "Be with wise men and become wise. Be with evil men and become evil" (Prv 13:20, TLB).[11]

Pray that God will be your resource for strength and wisdom when you encounter a fool.

"A wise man's heart guides his mouth, and his lips promote instruction" (Proverbs 16:23).

Many men die of heart trouble. But others die of a troubled heart. You probably won't see "troubled heart" listed on a death certificate, but it ought to be. It's real. Sometimes a friend will come up and say, "You look like your heart is troubled." It usually shows, not in chest pains, but in your face and body language.

What are the symptoms of a troubled heart? How about *anxiety?* You know, that sense of tension and feeling wired. It's often brought on by worry. And it does a real number on us. "An anxious heart weighs a man down, but a kind word cheers him up" (Prv 12:25). You actually feel as though a hundred-pound weight were pressing on your heart... and it's not indigestion.

And then there's *depression*—the feeling that hope has disappeared and everything is seen through a veil of gloom. Solomon talked about a "sorrowful" heart as well. "Even in laughter the heart may ache, and joy may end in grief" (Prv 14:13).

You may not be the one with a troubled heart. It may be a friend, spouse, fellow worker, or employee. They may smile and laugh on the outside, but on the inside they are anxious or depressed. They might need your permission to talk about what's troubling them. They may need you to draw it out of them as it states in Proverbs 20:5: "The purposes of a man's heart are deep waters, but a man of understanding draws them out." Help them talk. Listen to what they say without commenting. As it says in James, "Be a ready listener" (1:19, AMP).

Look back at the verse for today. The next verse gives you additional help in ministering to others. "Pleasant words are a honeycomb, sweet to the soul and healing to the bones" (Prv 16:24).

Troubled hearts can be healed. If yours is troubled, seek out a friend. If someone else is troubled, be a friend to him.

"The effective prayer of a righteous man can accomplish much"
(James 5:16b, NASB).

Lord,

I thank you for pursuing me with your love even when I wasn't interested. I thank you that you give me thoughts to guide me and that you strengthen my will through your Holy Spirit. Sometimes I think some things happen by chance, but I am learning that with you there is no "chance" or "accident". Thank you for the way your Spirit leads. Keep me from being blind to your Spirit's direction. I pray that each day I would grow more into the man that you would have me to be. I pray that I would become more like that man of men, your Son Jesus.

But I want to pray for more than just myself. There are so many others in need and I tend to overlook them.

I pray for those struggling with temptations right at this moment.

I pray for strength for the people who have tasks that are overwhelming them.

I pray for wisdom for the men and women who are struggling with decisions difficult to make.

For those overcome by debt or poverty;

For those experiencing the consequences of behavior done a long time ago and forgiven by you;

For those who at an early age were abused or never had a chance to experience life;

For families torn apart by divorce or death;

For those serving you in countries I don't even know about.

I pray that the concerns of my prayers would be less focused on me and more on the others you love, as well.

In Jesus' name,

Amen.[12]

SEPTEMBER 19

"The Lord God said, 'It is not good for the man to be alone. I will make a helper suitable for him'" (Genesis 2:18).

You're sitting there at home with the family. It's hot, so in addition to the TV, the stereo, the computer, the fridge, the stove, and the iron, you turn on the air conditioner. All of a sudden nothing is on. You're in semi-darkness and a sudden silence until everyone starts shouting, "What happened? What's wrong?" No more electricity. Why? Because you overloaded the circuits. It was too much for the circuit board to carry. It shut down. Sometimes wires actually burn up! Homes have caught on fire because of this and been destroyed... along with the people.

It happens at home in other ways. Sometimes it's a wife who collapses emotionally. Her feelings for her husband dry up. Or she doesn't get out of bed because she's immobilized by depression.

In some cases it's because of her husband. He overloaded the circuits by putting too much of a load on her. Some guys act like drill sergeants with their wives, snapping orders left and right. Some are perfectionists and everything has to be in order before they go to bed at night. And guess who has to keep everything in order? One of the most common ways to overload a wife is to come home and do nothing at all except eat, watch TV, and sleep.

That's not the way God intended it. A wife is a helper, created to be suitable to her man. She is not a slave or a servant. She was never meant to carry the burden. She needs a teammate, a lover, a provider, and an encourager. Enough said?

"Just as each of us has one body with many members, and these members do not all have the same function, so in Christ we who are many form one body, and each member belongs to all the others. We have different gifts, according to the grace given us" (Romans 12:4-6a).

Your church is like a body, with different members taking different roles in order for the body to function. This happens in business and it happens in the family, and it has to happen for the body to function smoothly. Sometimes you switch roles to help out someone else and let them take a breather. Perhaps the best way to demonstrate this is to look at the behavior of geese. These birds help each other during the rough times of life.

When they fly they do so in a V formation. As the bird flaps its wings, it makes flying easier for the bird behind it by creating an uplift of air. If one gets out of line it feels the resistance of the air. Flying in this way allows the flock to add 70 percent to its range. These birds fly hundreds or even thousands of miles this way.

Every so often the leader falls back in the V and another bird takes over the lead. Flying at the front takes the greatest strength, whereas the further back you go, the easier it is because of decreased wind resistance. The birds keep trading off and work in harmony with each other.

And which geese do you hear honking? It's not the leader as you might think. It's those in the back encouraging the others who are doing the hardest job.

If one bird becomes ill and has to drop out, two others follow it down to protect it. When it recovers the three take off and form their own V until they rejoin the main group.

The birds cooperate, trade off the hard jobs, encourage, support, and protect. It's a good example for all of us in the body of Christ.

"Brothers, I do not consider myself yet to have taken hold of it . But one thing I do: Forgetting what is behind and straining toward what is ahead" (Philippians 3:13).

Sometimes when you travel on an airline, you end up with excess baggage. The problem is, you're only allowed to check through so many bags. You can check in the excess, but it will cost you.

Many of us are going through life with some excess baggage and it's costing us. Not only that, it's robbing us... of joy, of being productive, and of achieving our potential.

We pack our excess baggage with numerous items. Some of us carry around hurts from our past—maybe an embarrassing incident in adolescence that keeps us from experiencing life to the fullest.

Some of us carry baggage from giving in to peer pressure when we were younger. We liked the result and soon it became a way of life...even into adulthood. We compromise our beliefs and values for the momentary approval of those around us, and soon we discover we're not really in charge of our lives, others are.

There's another item of excess baggage. A lot of men carry it, and often it's evident to others. It's a little three-letter word called *ego*. Ego is nothing more than an inflated, distorted sense of importance. I've seen it in men and so have you. They introduce themselves by their titles, their diplomas, by what they drive, what they've accomplished. They want you to identify them by what they've accomplished or accumulated rather than get to know them. They want others to think they're unique or special. So they tell them. But it usually has the opposite effect.

Excess baggage. Who needs it? There's a better way to live. It's God's way and it's free and clear!

"'For I know the plans I have for you,' declares the Lord, 'plans to prosper you and not to harm you, plans to give you hope and a future'" (Jeremiah 29:11).

There are three different kinds of men in this world. Which one are you?

The first are those who just get along in life. They have *no dreams* and *no plans*. They live for what's going on right now. Their lives are full of the same routine day after day, week after week, year after year. You've met some of them. Sometimes you go back to your high school reunion and you come away amazed at the lives of some of your classmates. Nothing has changed. And they don't seem to want their lives to change, either.

Other men are just full of *dreams...* but that's about all. There's *no action*. They talk a lot and tell everyone what they want to do. But somehow those dreams never get translated into reality. If you press them on how they're going to make their plans work, you'll hear excuses and perhaps blame.

The third group of men have *dreams with action*. They are the accomplishers. They look to God for direction, strength, insight, and wisdom. If you want some examples of men like this, look in the Bible.

Solomon had a dream to build a temple for God. He built it. Nehemiah had a dream to rebuild the walls of Jerusalem. He built them and made it possible for God's people to return and live there. Joseph interpreted Pharaoh's dream. He obeyed its message, and a nation was saved from starvation.

How about you? Do you have a dream? If not, ask God for one. He wants you to do something significant with your life... for him. And you can if you put that dream into action.[13]

"In peace I will both lie down and sleep, for you, Lord, alone make me dwell in safety and confident trust" (Psalms 4:8, AMP).

Sleepless nights—you know what they're like, especially those nights when you go to bed extra early because you have to get up at some unearthly hour. You lie there telling yourself to go to sleep. But sleep is like an elusive phantom. The more you try, the worse it gets. You toss and turn, disturbing your wife and causing her to wake up in a grumpy mood. We have all had to deal with sleeplessness at one time or another. It's no fun.

When you do sleep, is your sleep restful? Is it a time of recouping your strength, or do you awake just as exhausted as when you went to bed? If so, why? Some people have difficulty sleeping because they carry their fears and worries to bed with them. Have you experienced the peace the psalmist is talking about in today's verse? Do you give your fears and worries to Jesus Christ each night before you lie down? Do you say, "Lord, here are the burdens that I have carried all day long. I should have shared them with you earlier, but I do so now. I thank you that you will take my cares and that they don't have to plague my sleep. Thank you for the promise that you will carry my burdens. Thank you for the promise of your Word." If you haven't tried it before, what do you have to lose?

Here's another suggestion. If you watch the news on TV just before you go to bed, it may be having a negative effect on your sleep! Watching the bad news of the world isn't really conducive to rest. Talking about positive things, listening to some soothing music, reading a book or passages of the Scripture, or making love may make a difference in the way you sleep. What is your bedtime routine? Could it be better? God's Word can make the difference.[14]

"Many are the plans in a man's heart, but it is the Lord's purpose that prevails" (Proverbs 19:21).

Life is full of decisions—every day.

Some decisions are easy, such as what to eat for breakfast and whether to read the sports page or the comic page first. Other decisions are difficult—how to spend the last $100 in the checking account or how to tell your family you're not getting the promotion.

When you're a Christian there's another element involved in decision making—knowing God's will. Proverbs 16:1-4 seems to reflect the process many of us go through to get to God's will for our lives.

"To man belongs the plans of the heart..." (16:1). Sometimes we decide first what we're going to do and later we say, "Oh, by the way, God,..." We finally tell him about it (as if he didn't know).

"But from the Lord comes the reply of the tongue" (16:1). God responds to what we decide and sometimes in ways that surprise us. Has that happened to you?

"All a man's ways seem innocent to him, but motives are weighed by the Lord" (16:2). Have you ever pleaded with God to let you have what you want? Sometimes we beg him and try to justify why we want what we want. But he knows what's going on inside us. "Commit to the Lord whatever you do, and your plans will succeed. The Lord works out everything for his own ends" (16:3-4).

Give it to God. Tell him his decision is your decision and you'll do what he wants... in his timing. When you wait on him and listen to him, his desire can become the desire of your heart and life.

Are you facing an important decision today? You can decide by yourself—or you can get some divine guidance!

"A lazy mans sleeps soundly—and goes hungry!" (Proverbs 19:15, TLB).

When you hear the words *sluggard* or *slothful*, what image comes to mind? Maybe the same image as I see—a slug. A slimy, slithery, slow slug. They don't seem to get anywhere, do much, or have any purpose in life. You feel like stomping on the critters. The Hebrew word for this person is pretty much what I described—slow, hesitant, or sluggish. I'd call him lazy and in low gear.

This person seems to lack a Delco battery, of if he has one, it's dead. He needs a jump-start from someone else's cables. He is not a self-starter. "Some men are so lazy, they won't even feed themselves!" (Prv 19:24, TLB).

Maybe they don't know what to do or they're low on fuel! You wonder if they can even take care of the basic necessities of life! "But you—all you do is sleep. When will you wake up?" (Prv 6:9, TLB).

Lazy people rationalize and procrastinate. "'Let me sleep a little longer!' Sure, just a little more! And as you sleep, poverty creeps upon you like a robber and destroys you; want attacks you in full armor!" (Prv 6:10-11, TLB).

This kind of person seems to just go downhill. He wants things but lacks the oomph to go after them. "The lazy man longs for many things but his hands refuse to work. He is greedy to get, while the godly love to give!" (Prv 21:25, TLB). And he's full of irrational fears. He thinks the worst of situations. "The lazy man is full of excuses. 'I can't go to work!' he says. 'If I go outside I might meet a lion in the street and be killed!'" (Prv 22:13, TLB). He's his own worst enemy. "A lazy fellow has trouble all through life; the good man's path is easy!" (Prv 15:19, TLB). And he's got an inflated view of himself. He's a legend in his own mind. "He sticks to his bed like a door to its hinges! He is too tired even to lift his food from his dish to his mouth! Yet in his own opinion he is smarter than seven wise men" (Prv 26:14-16, TLB).

Not a pretty picture? No, but there's hope—tomorrow.[15]

"A lazy man sleeps soundly—and goes hungry" (Proverbs 19:15).

The sluggard is not a pretty sight, is he? Perhaps you wish he'd go off somewhere and not get in your way. But what if you work with one? What if he is one of your students in school or Sunday school? What if he works for you? "A lazy fellow is a pain to his employers—like smoke in their eyes or vinegar that sets the teeth on edge" (Prv 10:26, TLB).

When you give this person a job you think he's in a race with a snail and he's throwing the race! You'd like to get out a cattle prod and move him along. There is an answer to this problem. Never hire a sluggard, and if one works for you, write frequent reviews of his work so that if you need to fire him you can do so without fear of his suing you.

A sluggard can drive you up the wall because he leans on you for everything. He wants everyone to bail him out. "If you won't plow in the cold, you won't eat at the harvest" (Prv 20:4, TLB). He is too dependent.

The consequences of this lifestyle, according to Proverbs, include poverty. "A little extra sleep, a little more slumber, a little folding of the hands to rest means that poverty will break in upon you suddenly like a robber, and violently like a bandit" (Prv 24:33-34, TLB).

If you're lazy now, you pay later with interest. And the worst consequence is death. "The lazy man longs for many things but his hands refuse to work!" (Prv 21:25, TLB). He could die of starvation. Many people make this choice even today in our country! Whatever we put off doing comes back to haunt us. You can lose your job, your wife, your children by getting stuck in the area of rationalization and procrastination.[16]

Is there hope? There sure is. It's the same answer as for all our problems—an encounter with Jesus Christ. He can take the unmotivated and make them motivated. He can take the dependent and make them independent. It's happened before. It can happen again!

SEPTEMBER 27

"This, then, is how you should pray: 'Our Father in heaven, hallowed be your name'" (Matthew 6:9).

*H*allowed is not a word we use much anymore, not even in church. Some who use it aren't even sure what it means. The word *hallowed* seems heavy, austere, almost... sacred. To simplify it, what Jesus was saying was, "May your name be thought of or regarded as holy." God's name must be set apart and given the special place it deserves.

In God's Word, holiness is linked to things or persons that were set aside for God's service, such as the Sabbath or the priests. You and I are also to be "holy" because we belong to God, we "...who through faith are shielded by God's power until the coming of the salvation that is ready to be revealed in the last time" (1 Pt 1:5).

What comes to mind when you think of the word *holy*? Something austere, unattainable, unreachable? God is holy but accessible. And that's amazing when you realize that holiness means purity. We have contact with him because of his love for us.

How does he show his holiness? Well, get ready for this—you may be surprised—he shows it through *you*! Yes, through you. You are an instrument through whom he displays his holiness (see Matthew 5:16).

That's quite a responsibility. But we've been called to be holy, set apart, by the way we think, believe, speak, and behave. Don't think of it as a chore, but as an opportunity to draw others to the Father. You can be that instrument.[17]

"He who is slow to anger has great understanding" (Proverbs 14:29, AMP).

Scripture has clear implications for men concerning the proper control of anger. Proverbs, for instance, offers healthy guidelines for men dealing with anger.

"An angry man stirs up dissension, and a hot-tempered one commits many sins" (29:22).

"Do not make friends with a hot-tempered man, do not associate with one easily angered, for you may learn his ways and get yourself easily ensnared" (22:24-25).

In *The Man in the Mirror*, Patrick Morley describes a scenario that is familiar to many men.

> Anger resides behind the closed doors of most of our homes. Personally, I have never lost my temper at the office. I would never want my colleagues to think I couldn't control myself. But rarely a week goes by in which the sparks of family life don't provide good tinder for a roaring fire of anger.
>
> We put on a good show at the office and our social gatherings, but *how you are behind the closed doors of your own private castle is how you really are.* At the end of a long, hard day at the office, when you pull up the drawbridge to your own private castle, your family gets to live with the real you.
>
> Anger destroys the quality of our personal lives, our marriages, and our health. Angry words are like irretrievable arrows released from an archer's bow. Once released, traveling through the air toward their target, they cannot be withdrawn, their damage cannot be undone. Like the arrows of the archer, our angry words pierce like a jagged blade, ripping at the heart of their target.
>
> When anger pierces the soul of the home, the lifeblood of the family starts to drain away. You may notice that a secretary seems to find you attractive. You reflect on how your wife no longer appreciates you. It never occurs to you that it may be you, that if that secretary knew the real you—the angry you that lives secretly behind the closed doors of your home—she would find you about as desirable as a flat tire.[18]

That's kind of sobering, isn't it?

SEPTEMBER 29

"When someone becomes a Christian he becomes a brand new person inside. He is not the same any more. A new life has begun!"
(2 Corinthians 5:17, TLB).

Y ou're somebody. You became a somebody when you became a Christian. You became a new species. Your body didn't change (maybe you hoped it would!), your hair and eye color didn't change, you look and feel the same—but you're not. You're different. You were given a new identity at that time. Under your old identity you lived under a set of rules designed to help you get the most out of life. But with a new identity comes a new lifestyle.

You have a new set of directions for the way you behave. Here are a few of them:

Don't just pretend that you love others: really love them. Hate what is wrong. Stand on the side of good. Love each other with brotherly affection and take delight in honoring each other. Never be lazy in your work but serve the Lord enthusiastically. Be glad for all God is planning for you. Be patient in trouble, and prayerful always. When God's children are in need, you be the one to help them out. And get into the habit of inviting guests home for dinner or, if they need lodging, for the night. If someone mistreats you because you are a Christian, don't curse him; pray that God will bless him. When others are happy, be happy with them. If they are sad, share their sorrow. Work happily together. Don't try to act big. Don't try to get into the good graces of important people, but enjoy the company of ordinary folks. And don't think you know it all! Never pay back evil for evil. Do things in such a way that everyone can see you are honest clear through. Don't quarrel with anyone. Be at peace with everyone, just as much as possible. **Romans 12:9-18, TLB**[19]

"Let the peace of Christ rule in your hearts, since as members of one body you were called to peace. And be thankful" (Colossians 3:15).

Here is the story of one couple's adventure in developing spiritual intimacy:

For Esther and me, the best way to describe our life together is a covenant of love. We are both committed to walk as disciples of Christ, and this covenant binds us together in spirit, in purpose, and with integrity. Because of this common covenant, we have always been able to trust each other and to respect each other in our love as equally bearing the image of God.

Support for spirituality in our lives has come from reading the Word, from prayer, from worship, but especially from the dynamic of small-group relationships. Over the past twenty-five years we have shared in three such groups. These have enriched us and stretched our spiritual resources by offering fellowship and demanding accountability. This has been especially true for the past thirteen years working in the inner city, where we have been participants in a "covenant group" of thirteen persons, meeting each Thursday evening for sharing. We've shared everything from personal issues to a careful review of one another's financial resources and patterns of stewardship. We must be willing to be vulnerable with others and to search all the corners of our spirits.

Once, during a time of deep anguish over a problem in our family, three persons from our group came and asked us to permit them to do the praying for us during the next week; we were to relax and unhook from the emotional burden of prayer on this issue! This was a level of participation in the Spirit that provided therapy for our own spirits.

In our ministry we frequently meet ourselves in other persons while studying, counseling, and serving. We have sought to avoid a professionalism that makes the spiritual into an expression more than an experience, and have regularly sought the infilling of the Spirit to enable us to walk together in the fellowship of Christ.[20]

OCTOBER 1

"If you make the Most High your dwelling—even the Lord, who is my refuge—then no harm will befall you, no disaster will come near your tent" (Psalms 91:9-10).

Years ago there was a TV program called "The Fugitive," which captured the imagination of the nation. In the early 1990s it was made into a major motion picture starring Harrison Ford and Tommy Lee Jones. It's the story of a man running away from his home because of false accusations. It's a very intense film with a train wreck scene that brings you out of your theater seat.

Today there are people in our society who are fugitives for one reason or another. We see some of them on the streets, while others have hidden so well they are almost invisible.

What's interesting, though, is the number of men who are fugitives, even though they've remained at home. They may be living there physically but their hearts and minds are miles away. They pretend to listen to their families and participate in the routines of family life. These fugitives go through the motions, but they're on the run. The energy and effort it takes to be a functioning family member has been diverted elsewhere. Often it's been used up at work, in sports, hobbies, or sometimes on another woman.

Have you been or are you now in any way a fugitive? If so, you're a member of a very elite group. Moses was a fugitive for forty years and finally got his life straightened out. Look at how God used him.

David was a fugitive off and on because many people wanted to separate his head from his body. God still used him.

Then there was Jonah. Who was he running away from? You've got it—God. Perhaps we identify more with him than with the other two.

How about it? Are you running from God? If so, stop, turn around, and go home. He's not punitive. He's loving. Read Luke 13:31-35 and you'll see.

"And whatever you do, whether in word or deed, do it all in the name of the Lord Jesus, giving thanks to God the Father through him" (Colossians 3:17).

How will you leave this world? No, I'm not asking how you will die. Rather, how will you leave this world—a better place or the opposite?

The world is a better place because Michelangelo didn't say, "I don't do ceilings."

The world is a better place because Martin Luther didn't say, "I don't do doors."

The world is a better place because Noah didn't say, "I don't do arks."

The world is a better place because David didn't say, "I don't do giants."

The world is a better place because Jeremiah didn't say, "I don't do weeping."

The world is a better place because Peter didn't say, "I don't do Gentiles."

The world is a better place because Paul didn't say, "I don't do letters."

The world is a better place because Mary didn't say, "I don't do virgin births."

The world is a better place because Jesus didn't say, "I don't do crosses."

Will you leave the world be a better place than you found it? What will be your legacy? Will you discover and answer God's calling, both private and public?

Dwight L. Moody, the Billy Graham of the nineteenth century, one day heard these challenging words which marked the beginning of a new era in his life: "The world has yet to see what God will do, with, and for, and through, and in, and by, the man who is fully and wholly consecrated to Him."

He said "a man," thought Moody. He did not say a great man, nor a learned man, nor a rich man, nor a wise man, nor an eloquent man, nor a "smart" man, but simply "a man." I am a man, and it lies with the man himself whether he will, or will not, make that entire full consecration. I will try my utmost to be that man.[1]

Will you try your utmost to be that man?[2]

OCTOBER 3

"And taking with Him Peter and the two sons of Zebedee, He began to show grief and distress of mind and was deeply depressed" *(Matthew 26:37, AMP).*

Years ago there was a phrase that went, "Real men don't eat quiche." We found out that wasn't true. There's another myth that's been placed upon us as men, and it goes like this: "Real men don't get depressed." That's a myth, too. Men do get depressed. Christians get depressed. But too many men pretend their depression isn't there.

It's difficult for some men to admit to depression. They see it as a weakness rather than a symptom of something else. They may try to work harder to make it go away, but it doesn't work. If you're depressed or have been, you're not alone. Look at some of the great men of history who experienced depression.

Vincent van Gogh: first great impressionistic painter.

Peter Tchaikovsky: composed the classic *Nutcracker Suite* and other great Russian symphonies.

Wolfgang Amadeus Mozart: *the* musical genius of his day.

Robert Schumann: great romantic composer.

Ernest Hemingway: wrote *The Old Man and the Sea* and other great novels.

Fyodor Dostoyevski: author of *Brothers Karamazov* and the epic *Crime and Punishment.*

Theodore Roosevelt: President of the United States.

F. Scott Fitzgerald: American novelist.

James Forrestal: first Secretary of Defense.

Charles Spurgeon: great expository preacher.

David Brainerd: first missionary to the American Indians.

Here was a group of super-achievers, including some who spread the Word of God. And when you look at God's Word you find many others who experienced the normal response of depression. Jonah, Joseph, Jeremiah, Elijah—they all had their reasons for depression.[3]

Remember that depression is nothing more than a message system telling you that something else is going on in your life. Listen to that message.

continued on page 286

Depression denied will devastate you more. Depression admitted is the first step to recovery. Find a trusted friend and share what's been going on. You may be surprised to hear that he struggles with depression also. Jesus knows what you're going through. After all, he's been there.

"Now it is God who makes both us and you stand firm in Christ. He anointed us, set his seal of ownership on us, and put his Spirit in our hearts as a deposit, guaranteeing what is to come" (2 Corinthians 1:21-22).

You and your wife are out looking for a new car. You find a car mart, one of those places where there are new car dealers one after another. You begin looking. You start with Toyota, then Honda, then Buick, and finally end up at the BMW dealer. (If you do, let's hope you're making plenty of money!) You look, you discuss, you barter, you quibble, you decide, and then you buy... on time, of course! The first big step is the down payment. A down payment is a pledge that the rest of the amount will be paid. This could range from 5 to 20 percent of the actual cost. You pay it and now you have something to look forward to in addition to driving away in this quality car—four years of monthly payments! Great!

Well, a down payment was made on you, too. When you became a Christian you received a gift—the Holy Spirit. The Holy Spirit actually represents God's down payment to you. It's a promise that there are more payments to come—the reality of heaven. You *will* be going there. God is saying in this verse that there is a guarantee that you will receive all you have coming. That's your assurance. We don't have to worry (like the BMW dealer) that God might renege on his payment. You don't have to worry that your salvation will be repossessed. It's set. It's safe. It's sure. Full payment is there waiting for you. It's got a good sound to it, too... it's called eternal life![4]

"And you were also included in Christ when you heard the word of truth, the gospel of your salvation. Having believed, you were marked in him with a seal, the promised Holy Spirit" (Ephesians 1:13).

Seals are interesting, and I don't mean those ocean-going animals. Sometimes when you purchase a quality vase or art object there is a seal impressed on the base to indicate its authenticity—it's the real thing.

You find seals like this on many objects, including cattle. The owners of the herd have a roundup each year, bring in all the new calves, heat up the iron in the coals, and brand each one. This seal is a sign of ownership.

You too have been branded (if you want to look at it that way). You've been sealed as the Scripture states with the Holy Spirit. In a sense this seal is God's mark of ownership on you. You belong to him, not to yourself, your wife, your parents, or your work.

This seal does something else; it gives you security. No one else can put their brand or seal on you as cattle rustlers used to do. You are branded for good. And no one can take that seal off you, either. What happened to you took place on the inside.

Think about this: If you have a seal on you that comes from God, it means that what he has done for you is real, it's authentic. Your new birth *is* authentic. You have heaven to look forward to.

One more item. Remember the cattle owner? He dictates where the cattle go and what happens to them. He has authority over them. God has authority over us as well.

As you go through this day, rest in the security of being sealed! It puts a new perspective on the troubles of this life.[5]

OCTOBER 6

"Submit to one another out of reverence for Christ" (Ephesians 5:21).

If you're married, you and your wife are not compatible. That's just a fact of life. You may be becoming more compatible, but when first married, the differences are quite apparent. That's all right. They enhance a marriage relationship. These differences can be resolved if you learn to listen, lighten up, and not withdraw or pull the silent treatment. Perhaps the old adage about an animal bears repeating here. Remember the turtle? He only makes progress when he sticks his head out.

You will have conflicts. That's a given, but it's not the problem. Attacks and defensiveness win a war, but they are not good battle strategy for marriage. Consider your partner's point of view and learn to respond with, "That's a different way to look at this" or "Let me think about that for a minute."

Here are some passages to consider from the Word of God. How could each one of these be applied to your marriage relationship?

"Correct, rebuke, and encourage—with great patience and careful instruction" (2 Tm 4:2).

"Speaking the truth in love.... Therefore, putting away lying, 'Let each one of you speak truth with his neighbor.'... Do not let the sun go down on your wrath" (Eph 4:15, 25-26, NKJV).

"For even if I made you sorry with my letter, I do not regret it" (2 Cor 7:8, NKJV).

"Now no chastening seems to be joyful for the present, but painful; nevertheless, afterward it yields the peaceable fruit of righteousness to those who have been trained by it" (Heb 12:11, NKJV).

"Brothers, if someone is caught in a sin, you who are spiritual should restore him gently" (Gal 6:1).

"Exhort one another daily... lest any of you be hardened through the deceitfulness of sin" (Heb 3:13, NKJV).

"Make straight paths for your feet, so that what is lame may not be dislocated, but rather be healed.... [Look] carefully lest anyone fall short of the grace of God; lest any root of bitterness springing up cause trouble, and by this many become defiled" (Heb 12:13, 15, NKJV).

OCTOBER 7

"Rejoice in the Lord always" (Philippians 4:4, NIV).

Do you ever want to resign from life? You know, the days that Murphy's Universal Laws are in effect? Remember those laws?

"Nothing is as easy as it looks."
"Everything takes longer than you think it will."
"If anything can go wrong, it will."

Have you had a day when...
...you walk into the bathroom and the cat left a fur ball on the bathroom floor?
...during the night, to help out your wife, you change the baby's diaper, take it in the bathroom to drop it in the diaper pail, and it lands on your bare foot?
...you walk into the kitchen to discover the dog is eating your toddler's breakfast and the toddler is eating the dog food?
...you go to work and at the end of the day discover why everyone snickered when you walked by—your zipper was down?
The list goes on (by the way, all these happened to me!).
At times like these, you pray for patience—immediately. And speaking of patience, J.I. Packer once wrote,

Patience means living out the belief that God orders everything for the spiritual good of his children. Patience does not just grin and bear things, stoic-like, but accepts them cheerfully as therapeutic workouts planned by a heavenly trainer who is resolved to get you up to full fitness.

Patience, therefore, treats each situation as a new opportunity to honor God in a way that would otherwise not be possible, and acts accordingly. Patience breasts each wave of pressure as it rolls in, rejoicing to prove that God can keep one from losing his or her footing.[6]

OCTOBER 8

"Do not take revenge, my friends, but leave room for God's wrath, for it is written: 'It is mine to avenge; I will repay,' says the Lord" (Romans 12:19).

Have you ever wanted to get back at someone who's hurt you? Sure. We all have at one time or another. Some men get a great deal of satisfaction out of revenge.

Did you hear about the cranky old guy who was bitten by a dog? Not only that, it appeared the dog might have rabies. So the man was rushed to the hospital for treatment, and was kept there to see if further treatment were needed. An intern walked by the man's room and saw the man muttering to himself and staring into space. But he was also writing something on a piece of paper and the intern thought he was writing a will. The man said, "Now, in case I get rabies, I'm making a list of the people I want to die before I kick off." This man was poisoned, all right—by hate and revenge. And he didn't get it from a dog bite.

Settling the score is not our right. Vengeance comes from bitterness, which can kill us.

At one time or another we all may feel we have a right to get back. Well, if anyone has felt that way it was Joseph. His brothers sold him into slavery (see Genesis 37-50). But when they were finally reunited, he explained why he didn't try to get back at them. "'So then, don't be afraid,' he said. 'I will provide for you and your children.' He reassured them and spoke kindly to them" (Gn 50:21).

Let God be who he is and do what he does. "Do not take revenge, my friends, but leave room for God's wrath, for it is written: 'It is mine to avenge; I will repay,' says the Lord" (Rom 12:19).

What he wants from us is to forgive. It's the only sure way to resolve issues.[7]

"By faith he left Egypt, not fearing the king's anger; he persevered because he saw him who is invisible" (Hebrews 11:27).

Many of the Old Testament men had character traits worth imitating. It doesn't mean they were perfect. Far from it. We can breathe a sigh of relief for that. But we can still learn from them.

What would you think about a guy who was so stubborn that even when the ruler of his country started hassling him, he wouldn't budge? He stood his ground. What would you think about a man who wouldn't budge from what he believed in and wanted to do, even when thousands of people he was supposed to lead disagreed with him? And they weren't silent in their disagreement. They were verbal! They griped and complained and blamed, and finally... rebelled. And to make it worse (maybe you've been in this pressure cooker), his own family, his brother and sister, got on his case and became his personal critics. But this guy wouldn't budge even one inch. Talk about stubborn. Or was he?

Scripture uses another word to describe Moses. He *endured.* He wouldn't cave in or throw in the towel. When someone is having a hard time we often say, "Hang in there." That's exactly what Moses did. Look at how other translations put it.

The *Living Bible* says, "...he kept right on going."
The *New English Bible*: "...he was resolute."
The *Amplified*: "...he held staunchly to his purpose."
Moffatt's rendering: "...he never flinched."

Chuck Swindoll says that we should...

Stand firm when conspirators seem to prosper. Stand firm when the wicked appear to be winning. Stand firm in times of crisis. Stand firm even when no one will know if you compromised. Stand firm when big people act contemptibly small. Stand firm when petty people demand authority they don't deserve. Stand firm... keep your head... stay true... endure![8]

OCTOBER 10

"Treat others as you want them to treat you.... Never criticize or condemn—or it will all come back on you. Go easy on others; then they will do the same for you. For if you give, you will get! Your gift will return to you in full and overflowing measure, pressed down, shaken together to make room for more, and running over. Whatever measure you use to give—large or small—will be used to measure what is given back to you" (Luke 6:31, 37-38, TLB).

Interesting verses, aren't they? There's a principle there—the rubber band principle. What you do and give to others is going to come back to you. It's like a boomerang. You get ticked off at that guy who cut in front of you on the freeway and you make a threatening gesture (or worse!). You know what will happen. Did you really think he'd be sorry, wave happily, or apologize? In your dreams! He'll dish it out right back to you.

It works that way all the time. If you frown and scowl around other people, guess what? You'll get the same back. If you want the people you work with to be critical and rude, griping and complaining, all you have to do is treat them that way. People tend to mirror back what they see. They're like parrots repeating what they hear.

You can exert a tremendous amount of influence on others by your words and behavior.

We're called to model the behavior that we want in others. That's what Luke 6:31, 37-38 is all about.

So... why don't you describe the kind of people you want around you. Be specific. Identify those responses. Just remember, they're waiting for you to set the tone.

Go ahead; you can do it. After all, if God called us to model right behavior, it's possible. He's the one to make it all happen.

"I will give them an undivided heart and put a new spirit in them; I will remove from them their heart of stone and give them a heart of flesh" (Ezekiel 11:19).

The picture on the TV monitor wasn't pretty. It showed a cavity in the man's chest where his heart had been. The surgeon had just lifted it out and placed it in a steel dish. The heart was worn out, defective, and now dead. It was going to be discarded. The team of physicians had taken a new heart from a special container and it was now being placed in the chest cavity. Soon it would be sewn in place.

Some men don't want to hear about this process. But let's face facts. Some of us will have a heart attack. Some of us will have bypass surgery. And a few will have a heart transplant (if there's a heart available).

You see, half a million adults and six thousand children will die this year because of defective hearts. And of those whose hearts are so bad they need a transplant, 90 percent of them will die before they receive one. There are just not that many available. Many men just sit around waiting, hoping that someone chose to be a donor while they were alive. They want their defective heart replaced by a healthy, beating, massive muscle that will adjust to their body.

Actually, we all need a heart transplant. Ours has a disease called sin. It can destroy our life and keep us separated from God. Jesus died but in his death he is saying, "I want to give you a new heart, a clean heart, a healthy heart, free from sin!" And when you accept this, there is no fear of this transplant being rejected. It's a perfect fit; we have a new lease on life.[9]

"Only conduct yourselves in a manner worthy of the gospel of Christ" (Philippians 1:27, NASB).

As a follower of Jesus Christ, are you doing that? I mean are you following him in what you do and how you respond to others? Consider these four examples from Jesus' life.

Jesus had compassion. We see his compassion expressed in Mark 8:2: "I feel compassion for the multitude because they have remained with me now three days, and have nothing to eat." His concern was to alleviate suffering and meet the needs of the people. In what way can you demonstrate compassion to others around you?

Jesus accepted people. When Jesus first met people, he accepted them as they were. In other words, He believed in them and what they would become. The characteristic of acceptance is seen in John 4, John 8, and Luke 19. When Jesus met the woman at the well, he accepted her as she was without condemning her. He accepted the woman caught in adultery and Zacchaeus, the dishonest tax collector, as well. Who needs your acceptance today?

Jesus gave people worth. People were Jesus' top priority. He established this priority and gave them worth by putting *their* needs before the rules and regulations the religious leaders had constructed. Sometimes we fall into that trap. He involved himself in the lives of people who were considered the worst of sinners, and he met them where they had a need. In so doing, he helped them elevate their sense of self-worth.

One of the ways Jesus gave worth to people was by showing them their value in God's eyes, by comparing God's care for other creatures with God's care for them: "Are not two sparrows sold for a cent? And yet not one of them will fall to the ground apart from your Father" (Mt 10:29, NASB).

Jesus encouraged people. "Come to Me, all who are weary and heavy laden, and I will give you rest. Take My yoke upon you, and learn from Me, for I am gentle and humble in heart; and you shall find rest for your souls. For My yoke is easy, and My load is light" (Mt 11:28-30, NASB).

One of the ways we can encourage others is to introduce them to Jesus.

OCTOBER 13

"Don't grumble about each other, brothers. Are you yourselves above criticism? For see! The great Judge is coming. He is almost here. [Let him do whatever criticizing must be done.]" (James 5:9, TLB).

Does griping ever get to you? Some people are never satisfied, never grateful. They perpetually grumble and complain. They always want more, less, or something different. You've probably heard plenty of griping at work or perhaps right in your own family. You're not alone. In Numbers 11, Moses got an earful.

> The people were soon complaining about all their misfortunes, and the Lord heard them.
>
> Then the Egyptians who had come with them began to long for the good things of Egypt. This added to the discontent of the people of Israel and they wept. **Numbers 11:1, 4-5, TLB**

You may have to hear the griping of one, three, or even several people. Moses had a couple million to contend with. So, what did he do? He complained to God. He let God know exactly how he felt.

> Moses said to the Lord, "Why pick on me, to give me the burden of a people like this? Are they *my* children? Am I their father? Is that why you have given me the job of nursing them along like babies until we get to the land you promised their ancestors? Where am I supposed to get meat for all these people? For they weep to me saying, 'Give us meat!' I can't carry this nation by myself! The load is far too heavy! If you are going to treat me like this, please kill me right now; it will be a kindness! Let me out of this impossible situation!" **Numbers 11:11-15, TLB**

Well, God fed the people with quail but he also sent a plague. At times you've probably wanted to send one, too, when people complain.

What can you do when others gripe and grumble? It's simple.

1. Don't follow their example.
2. Ask God for wisdom.
3. When people complain, let them know you hear them so they don't have a need to repeat themselves. Then ask them for two possible solutions to the problem. Who knows? They may solve it themselves!

"The good man is covered with blessings from head to foot, but an evil man inwardly curses his luck" (Proverbs 10:6, TLB).

Have you ever used the word *wicked*? We use it to describe all kinds of situations, such as: "He's got a wicked left hook," "He throws a wicked curve ball," "We live in a wicked world."

Our world is full of wicked people no less than it was during Solomon's time. How would you describe a wicked person? Think about it for a minute. In the Old Testament the words used to describe this kind of person include: rejecting God, idolatrous, abusing others as well as property, violent, greedy, oppressive, oppressing the poor, and thinking nothing of murdering another person. Morals? They don't know the meaning of the word.

Take a look at the daily paper. It's full of all the events just described. But do we call these events wicked? Not usually. There's a lot more emphasis on either rationalizing the behavior, blaming others for the cause, or looking for ways to sugar coat what was done.

Some people are blatantly wicked, but others are clever about it. They know what to say, when to say it, and how to say it. They're subtle. Proverbs says, "A wicked man shows a bold face" (21:29, NASB). They have the ability to portray someone they really aren't. They're deceptive.[10] You've heard the phrase "all things to all people." That's the way the wicked operate. "Blessings crown the head of the righteous, but violence overwhelms the mouth of the wicked" (Prv 10:6).

Did you catch that? They're able to cover up violence! Sometimes their lifestyle is attractive. Sometimes they seem to get away with so much that it doesn't seem fair. But remember this: "Don't envy the wicked. Don't covet his riches. For the evil man has no future; his light will be snuffed out" (Prv 24:19-20, TLB).

OCTOBER 15

"When a good man speaks, he is worth listening to, but the words of fools are a dime a dozen" (Proverbs 10:20, TLB).

You see them on TV all the time. They're interviewed on talk shows and in the tabloids, and even on *Entertainment Tonight* and other classy shows. They talk about their major business deals, their eighth marriage, how they were caught with a hooker or someone else's spouse, and we shrug our shoulders and just seem to accept it as part of life. You'd probably never call what they do wicked. But God would.

There are a lot of people in small and large businesses, in the government, and in the entertainment industry, just to name a few, who would do anything, use anyone, to get what they want. They seem to have no sense of morality. So, what should we do about them? There are several things to remember that can give us some hope.

First, don't play with the thought of joining them, don't ever envy them. "Don't do as the wicked do. Avoid their haunts—turn away, go somewhere else" (Prv 4:14-15, TLB).

Second, don't let them get to you. You don't have to be afraid of them. "You need not be afraid of disaster or the plots of wicked men, for the Lord is with you; he protects you" (Prv 3:25-26, TLB).

Third, they will get what they deserve. "Reverence for God adds hours to each day; so how can the wicked expect a long, good life?" (Prv 10:27, TLB).

Fourth, you as a righteous man will survive. They won't. "Evil men shall bow before the godly" (Prv 14:19, TLB).

Fifth, you have a responsibility to do something about what they do. Take a stand. Speak out and speak up. When you see sin, confront it. You may not be popular in men's eyes, but who needs their adulation anyway?

Some of what goes on today happens because we've let it happen. Once again, Proverbs tells you what to do: "Blessings shall be showered on those who rebuke sin fearlessly" (Prv 24:25, TLB).

"Do not merely listen to the word, and so deceive yourselves. Do what it says" (James 1:22).

L ord,

I praise you for understanding me and my struggles. I admit that I have numerous faults that still interfere with living my life as you want. Forgive me for my conscious and purposeful acts of sin, as well as those which seem to creep in even though I'm fighting against them.

Help me not to say one thing with my words and another with my actions.

Help me not to criticize others for the same faults I see in myself.

Help me not to demand standards from others which I make little or no effort to fulfill.

Help me not to play and skirt around temptations that I know are my weakness.

Help me to deal with the inability to say yes or no and to be definite in my commitments.

Help me with my stubbornness and reluctance to give up habits which I know are wrong and break my relationship with you.

Help me to quit trying to please both worlds; forgive me for pleasing others and myself first rather than you.

Help me to be consistent and live the week the way I live on Sunday morning.

Help me to kick out anything in my life that keeps me from giving you all of me.

Thank you for hearing, for responding, and for working in my life.

In Jesus' name,

Amen.[11]

"You made him a little lower than the heavenly beings and crowned him with glory and honor" (Psalms 8:5).

Most of us like to be successful. Some of us, however, turn success into a requirement. When this happens, we become preoccupied with the pursuit, not of excellence, but of perfection. The greater the degree of pursuit, the lesser the degree of joy. Perfectionism becomes a mental monster.

To prove they are good enough, perfectionists strive to do the impossible. They set lofty goals and see no reason why they should not achieve them. Soon they are overwhelmed by the arduous task they have set for themselves. The standards of a perfectionist are so high that no one could consistently attain them. Yet their worth, they think, is determined by attaining these goals.

We as believers are called to be perfect. But it is a call to continue to grow and mature. It does not mean never making a mistake. It means looking at ourselves objectively, accepting and recognizing our strengths and talents as well as the areas of our life in which we are lacking.

One author said, "We must stop being picture straighteners on the walls of life before we can find and bring joy in life."[12]

It's not so terrible to be average. In fact, the world is full of mostly average people. *Average* means we accept our strengths and weaknesses and do what we can to change the weak areas.

We can be average and yet be adequate. Adequacy is a free gift to us and always has been. Any shortage in our lives has been paid for by God's free gift. Let's begin to express ourselves out of our sense of adequacy, instead of striving to become adequate. Let's let loose of the criterion of human performance, for God calls us to be faithful, not perfect. This is the standard—faithfulness!

"Then Job replied: 'I have heard many things like these; miserable comforters are you all! Will your long-winded speeches never end? What ails you that you keep on arguing? I also could speak like you, if you were in my place; I could make fine speeches against you and shake my head at you" (Job 16:1-4).

You're having a rotten, lousy day. Nothing has gone right. One thing after another seems to pile up on you. How could anyone have so much difficulty at one time? It's like your world is crumbling around you.

Fortunately, you have some friends to comfort you. Or at least you thought they were your friends. At first, they didn't say anything. They were just there silently in their support of you, and it helped. Then they began to talk, and you wished they hadn't! One of them told you to remember the advice you gave to others in the past. That didn't help too much, but this friend went on with the clincher. He had the audacity to tell you that he'd had a vision showing him that your suffering was the result of some sin. Imagine a friend telling you your problems were caused because of some sin you committed! Isn't that great? Then he told you that you sounded like a fool and what you needed to do was repent! To make matters worse, he said these problems were blessings in disguise.

Great! Just when you need comfort, empathy, and support, what do you get? Theology. And as you argue with your friends, their insensitivity grows. It's as though you need to argue with their theology. Well, if this has happened to you, you're not alone. Remember Job? You can read about it in Job 4 and 5.

When a friend is hurting he needs comfort, not theology. He needs you to listen, not give advice. "Understand this, my beloved brethren. Let every man be quick to hear, (a ready listener,) slow to speak, slow to take offense *and* to get angry" (Jas 1:19, AMP). He doesn't need criticism, he needs encouragement. Be there. Be silent, be available, be sensitive.

OCTOBER 19

"How I long for the months gone by, for the days when God watched over me, when His lamp shone upon my head and by His light I walked through darkness!" (Job 29:2-3).

One of the worst experiences any of us could have is to be or feel abandoned. Sometimes this happens to us as children. The result is that we live with the fear of abandonment the rest of our lives.

There may be times when you feel God has abandoned you. You're not alone. So did Job. He lost it all—his property, servants, livestock, children, and health—and he experienced intense pain. But the worst experience of all was God withdrawing the assurance of his presence. We all experience this at some time or another. Some have called this "the dark night of the soul." Many have felt that God has actually deserted them.

Is it true that God actually deserts? No, he doesn't. But in the midst of suffering, like Job we could begin thinking that he has. God doesn't desert us. What he does is make us sensitive to his absence so we look for him with a greater intensity and cry out for him.

Job accused God of forsaking him (Jb 30:21). It was like saying, "God, you're unfair!" Have you ever asked God, "Why?" again and again as Job did? Your "why" question is actually more of a cry of protest against what has happened. Was God obligated to answer Job's questions? No. Is he obligated to answer our questions? No.

Elihu gave Job some good advice (chapters 32-37) that's applicable for us today. We can focus on what we think God hasn't done and what we think he should do OR we can dwell on who he is and his majesty. You may even think God's ways are wrong. They're not, they're just different and mysterious. Consider the dark days a greater opportunity to trust him even more.[13]

OCTOBER 20

"My God, my strength, in whom I will trust; my shield and the horn of my salvation, my stronghold" (Psalms 18:2, NKJV).

All of us would like to be men of strength. It's just part of being masculine. When you think of strength, what comes to mind first? Probably physical strength. We usually measure our strength from a physical perspective. Pumping iron, running laps, doing curls, walking fifteen miles in three hours. We measure our ability in terms of endurance and strength—by what we can do physically.

Physical fitness is a big business. Just check out the sports club ads in the Monday edition of the paper for examples of strength and perfect proportions. But to look like that (and some of us never will, no matter what we do) takes time.

There are other kinds of strength: strength of character, emotional strength, spiritual strength.

What are your personal strengths? Have you ever identified them? How are they being used? In what way would you like to be stronger?

The psalmist states that God is his strength. The word *stronghold,* as it was used in the Old Testament, meant "a place of refuge" where you would be secure. No one could break in and penetrate this place. David spoke frequently of God as his stronghold. It's a descriptive term for God. And David did the one thing with God that gave him strength. It's the same step that will give each of us the strength we need. He spent time alone with God. That's what we must do—clear the clutter from our minds and reflect upon him.

If you want real strength—spiritual strength—go to the trainer who can get you into condition. The Stronghold. Invest your time with him. You'll discover a strength that will amaze you.

"I am speaking in human terms because of the weakness of your flesh" (Romans 6:19, NASB).

We're weak. We've all got our Achilles' heel that we don't like to admit. We try to compensate for physical weakness by working out hour after hour, joining health clubs, taking vitamins, going to the health food store for supplements. Even with all our preparations, defenses, and building walls of resistance, there could be something that might bring us to our knees.

We're like Superman in a way. Remember him? I knew about him in the forties when I was a kid (yes, I'm that old. So...). The man of steel, faster than a locomotive, who could leap tall buildings. Nothing, but nothing, could get to him... except kryptonite. It was a substance from his home planet. It could not only weaken him, it could kill him with prolonged exposure. Perhaps you too remember the scenes when he tried to leap or run or fly and he couldn't because of exposure to kryptonite. He was weakened.

If even Superman had a weakness, is there any hope for us? There are many varieties of kryptonite out there. Some of it is attractive, too. More money, a bigger house, the BMW, popularity with the guys, glances from attractive women. We've all got our weaknesses. What's yours? When you admit it, face it, confess it, and ask Jesus Christ to help you, it loses its power. And that weak area of your life begins to diminish.

There is a state of weakness that is positive, though. It's when we acknowledge that we really are insufficient and weak in the flesh and we lean upon the suffering of Christ that real strength comes.

> But he said to me, *"My grace is sufficient for you, for my power is made perfect in weakness."* Therefore I will boast all the more gladly about my weaknesses, so that Christ's power may rest on me. That is why, for Christ's sake, I delight in weaknesses, in insults, in hardships, in persecutions, in difficulties. For when I am weak, then I am strong. **2 Corinthians 12:9-10**

"Be still before the Lord and wait patiently for him..."
(Psalms 37:7a).

Would you like to get more out of your life, enjoy it more, feel relaxed, and be productive? If you said yes, consider these suggestions. This is the program Type-A men learn to follow to change their life. We'll consider these today and tomorrow.

Begin each day by asking God to help you prioritize those items that need to be done. Do only those items for which you really have time. If you feel you can accomplish five during the day, do only four. Try to accomplish only one thing at a time.

Each day think about the cause for any potential time urgency. Write down one of the consequences of being in a hurry. If you begin to feel pressured about completing your tasks, ask yourself: *Will completing this matter three to five years from now? Must it be done now? If so, why? Could someone else do it? If not, why?*

Make a conscious effort to become a "ready listener" (see James 1:19, AMP). Ask questions to encourage others to continue talking. When someone is talking, put down your newspaper, magazine, or work and give that person your full attention.

Reevaluate your need for recognition. Instead of looking for the approval of others, tell yourself in a realistic way, "I did a good job and I can feel all right about it."

Try to relax without feeling guilty. Give yourself permission to relax and enjoy yourself. Play some soft background music at home or at the office to give a soothing atmosphere. Begin to read magazines and books which have nothing to do with your vocation. (But don't see how many different books you can read—or brag to others about your "accomplishment.")

Begin to look at the Type-A behavior of others. Ask yourself, "Do I really like that person's behavior and the way he or she responds to people? Do I want to be that way?"

Attempt to plan your schedule so that you drive or commute when traffic is light. Try to drive in the slow lane of the highway or freeway. Try to reduce your tendency to drive faster than others or just as fast. Let others pass you!

OCTOBER 23

"Be still before the Lord and wait patiently for him" (Psalms 37:7a).

Let's continue the suggestions for living a balanced, stress-free, non-Type-A lifestyle.

Begin your day fifteen minutes early and do something you enjoy. If you tend to skip breakfast or eat standing up, sit down and take your time eating. Look around the house or outside and fix your interest upon something pleasant you have been overlooking.

Think about what your values are. Where did they come from and how do they fit into the teaching of Scripture?

Each day try to spend a bit of time alone. Whatever you do at this time, do it slowly in a relaxed manner.

Begin to develop some interests and hobbies that are totally different from what you do for a living. Experiment a bit.

Periodically decorate your office or work area with something new. Take pride in what you do to express yourself, and run the risk of being different.

As you play games or engage in sports, whether it be racquetball, skiing, or cards, do it for the enjoyment of it and do not make it a competition. Begin to look for the enjoyment of a good run, an outstanding rally, and the good feelings that come with recreation, which you have been overlooking.

Allow yourself more time than you need for your work. Schedule ahead of time and for longer intervals. If you usually take half an hour for a task, allow forty-five minutes. You may see an increase in the quality of your work.

Evaluate what you do and why you do it.

In one of his sermons, Dr. Lloyd Ogilvie, Chaplain of the U.S. Senate, raised two interesting questions that relate to what we are doing and how we are doing it. "What are you doing with your life that you couldn't do without the *power of God?*" and "Are you living life out of your own *adequacy* or out of the abundance of the riches of Christ?" Both questions are something to think about.

"I do not understand what I do. For what I want to do I do not do, but what I hate I do" (Romans 7:15).

Failure! The word we dread. Some of us don't allow it in our vocabulary. Failure is what happens to others, or so we hope, but it hits all of us at times.

The word *failure* means "to deceive or disappoint." The words *fallacy* and *fallible* come from the same source. *Webster's Dictionary* says failure is "the condition or fact of not achieving the desired end."[14] But is failure just the absence of success? Is it simply a matter of bombing out, of not completing what we set out to attain? Perhaps not.

Many men have achieved significant goals, but found no satisfaction in them. It really didn't matter after all. This is a side of failure. It's like climbing a path up a mountain and making it to the top, only to find out you climbed the wrong mountain! Failure is not just the pain of a loss but the pain of a new beginning as well.

When you experience failure, do you judge *yourself* as having failed or what you *did* as having failed? The difference is crucial. We can let failure devastate and cripple us, or we can look at Scripture and see how God used people who failed such as Noah, Abraham, Jacob, Moses, and others to accomplish his purposes. Think about this perspective on failure from a Promise Keeper speaker, Dr. Gary Oliver:

> What apart from God feels like a failure can, in His skilled hands, become a part of His provision for our growth. We can't be successful in the Christian life if we deny the existence of failure. If we learn how to value it, understand it, and take it to the foot of the cross, we can become wiser and stronger because of it.[15]

What can you do to reconstruct the way you view failure?

"As it is written: 'There is no one righteous, not even one: there is no one who understands, no one who seeks God. All have turned away, they have together become worthless, there is no one who does good, not even one.' 'Their throats are open graves: their tongues practice deceit.' 'The poison of vipers is on their lips.' 'Their mouths are full of cursing and bitterness.' 'Their feet are swift to shed blood: ruin and misery mark their ways, and the way of peace they do not know.' 'There is no fear of God before their eyes'" (Romans 3:10-18).

This is a strong passage. It hits hard. It should. It describes a man who has *no* reverence for God.

Reverence, a word that *doesn't* mean being quiet and reserved in worship service. Reverence is standing in awe of who Almighty God really is. It's recognizing that he is all powerful, not us.

In Exodus 3:5-6 God called Moses by name, and what did Moses do? He hid his face. He was afraid to look at God. He had a godly fear, a reverence.

There are benefits in reverencing God. Are you aware of that?

First of all, it's the beginning of wisdom. "The fear of the Lord is the beginning of knowledge, but fools despise wisdom and discipline" (Prv 1:7).

Second, it will give you greater confidence in your life. "He who fears the Lord has a secure fortress, and for his children it will be a refuge. The fear of the Lord is a fountain of life, turning a man from the snares of death" (Prv 14:26-27). When you have confidence in God, your own level of confidence grows because you realize you're not going through life alone.

Third, when you reverence God you have a more exciting and prolonged life. "The fear of the Lord adds length to life, but the years of the wicked are cut short" (Prv 10:27). "The fear of the Lord leads to life: Then one rests content, untouched by trouble" (Prv 19:23).

Many men are putting in hours and hours a week, as well as spending money, to keep themselves in shape. That's great. But they're missing one element—reverencing God. It's the ultimate workout.[16]

"But even the Son of Man did not come to be served, but to serve, and to give His life as a ransom for many" (Mark 10:45).

"This is a test. Take out a pencil and a piece of paper. You've got ten minutes to complete it." Remember those hated words in high school and college? Those sneak quizzes they'd drop on you on the days after the night you didn't crack a book? Well, guess what? Today you're going to have a quiz. But good news, no grades or penalties.

There are three words for you to define. The first is *ransom*. Do you know what it means? *Ransom* is a word built on the concept that something has been lost or taken and now has to be paid for in order to be set free. That's exactly what Jesus did for us in a voluntary way.

Watch out for the next word. It's *propitiation*. It's a word to denote an appeasement. God's wrath against sin needed to be appeased. This was done by Jesus' death and suffering on the cross for our sins. God is a just and holy God, and the penalty needed to be paid. God stepped in and sent his Son as the payment which appeased his wrath.

The last word may get you. It's *expiation*. This sounds like a combined English/Theology class, doesn't it? True, but it's important to understand what took place to give us the freedom we have.

When Jesus suffered and died, his suffering purged our sins. That is what expiation is all about. It has to do with the act of removing our guilt by paying the penalty for sin. Your penalty and mine were put on Jesus. He took our punishment. God has been satisfied.

Did we deserve it? No. Was God satisfied? Yes. And one other thing: God didn't have to do this, he chose to because he loves us.[17]

"Give thanks in all circumstances, for this is God's will for you in Christ Jesus" (1 Thessalonians 5:18).

How do you handle the "gifts" life gives you? Like when you get an ugly sweater for Christmas instead of that power saw. Or when the one Saturday you can play golf or tennis it rains for three hours and you spend the time in the clubhouse talking with your friends. Or when you go to the doctor to check on those aching joints and are told you have arthritis and it will continue to intensify.

Paul said to give thanks in all circumstances. He's talking about an attitude called gratitude. Paul shows us what he means in this passage:

> I have cheerfully made up my mind to be proud of my weaknesses, because they mean a deeper experience of the power of Christ. I can even enjoy my weaknesses, suffering, privations, persecutions and difficulties for Christ's sake. For my very weakness makes me strong in him."
>
> **2 Corinthians 12:9-10, Phillips**

If you want happiness, you must be grateful for whatever you receive in life, whether it is good or bad.

Years ago a soldier put it well.

I asked God for strength that I might achieve.
I was made weak that I might learn humbly to obey.
I asked God for health that I might do greater things.
I was given infirmity that I might do better things.
I asked for riches that I might be happy.
I was given poverty that I might be wise.
I asked for power that I might have the praise of men.
I was given weakness that I might feel the need for God.
I asked for all things that I might enjoy life.
I was given life that I might enjoy all things.
I got nothing that I asked for
but everything I had hoped for....
Almost despite myself my unspoken prayers were answered.
I am among all men most richly blessed.

—Unknown Confederate Soldier

"For I know the plans I have for you,' declares the Lord. "Plans to prosper you and not to harm you, plans to give you a hope and a future"' (Jeremiah 29:11).

S ome days will be bad. You will feel as if life is crumbling around you. That's when you question God. The three questions most often asked by those in hard times:

"Why, God, why?"

"When, God, when?"

"Will I survive, God?"

Of those three questions, the most common question of all is: Why? Why me? Why now? Why this? Why, God, why? You're not the first person in crisis to ask why, and you won't be the last.

Remember Job, the man who lost it all in just one day? One devastating crisis after another. Everything went—his family, possessions, wealth, and health. After several days of silence he began asking the questions many of us ask.

"Why didn't I die at birth?"

"Why can't I die now?"

"Why has God done this to me?"

He threw the question, "Why?" at God sixteen times. Each time there was silence. And you know... silence was probably the best answer. I know that sounds strange, but if God had given Job the answer to this question right away, would he have accepted it? Would you? Or would you argue against his answer? You probably wouldn't understand God's reason at the time. By not having the answer, we have the opportunity to learn to live by faith.

God does not explain all suffering in the world or the meaning of each crisis that occurs.

What God allows us to experience is for our growth. God has arranged the seasons of nature to produce growth, and he arranges the experiences of the seasons of our lives for growth also. Some days bring sunshine and some bring storms. Both are necessary.

He knows the amount of pressure we can handle. First Corinthians 10:13 tells us he will "not let you be tempted beyond what you can bear." But he does let us be tempted, feel pain, and experience suffer-

continued on page 312

ing. Sometimes he gives us not what we think we need or want but what will produce growth.

When your question changes from "Why?" to "What?" then you will have the answer.

"When you were dead in your sins and in the uncircumcision of your sinful nature, God made you alive with Christ. He forgave us all our sins" (Colossians 2:13).

D r. Harold Sala, in his book *Things Can Be Different Today*, shares a fascinating story of how Jesus changed lives.

Things didn't go quite as airline officials had planned on that July morning when American Airlines inaugurated their new flight #673. They were to have company dignitaries along with several public officials honor the first passenger with a news photo and speeches. Everything was fine, until they handed passenger Ron Rearick a plaque commemorating his flight. Here the script fell apart.

Upon receiving the presentation, Rearick presented the airline official with a copy of *Iceman*, the story of his life. The official took a quick glance; then was horror-struck. On the cover was a block of ice on which was pictured the profile of the man who stood on the platform that day. The back cover was a photo of Rearick and these words: "In 1972 Iceman hijacked United Airlines for one million dollars. He was sentenced to 25 years at McNeil Island Federal Prison. No one wanted him out. Not the state! Not the FBI! Not the public! But Iceman was freed by a higher court! Read the true story of Ron Rearick. He was the Iceman!"

Suddenly the politicians moved from view of the TV cameras. The airline officials went into a huddle. This was the man, all right, the same one who had been labeled an "habitual criminal." Here he was being honored by another airline as the first passenger on the new flight. Rearick walked over. "By the way, I'm not in the business anymore. I'm on your side now."

The real story is not that an extortionist by some quirk of fate had become the honored passenger on an inaugural flight by another airline; the real story is that this hardened criminal had met Jesus in prison and his life was transformed. After a twenty-five-year career in crime, Rearick, alias Iceman, became Ronald Rearick, B.A. (born again). Today he's an ordained minister and speaks before thousands, telling them about his changed life. God is no respecter of persons. What he's done for Rearick, he'll do for you. He's still in the business of changing lives.[18]

"Meanwhile, the older son was in the field. When he came near the house, he heard music and dancing. So he called one of the servants and asked him what was going on. 'Your brother has come,' he replied, 'and your father has killed the fattened calf because he has him back safe and sound.' The older brother became angry and refused to go in. So his father went out and pleaded with him" (Luke 15:25-28).

The elder brother was all business. He was a serious guy working in the fields. And there's a good reason for that. He was the oldest son. He would receive two-thirds of the inheritance. It was his and he saw it as such.

But was he ever indignant when he learned the reason for this big party! His brother, the playboy who wasted his inheritance, had come home, and now his father was treating him like nothing had happened. In verses 29 and 30 he accuses his brother of some things no one had mentioned. Could it be these were fantasies the older brother had?

Look at the self-righteous elder brother. His status with his father was based on how well he served and obeyed. He was proud of who he was and what he had done. Pride soon leads to arrogance, and this leads to judgmentalism. When we are proud we look down on the less fortunate. If they haven't worked as hard as we have, they don't deserve what we have.

How do you feel when someone you think is undeserving is elevated like the younger son? Do you resent missing out on living the life of a prodigal?

Is there an "elder" brother living and lurking within you?

Sure, there are many prodigals in life. They're obvious. But anyone can be a prodigal and not even show it, even an elder brother.[19]

"Many waters cannot quench love; rivers cannot wash it away. If one were to give all the wealth of his house for love, it would be utterly scorned" (Song of Songs 8:7).

In over thirty-five years of marriage one of the discoveries that Joyce and I have made is this: Developing our spiritual intimacy is the foundation for a lasting marriage. And it is more than doing activities together; it's an attitude or an atmosphere within the marriage relationship. It's the feeling of freedom that you can connect at any time and in any way about spiritual matters or issues. There is no walking on eggshells about sharing or raising a question. You live your lives in the confidence that you are connected spiritually.

In terms of the specifics of our spiritual growth together, we each maintain our own personal devotional life. This involves daily prayer with a specific list of prayer requests. We read from both the Old and New Testaments as well as devotional reading. Some days we read separate material, but on others it is the same. Our worshiping together at church is very important to us, and frequently we talk about our response to the music or message as we drive home.

Perhaps sharing the mutual grief over the life and death of our retarded son during the past twenty-seven years was a factor that brought us together spiritually. Through this we learned to share our hurts, concerns, frustrations, and joys together. What has ministered to us both at these times was worship—not only at church, but at home through worship music from a multitude of Christian artists and numerous musical and inspirational videos. We have found that our personal and corporate walk with the Lord must be a priority and a commitment just as much as our wedding vows.

NOVEMBER 1

"Finally, brothers, whatever is true, whatever is noble, whatever is right, whatever is pure, whatever is lovely, whatever is admirable— if anything is excellent or praiseworthy—think about such things" (Philippians 4:8).

The label is everything. We're taught to check the labels of food items in the store. We won't buy clothes or even golf clubs if they don't have the right label. We depend on labels, and they have their place... except in marriage.

Negative thoughts and labeling never provide a full picture of your wife. They are limited, biased, and slanted in one direction. More important, they interfere with one of the ingredients most essential for a marriage to change, progress, and move forward. It's called forgiveness. Negative labels and thoughts block forgiveness. You have to see your wife in a new light for forgiveness to occur. Can you forgive a person you label as callous, selfish, controlling, insensitive, manipulative, unbending, crazy, etc.?

Labels are false absolutes. They are developed to describe those who are different. They're used to make it easier to justify ourselves and to keep us from thinking. If we used our minds constructively, we would be able to see both sides of a person. Labels limit our understanding of what is occurring in a marriage, for we see the label as the cause of the problem. Why look elsewhere?

Labels also keep us from looking at our part in the problem. We use labels to avoid looking in the mirror for fear of what it will reflect. When you treat your wife as *if* she is a certain way and possesses a particular quality, she may begin to act that way. Our negative expectations often become self-fulfilling prophecies and we end up cultivating what we don't want to grow.

Do you and your spouse label each other? Are the labels positive and motivating or negative and debilitating? Are there generalizations attached to descriptions such as *always* or *never*? If you do label your wife, perhaps you could learn to correct the label and in your heart and mind give her an opportunity to be different. It could make a difference in your marriage.[1]

"Husbands, love your wives, just as Christ loved the church and gave himself up for her" (Ephesians 5:25).

We need men today who are leaders—leaders in the home, the workplace, the community, and our churches. Since there are different ways to lead and different styles of leadership, let's see what we can learn from leaders themselves about leadership. British Field Marshall Bernard Montgomery describes it this way: "Leadership is the capacity and will to rally men and women to a common purpose and the character which inspires confidence."

Former President Harry Truman said, "A leader is a person who has the ability to get others to do what they don't want to do and like it." If you can do that, what an ability! It means overcoming resistance and defensiveness. It means creating an openness on the part of a person to consider what you are suggesting and substitute it for what they believe or do. To be this kind of leader you need to listen, believe in what you feel needs to be done in a non-obnoxious manner, and show the positive benefits of what you are suggesting.

Another leader, Fred Smith, said simply, "Leadership is influence." There are some people in positions of leadership who don't lead. If you're not affecting the thoughts and actions of others, you're not leading. Someone said, "He who thinks he leads and has no one following him is only taking a walk."

True leadership is modeling. It's leading the way, showing what to do in a sacrificial way. That's the biblical way. That's God's way.[2]

"My times are in your hands..." (Psalms 31:15, NKJV).

Take a look at your hand right now. What do you see? Is it smooth or calloused, squat or long, strong or weak? Can you imagine going through life without the use of one or both of your hands? We are totally dependent upon our hands.

The word *hand* has great significance in Scripture. The phrase "the hand of the Lord" is used frequently. Do you know what it means? It's a figure of speech that uses the word *hand* for the "providence, presence, and power of the Lord."

We use the word as a compliment: "I've got to hand it to you." Many of the statements we make about a person's ability and activity relate to our hands, and sometimes in a humorous way, such as, "Can you lend me a hand?" In many naval war movies, we've heard the phrase "all hands on deck." We ask someone to help us by saying, "Can you take this off my hands?" We refer to a worker as a "hired hand." We see someone begging and say, "He wants a hand-out."

Hands can be used for good or evil. The same hand that gently caresses a wife's face can be used to deliver a stinging slap.

One day on the Sabbath Jesus met a man with a withered hand. "And behold there was a man with a withered hand" (Mt 12:10, NASB). The original Greek means "a man who had his hand withered." It wasn't a birth defect but perhaps a burn or an accident. He couldn't use his hand. It had become a burden, a restrictive portion of his body, limiting his life. He looked to Jesus for healing—and he got it. "Then he said to the man, 'Stretch out your hand.' So he stretched it out and it was completely restored, just as sound as the other" (Mt 12:13).

Are your hands complete? Are they handicapped in any way? Do they hinder you? Are they being used to further Christ's kingdom? Is there any way in which they are withered? If so, reach out and allow Jesus Christ to touch you so that your hands can be an instrument of healing to other people.[3]

"Love the Lord your God with all your heart and with all your soul and with all your mind and with all your strength. The second is this: Love your neighbor as yourself. There is no commandment greater than these" (Mark 12:30-31).

L ove is a choice. Yes, there may be feelings of love at times, but they come and go. It is a choice—especially agape love. This word is used in one form or another over two hundred times in Scripture. If you're married it's the type of love that will make your marriage come alive. You can't do it on your own, though. It's difficult. You need God infusing you with this love and the strength to be consistent with it. If you want to know what it's like, look at Jesus. There are three words that describe how Jesus loves us and how we're to love others.

He loves us unconditionally. He loves you with no conditions, no restrictions. No matter how wild you are, how bad you are, how mad you are, how vile you are, he loves you. Remember this: How you behave doesn't earn you any more of God's love. The man who murdered his wife and three children? Jesus loves him as much as he loves you and me. That's unconditional love.

He loves us willfully. Do you understand what this means? He loves you because He *wants* to love you. He wasn't forced to go to the cross for you, he chose to. He chose to touch lepers, he chose to heal the sick, he chose to die. How do we love others? By choosing to. And if that's difficult, as it will be sometimes, pray for a change of heart and attitude.

He loves us sacrificially. Sacrificial love gives all, expecting nothing in return. It's a costly love. It's not an easy love. It takes something from us. It takes us out of the comfort zone. How could you love someone sacrificially today? When you've decided, go ahead and do it. In doing so, you become a bit more like Jesus.[4]

"We love because he first loved us" (1 John 4:19).

L et's continue to think about agape love again today, especially agape love in marriage.

Agape is self-giving love, the love that goes on loving even when the other person becomes unlovable. In a marriage, agape can keep erotic love alive or rekindle erotic love that has been lost. *Agape love is not just something that happens to you; it's something you make happen.*

When the Bible states that God is love, it uses the word *agape*. John wrote, "God so loved (agape) the world, that he gave his only begotten Son" (Jn 3:16). *Agape* gives. *Agape* sacrifices. *Agape* initiates. *Agape* loves whether or not the object deserves that love. "But God demonstrates His own love toward us, in that while we were yet sinners, Christ died for us" (Rom 5:8, NASB).

Let's get practical now in a marriage and consider what *agape* is all about.

Agape is kindness. It is being sympathetic, thoughtful, and sensitive to the needs of the other person. It is...

- squelching the urge to ask whether she's eating more chocolates lately.

- listening when she wakes up and wants to talk at 2:35 A.M.

- helping to put the children to bed, even during the fourth quarter of the TV football game.

Agape is forgiving. It tries to be content with those things that don't live up to expectations. It is...

- being patient when she squeezes the toothpaste tube from the wrong end for the 837th time.

- not making nostalgic comments about your mother's fine cooking.

- learning to love *all* her relatives—even Uncle Howard!

NOVEMBER 6

"The fool says in his heart, 'There is no God.' They are corrupt, their deeds are vile; there is no one who does good.... All have turned aside, they have together become corrupt; there is no one who does good, not even one" (Psalms 14:1, 3).

Have you ever been on the receiving end of slander? It can hurt you and your reputation for years to come. Slander demonstrates graphically the proverb, "Death and life are in the power of the tongue" (Prv 18:21, NASB). Slander destroys reputations, friendships, and trust, as well as a person's potential for the future. It's a twisting of the truth to do in another person, usually for the slanderer's benefit.

Slander is all around us. Listen to the news. Read the headlines on those tabloids at the checkout stand. What they are engaging in is character assassination. The slanderer looks at another person as though they were under a microscope. What are you looking for? Imperfection, weaknesses, cracks in the person's character. And then the plan is to turn the microscope into a verbal magnifying glass and share it with the world. Even if there isn't an ounce of truth to what is said, the damage is still done. It's the same as a judge in a trial saying to the jury, "Disregard that last comment." The damage has already been done.

A man after God's heart doesn't give in to the temptation to elevate himself by demeaning another person. He looks for truth. He looks for the person's character qualities and talks about those rather than the defects. When he hears others bad-mouthing someone, not only does he refrain from passing it on, he challenges the one who's talking to verify that what is being said is actually accurate.[5]

Nobody needs slander. So... when you learn something good about another person, share it. When you learn something bad about someone, forget it.

"The rich man's wealth is his only strength. The poor man's poverty is his only curse" (Proverbs 10:15, TLB).

Would you like to be wealthy? Let's be honest. Who wouldn't? Somewhere within us is that dream of having all the money we want so we will never be in need and can buy whatever we want!

We don't want to wait for wealth. We want it now. I see it all the time when I counsel young couples before they marry. They want to start out economically at the same level as their parents, even though it took their parents twenty-five or thirty years to get there. The reality is that when they marry, they will probably have to step down a notch or two economically!

Proverbs has much to say about being wealthy. You'll find that the teachings in this book go a bit counter to the way people think today. If you're interested in becoming wealthy, take some advice from Proverbs. "Lazy men are soon poor; hard workers get rich" (Prv 10:4, TLB). Perhaps the old TV commercial from "Smith-Barney" took its closing line from this passage. It said, "We make money the old-fashioned way—we earn it." That's what Proverbs is saying. Work for it. Earn it.

There's another way wealth comes. "True humility and respect for the Lord lead a man to riches, honor and long life" (Prv 22:4, TLB).

Humility doesn't seem to fit the profile of society's wealthy, especially when you consider the wealthy in the sports or entertainment industry. It's just the opposite. Or is it? Those who get press are the ones we know about. There are many others we don't see who have found that the wisdom of Proverbs is true. And speaking of wisdom, that's another way to be wealthy. "Any enterprise is built by wise planning, becomes strong through common sense, and profits wonderfully by keeping abreast of the facts" (Prv 24:3-4, TLB).

This will give you something to consider.[6]

"If you must choose, take a good name rather than great riches; for to be held in loving esteem is better than silver and gold" (Proverbs 22:1, TLB).

Imagine with me for a moment that you're on a major TV quiz show and you're on a winning streak. One question to go and you make it to the top. The question is asked, you give the answer. It's correct! You've done it! But all of a sudden the announcer says, "We have one more question for you." You're shocked! It shows on your face. But the announcer goes on. "You've won but now you've got a choice of prizes. You can have all this wealth—the money, the boat, the new car, the European trip—or you can have integrity. Which do you want?" Silence. Dead silence. Perhaps you're wondering even now which you would take. You may even ask, "Why not both?" But if you had to choose, which one would you take?

That may be a tough one for you, especially as you look at the bills, the house, what the kids need, etc. We all have a need for money. Much of it is justified. But sometimes we place too high a value on wealth and moving up!

Think for a moment: does wealth bring us closer to God or might we tend to drift away? It's easier to become enamored with our own ability when we're financially comfortable unless we remember that whatever we have really belongs to God. It's not wrong to have money. God never condemns wealth. Not at all. In fact there are many wealthy men who give 50 percent of what they make to the Lord's work. They've discovered not only wealth but integrity too.

Proverbs leaves us with some thoughts about this issue:

"Better to be poor and honest than rich and a cheater" (Prv 28:6, TLB). "Better to be poor and honest than rich and dishonest" (Prv 19:1, TLB). "A little, gained honestly, is better than great wealth gotten by dishonest means" (Prv 16:8, TLB).

"Mocking the poor is mocking the God who made them. He will punish those who rejoice at others' misfortunes" (Proverbs 17:5, TLB).

"Anyone who oppresses the poor is insulting God who made them. To help the poor is to honor God" (Proverbs 14:31, TLB).

What does God think about that guy in tattered, dirty clothes standing on the corner with a scrawled sign, "Homeless—will work for food"? What do you think of him?

Good question. Few of us have ever been poor. We don't know what it's like. Let's be blunt. God is for the poor. He looks out for them. "Don't rob the poor and the sick! For the Lord is their defender. If you injure them he will punish you" (Prv 22:22-23, TLB). "Everyone enjoys giving good advice, and how wonderful it is to be able to say the right thing at the right time!" (Prv 15:23, TLB).

If God is for the poor, then what is our responsibility? Sometimes the poor are victimized by others. They can't defend themselves as well. Other poor people rip them off. Perhaps we do, too, when we give them a dollar, knowing it won't buy a meal. Or perhaps we have them work for us, thinking they don't have to be paid as much as a regular worker. Proverbs says this shouldn't happen. "Listen to your father's advice and don't despise an old mother's experience" (Prv 22:22, TLB). "They devour the poor with teeth as sharp as knives" (Prv 30:14, TLB).

There's just one thing to do. We have to take responsibility to help the poor. "Happy is the generous man, the one who feeds the poor" (Prv 22:9, TLB). "When you help the poor, you are lending to the Lord—and he pays wonderful interest on your loan!" (Prv 19:17, TLB). "He who shuts his ears to the cries of the poor will be ignored in his own time of need" (Prv 21:13, TLB). "If you give to the poor, your needs will be supplied! But a curse upon those who close their eyes to poverty" (Prv 28:27, TLB).

Take a minute to read Matthew 25:31-46. It sheds a new light on the poor.

"But even if he does not..." (Daniel 3:18).

Three men were in deep trouble. Here's the story. Nebuchadnezzar told Shadrach, Meshach, and Abednego that if they didn't bow down and worship his gods, he would fry them. You know, crank up the heat in the furnace and invite them in. How did they respond?

> Shadrach, Meshach and Abednego replied to the king, "O Nebuchadnezzar, we do not need to defend ourselves before you in this matter. If we are thrown into the blazing furnace, the God we serve is able to save us from it, and he will rescue us from your hand, O king. But even if he does not, we want you to know, O king, that we will not serve your gods or worship the image of gold you have set up." **Daniel 3:16-18**

Each of us has our own dreams, desires, expectations, and hopes. If these come about we say, "Everything is all right. I can handle life and I'm content. Now I can have the peace and stability I was looking for."

For many of us our faith is dependent upon getting God to do what we want. However, this is not the biblical pattern. It's all right to say, "I hope it turns out that way." "I hope the escrow doesn't fall through." "I hope he pulls through the operation." But we must also learn to say, "I hope... but even if it doesn't turn out that way, *it will be all right.*"

Each of us has his own "fiery furnace" to face at one time or another. When such a time hits, we'll experience the normal emotional responses that are part of the healing process and then, with God's strength and stability, face the results. God does not always send in a rescue squad to get us out of the difficulty. (He doesn't always extinguish the fire in the furnace.) He does come in and say, "Let's go through this together." God gives us the grace to live life. And grace is really God's assurance that life can be all right when everything in it is all wrong.

Things will be better tomorrow, but better from *God's perspective.* Saying "even if he doesn't" means we are willing to leave the results to God.

NOVEMBER 11

"The eye is the lamp of the body. If your eyes are good, your whole body will be full of light. But if your eyes are bad, your whole body will be full of darkness. If then the light within you is darkness, how great is that darkness!" (Matthew 6:22-23).

"Dream on!" That's a common expression we use to let someone know whatever they're saying is not possible. When we say someone is a "real dreamer," it's not usually a complimentary remark. But there's nothing wrong with having dreams for yourself or even for others. We need vision and often that comes from dreams.

Perhaps you've seen *Man of La Mancha*, the musical about Don Quixote, a crazy old man. The story takes place about one hundred years after the age of chivalry. Even though there were no more knights, Don Quixote thinks he is one. So he puts on a suit of armor and rides out into the world to fight against evil. He wants to protect those who are weak. He has a little servant whom he brings along as his squire. When they stop at an inn used by mule traders, Don Quixote calls the innkeeper the lord of the castle. In this inn he meets a pathetic, abused girl who cleans up after everyone and is misused by the profane mule traders. But our hero renames her. He calls her Dulcinea and begs for her handkerchief to carry with him as a token into battle. You probably remember scenes of Don Quixote on his horse charging windmills and trying to slay them with his lance.

But at the end of the play, as he's dying, he no longer has these delusions. In a very gripping scene, every person he has renamed comes to his bedside. They plead with him *not* to change. Why? It was simple. The excitement he had about their future transformed them into the very people he imagined. His strange dreams shaped their lives. That's what dreams can do.

So... dream on.

NOVEMBER 12

"Let marriage be held in honor among all, and let the marriage bed be undefiled" (Hebrews 13:4a, NASB).

Sex—we think about it a lot. Why not? We were created as sexual beings. Sex wasn't man's invention but God's idea. So... why not thank him for it in a prayer like this:

Lord, it's hard to know what sex really is—
Is it some demon put here to torment me?
Or some delicious seducer from reality?
It is neither of these, Lord.
I know what sex is—
it is body and spirit,
it is passion and tenderness,
it is strong embrace and gentle hand-holding,
it is open nakedness and hidden mystery,
it is joyful tears on honeymoon faces, and
it is tears on wrinkled faces at a golden wedding anniversary.
Sex is a quiet look across the room,
a love note on a pillow,
a rose laid on a breakfast plate,
laughter in the night.
Sex is life—not all of life—
but wrapped up in the meaning of life.
Sex is your good gift, O God,
to enrich life,
to continue the race,
to communicate,
to show me who I am,
to reveal my mate,
to cleanse through "one flesh."
Lord, some people say
sex and religion don't mix;
but your Word says sex is good.
Help me to keep it good in my life.
Help me to be open about sex
and still protect its mystery.

continued on page 328

Help me to see that sex
is neither demon nor deity.
Help me not to climb into a fantasy world
of imaginary sexual partners;
keep me in the real world
to love the people you have created.
Teach me that my soul does not have to frown
at sex for me to be a Christian.
It's hard for many people to say, "Thank God for sex!"
Because for them sex is more a problem
than a gift.
They need to know that sex and gospel
can be linked together again.
They need to hear the good news about sex.
Show me how I can help them.
Thank you, Lord, for making me
a sexual being.
Thank you for showing me how to treat others
with trust and love.
Thank you for letting me talk to you about sex.
Thank you that I feel free to say:
"Thank God for sex!"[7]

NOVEMBER 13

"Let your eyes look straight ahead, fix your gaze directly before you. Make level paths for your feet and take only ways that are firm. Do not swerve to the right or the left; keep your foot from evil" (Proverbs 4:25-27).

Keep your eyes straight ahead, says the writer of Proverbs. There are some good reasons for that admonition. You've probably already figured them out. For instance, you've seen guys at the beach with their wives. They strain their necks and turn their heads frequently, checking out the abundance of bikini-clad bare skin. Have you ever noticed the expressions on the faces of their wives? Sometimes it ranges from the deepest hurt imaginable to "You check out one more woman and you're dog meat, fella." It's probably one of the greatest insults a husband could lay on his wife, to gaze at another woman while his wife watches. It sends plenty of messages to his wife—the wrong kind. Those glances should be reserved for her!

There's another reason why our eyes stray. It's called envy, and don't think this is just a problem for women. We struggle with it as well. When you're envious, you're not content. "More" is the byword. "Better and bigger" is the theme song. If you have a computer, what kind is it? How many megabytes? How do you react when you see a guy with one that runs circles around yours? Did your level of satisfaction go up or down? Did that little sensation of "I want it; I want what he's got" come into play? When envy hits, rationalization is refined. We have the "best" reasons in the world for having what others have—all but the good reasons.

Whether it's golf clubs, power equipment, or the make and year of our cars, the potential for envy is there. And when it hits, just remember, you're allowing yourself to be dominated and controlled by what the other guy has. That's a worse experience than envy. And it wouldn't happen if we were looking ahead rather than to the side. Don't fix your eyes on what others have, fix your eyes on Jesus, the author and finisher of our faith.

"No servant can serve two masters. Either he will hate the one and love the other, or he will be devoted to the one and despise the other. You cannot serve both God and Money" (Luke 16:13).

When I was a kid in the forties, I lived in the hills of Hollywood, California. It was a long way up that steep road to get to my house. So as soon as the school bus dropped me off, out came my thumb to snag a free ride. It beat walking. And it usually worked. Back then we knew most of the people and it was safe. I rode in Model As with rumble seats, or stood on the running board of a car, hanging onto a window and hoping my parents wouldn't find out. You may not even know what a rumble seat or a running board is! If not, ask a "mature" (older) man who's in the know.

Times have changed. It's too dangerous now to hitch a ride or to pick up a hitchhiker.

But consider the hitchhiker for a moment. He wants a free ride. He has no responsibility at all for the vehicle. He doesn't have to buy a car, pay for insurance, upkeep, or gas. Have you ever met a hitchhiker who volunteered to chip in for gas? Not likely. He wants a free ride, a comfortable ride, a safe ride, and sometimes imposes upon you to take him out of your way. It's as though he expects you to do this for him.

There are a lot of spiritual hitchhikers today. They know the Lord, but they want a free ride. They want all the benefits of being a Christian but none of the responsibilities or the costs. No accountability, no commitment, no willingness to serve. And if it begins to cost, or decisions have to be made to give up the free ride, they bail out.

The decision to serve God or serve themselves is a big one. We can't serve both. We can hitchhike in our faith or we can serve our God. And actually, the ride is better with Him.[8]

"So I say live by the Spirit, and you will not gratify the desires of the sinful nature. For the sinful nature desires what is contrary to the Spirit, and the Spirit what is contrary to the sinful nature. They are in conflict with each other, so that you do not do what you want. But if you are led by the Spirit, you are not under law" (Galatians 5:16-18).

Lord,

You have given me everything good in my life. Remind me that I haven't done it and that I'm not you. I pray now for a greater sense of responsibility.

Help me to remember my sense of responsibility to myself.

Help me never to do anything so I lose my self-respect.

Help me never to let myself down by doing anything which attacks or destroys another person.

Help me never to do anything that I would spend the rest of my life regretting.

Lord, I want to always remember my responsibility to my friends, to those I love, and to those who love me and those who don't.

I want to be faithful so I don't disappoint those who love me.

Help me not to fail anyone who depends on me.

Keep me from being a source of grief to others.

Lord, sometimes it's difficult to be faithful, but I know that you can keep me faithful. Thank you that it's not just up to me!

Help me not to be a man who remembers my rights and forgets my responsibilities.

Help me not to be a man who wants to get everything out of life without putting anything into it.

Help me not to be a man who doesn't care what happens to others.

Remind me that I am responsible to you and will answer to you for the way I use what you have given to me.

And help me each minute of the day to remember how much you love us and how Jesus died for me. I praise you.

Amen.[9]

NOVEMBER 16

"The Lord is my shepherd, I shall not be in want" (Psalms 23:1).

Y ou've heard the hyped-up announcements on TV, offering you great deals and values. You believe every word they say, right? Only if you're gullible. What if someone came to you and said, "I want you to have this gift. Here it is: rest, peace, restoration, guidance, courage, companionship, constant comfort, protection, power, abundance, and security." Would you believe the offer? This one you can trust. Here is the way Chuck Swindoll describes the promises of the 23rd Psalm.

I shall not lack **rest** or **provision**—why?
He makes me lie down in green pastures.
I shall not lack **peace**—why?
He leads me beside quiet waters.
I shall not lack **restoration** or **encouragement** when I faint, fail, or fall—
      why?
He restores my soul.
I shall not lack **guidance** or **fellowship**—why?
He guides me in the paths of righteousness.
I shall not lack **courage** when my way is dark—why?
Even though I walk through the valley of the shadow of death, I fear no evil.
I shall not lack **companionship**—why?
For Thou art with me.
I shall not lack constant **comfort**—why?
Thy rod and Thy staff, they comfort me.
I shall not lack **protection** or **honor**—why?
Thou dost prepare a table before me in the presence of my enemies.
I shall not lack **power**—why?
Thou hast anointed my head with oil.
I shall not lack **abundance**—why?
My cup overflows.
I shall not lack perpetual **presence**—why?
Surely goodness and mercy shall follow me all the days of my life.
I shall not lack **security**—why?
And I will dwell in the house of the Lord forever.[10]

NOVEMBER 17

"Enter his gates with thanksgiving and his courts with praise. Give thanks to him and praise his name" (Psalms 100:4).

Thanksgiving Day. But wait a minute. Every day is a thanksgiving day. Every day of our life is to be a day of gratitude. Thanksgiving is more than a day of football games, reunions, and eating turkey.

Gratitude is a quality or feeling of being grateful or thankful. It's being appreciative of what you have received.

Have you ever made a list of all you've received that you are thankful for? I mean an extensive list that you keep adding to daily for a month. It's a great family activity for Thanksgiving Day. You could also turn on a tape recorder during the family meal and capture all the interaction! You'll have some choice memories in years to come.

Wouldn't it have been an experience to be there on that first Thanksgiving Day? The pilgrims knew what gratitude was, at least those who were still alive. Many had died on the ship and in the harsh new country. They were grateful because now they were free. They weren't oppressed anymore for what they believed. Sure, they faced hardships we don't know anything about. But you've got your own hardships too. Being thankful doesn't happen without difficulties; being thankful happens in the midst of difficulties.

God can give us a grateful heart if we ask... and he does want to hear about our gratefulness to him. After all, he gave his all for us.[11]

"Though an army besiege me, my heart will not fear; though war break out against me, even then will I be confident" (Psalms 27:3).

There is something we as men don't want to admit. Yeah, there really is. Fear. A man isn't supposed to be afraid. Whoever started that myth didn't understand human nature.

We're all afraid at one time or another. Those who say they're never afraid, take their pulse, quick! They could be cadavers.

What are you afraid of? If you need some help identifying your fears, here are some suggestions: failure, heights, crowds, disease, rejection, macho men, wimpy men, strong women, unemployment, death, a call from the IRS, a summons from your boss, financial reversal, war, and the list goes on.

Fear hits us at the worst time, at our weakest point, and goes to work on our minds. It's like a sickness that won't go away.

Chuck Swindoll has some helpful words about fear.

David's 27th psalm is known to contain an unusually effective antitoxin. With broad, bold strokes, the monarch of Israel pens a prescription guaranteed to infuse iron into our bones. He meets Fear face-to-face at the door of his dwelling with two questions:

Whom shall I dread?

Whom shall I fear?

He slams the door in Fear's face with the declaration:

My heart will not fear… in spite of this I shall be confident (v. 3).

He then whistles and hums to himself as he walks back into the family room, kitchen, office, or bedroom reminding himself of the daily dosage required to counteract Fear's repeated attacks:

PRAYER: I have asked from the Lord (v. 4).

VISION: I behold the beauty of the Lord (v. 4).

GOD'S WORD: I meditate in His temple (v. 4).

GOD'S PROTECTION: In the day of trouble He will conceal me/hide me/ lift me (v. 5).

MOMENT-BY-MOMENT WORSHIP: I will sing (v. 6).

REST: I had believed…wait for the Lord (vv. 13-14).

DETERMINATION: Let your heart take courage (v. 14).[12]

Read this psalm each day. Learn to live by its truths. It's a wonderful antidote for fear.

"Beloved, never avenge yourselves, but leave the way open for [God's] wrath; for it is written, Vengeance is Mine, I will repay (requite), says the Lord" (Romans 12:19, AMP).

Anger is mentioned 455 times in the Old Testament. And 375 times it refers to God's anger! In the New Testament six different Greek words are used for anger. One of them is found in Ephesians 4:26, where we are advised not to let the sun go down upon our wrath. The word in that verse refers to anger that is accompanied by irritation, exasperation, and embitterment. It can be easily expressed in attitude, speech, and behavior. Out of it can come a resentment that will hurt you more than it hurts others. Resentment carries with it the tinge of revenge—wanting to get back at another person or get even. This type of anger needs to be gotten rid of quickly.

In Dr. S.I. McMillen's book, *None of These Diseases,* the story is told of a visit Dale Carnegie made to Yellowstone National Park. While observing the grizzly bears feeding, a guide told him that the grizzly bear could whip any animal in the West with the exception of the buffalo and the Kodiak bear. That very night as the people sat watching a grizzly eat, they noticed there was only one animal the grizzly would allow to eat with him—a skunk. Now the grizzly could have beaten the skunk in any fight. He probably resented the skunk and wanted to get even with it for coming into his own feeding domain. But he didn't attack the skunk. Why? Because he knew the high cost of getting even! It wouldn't be worth it.

Many of us have not learned that important lesson. We spend long days and longer nights dwelling on our resentments and even plotting ways to strike back, to our own detriment.

There is a price to pay for this kind of anger. It can lead to severed relationships with God and other people, even those to whom the anger is not directed. And for those who harbor these feelings, the result may be strokes, heart attacks, high blood pressure, hypertension, colitis, or ulcers. The question is, "Is it worth it?"

"We have different gifts, according to the grace given us. If a man's gift is prophesying, let him use it in proportion to his faith" *(Romans 12:6).*

Take heart. There are many different styles of responding to life. You don't have to be a replica of all the other men you've known. God wants you to have the freedom to express your unique personality in what you do.

Let's consider for a moment how your spiritual gifts may be reflected in your life. Romans 12:6 says, "Having then gifts...." The word *gift* in Greek is *charisma*. The root of this Greek word means "joy" or "gladness." The seven gifts described in Romans 12 are to be considered gifts of joy. So if you are aware of your gift and use it, the result is you will be a person bringing joy and gladness. And your gift is just that... it's a gift from God. There are seven such gifts.

The first gift mentioned is prophecy. It means to "speak out" or to "declare." It also has the connotation of proclaiming in a very direct manner. A person reflecting this gift will be seen as one who is telling, declaring, or speaking out about something. This could be your gift, or it could be your wife's or a friend's. A person with the gift of prophecy doesn't waver. The truth is spoken without much hesitation. The prophetic person acts on whatever is right, sometimes without concern over the consequences. Other people know where the prophet stands and can trust that person's word because he or she doesn't waver. The prophet is usually a person of action—persuasive and even competitive.

People with the gift of prophecy attract other people, but can also push them away. They have strong convictions and the unusual capacity to stand alone.

Well, what about it—is this your gift? Someone else's in your family or circle of friends? If so, how can it be used in the most positive way to bring honor and glory to God? It's something to talk about.[13]

"We have different gifts, according to the grace given us.... If it is contributing to the needs of others, let him give generously" (Romans 12:6a, 7b).

Generosity. Perhaps that's the best word to describe a person with the gift of giving. In most of the translations the verse is translated, "he who gives, with liberality." The original Greek word means "to share a thing with anyone, or to impart." Once again *Webster's Dictionary* gives us food for thought. Some of the definitions for "giving" are "to be the source, produce; supply; as, cows give milk."[14] A cow cannot *not* give milk. That's its function. And it's the same with any person with this gift. They can't help but give. Their whole lifestyle is that of giving. It's a natural habit and is built in.

Giving means something a bit foreign to the thinking in our culture today. The person gives by turning over possessions or control of something to another person with no strings attached. There is no cost to them. There is no bartering. It's given freely. They also look for ways to give without drawing attention to themselves. And they gain enjoyment in giving without the pressure of an appeal. A husband looks for ways to give to his wife without his wife demanding, expecting, or using some ploy to get her way.

Giving sets a wonderful example for children, because they can gain an understanding of how God gives through their parents. And parents usually encourage their children not only to give but to express gratitude for what they receive through verbal and written responses. There is also a contentment on the part of the givers to be satisfied with whatever they have in life, whether a little or a lot.

If neither parent has the gift of giving it's possible to find others who can be involved with their children so they can be exposed to a wide variety of God's gifts. Keep in mind, all gifts have a purpose, and one isn't any better than another. Even if generosity isn't our natural gift, we can all learn to give in some way.[15]

NOVEMBER 22

"We have different gifts, according to the grace given us.... If it is encouraging, let him encourage" (Romans 12:6a, 8b).

Are you an exhorter? A what? You know, a man whose gift is exhortation. Not yelling or pushing or prodding, but an exhorter. Most people do not really understand what this gift is. Frequently it's equated with preaching, but that's not the case.

Various versions of the Bible express it differently. For example, the *King James* version describes it as "he that exhorteth" (v. 8). In the *Berkeley* version this person is described as "the admonisher." In the *Williams* version the person with this gift is described as "one who encourages others." J.B. Phillips in his modern English version describes this gift as one used in "stimulating" the faith of others. Elsewhere in the New Testament it's used to convey the idea of consolation, comfort, and entreaty.

So... if a man has this spiritual gift, it will be very natural to see him admonishing, advising, encouraging, and stirring up the faith and self-worth of others. Family members will feel encouraged and cheered by his words of encouragement. They will feel fortified because of his noncritical listening as well as his belief in their capabilities. They know that he's available whenever needed.

This gift is often manifested by taking the time to explain, amplify, or clarify situations for others. A balanced exhorter is one who knows enough not to get so personally involved that it jeopardizes his time, knowledge, or... finances! He also knows not to allow others to develop an unhealthy dependency upon him.

Is this your gift? Your spouse's? Your child's? All of us as parents need to be people of encouraging words, especially as reflected in this verse: "Anxiety in a man's heart weighs it down, but an encouraging word makes it glad" (Prv 12:25, AMP). If this is your gift, it will come naturally. Use it to build up others and glorify the Lord.[16]

"[He whose gift is] practical service, let him give himself to serving; he who teaches, to his teaching" (Romans 12:7).

A person whose gift is serving has an approach to life that is devoted to meeting the needs of others. In fact, some who have this gift seem to anticipate and care for some needs even before they are evident. Some people don't particularly care for this gift. They'd rather be served!

The word *practical* has rich and deep connotations. It means, "designed for us; utilitarian; concerned with the application of knowledge to useful ends; or concerned with, or dealing efficiently with everyday activities."[17]

While all Christians might reflect some of the meaning of this gift, for some their entire life is devoted to this calling. Various Bible translations all convey the idea of "giving assistance or advantage to another person." And it is done with a sense of joy and delight, not grudgingly.

Those who live with a person who has this gift will see an example of cheerfulness in meeting needs. Verbalizing concerns may be a part of this, but doing is their forte.

All of us need to be givers in some way. This is the calling to everyone who claims Jesus as Lord of their life. But a spiritual gift is different. There needs to be both a joy in giving as well as knowing how not to neglect your own needs. Who do you know with this gift? If it's yours, how can you use it for the glory of God?[18]

"We have different gifts, according to the grace given us.... If it is showing mercy, let him do it cheerfully" (Romans 12:6, 8).

Do you know someone who especially enjoys informal social gatherings, or someone who is sensitive to the atmosphere of a get-together? Or perhaps they like to listen to a speaker who is very emotional compared to someone who is logical. Have you run into the highly sympathetic person, one who may even cry easily? What about the one who is very tactile, always touching others? This person reflects empathy, compassion, sympathy, and is highly attentive while listening sincerely. These people have the gift of mercy.

People with this gift seem to have an antenna that picks up the emotional response of others. They want harmony in their home and at work. They go out of their way to soothe those in disaster. Physical contact is highly valued in all of their relationships. They seem to be able to read the body language of others very well. There are some limitations, though, as with the other gifts. Being so caring makes it sometimes difficult to discipline, confront, or correct others. Sometimes there is too much toleration of situations that could hurt. And they are often swayed and influenced too easily.

Family members know they are loved, understood, and accepted because their feelings are validated and accepted. Mercy means "to console or to succor one afflicted." The *Amplified Bible* says, "He who does acts of mercy, with genuine cheerfulness and joyful eagerness." There is the true manifestation of this gift. It leaps from their heart. There's no resistance to doing. They don't begrudge.

Sometimes people with a different gift wonder, "How can you keep doing what you do?" Well, they can't by themselves. After all, like the other characteristics you've read about, mercy is a gift. And what do we do when we receive a gift? Rejoice. Be thankful. And use it![19]

"We have different gifts, according to the grace given us.... If it is teaching, let him teach" (Romans 12:6a, 7a).

Some men instill within others a quest for knowledge and a thirst for learning. It could be with their children or with others at work. It's as though they are able to turn every situation into a classroom. These individuals have been given the gift of teaching. For them it's very natural and happens constantly. The word *teach* means "to train,... to give lessons to (a student or a pupil); to guide the study of; to instruct,... to give lessons in,... to provide with knowledge, insight."[20]

If you have this gift, you are usually sharing information or knowledge with a joyful attitude. It's easy. It's natural. The opportunities are unlimited. A child raised in this type of home will have an abundance of stimuli such as books, tape recorders, and other research material. An executive will provide the same for his employees. These men usually surround others with whatever will assist them in learning.

Wise men know the value or strength of their gift as well as the weakness of its overuse. For example, a wise teacher does not overburden others with too many details and thus douse their enthusiasm. When a person asks the time, you don't tell them how the watch was made! A wise man with this gift allows for individual differences within others and looks for teachable moments. He also works with others to help them discover their own uniqueness or giftedness. If this is your gift, rejoice in it and use it.[21]

NOVEMBER 26

"We have different gifts, according to the grace given us. If a man's gift is... leadership, let him govern diligently" (*Romans 12:6a, 8b*).

R uling is not limited to kings and presidents. We all have to rule to some degree, but the one with this spiritual gift is quite obvious. He or she is usually organized, structured, and likes to get things done. Sometimes others refer to the person with this gift as "the boss" or perhaps "bossy." But it is a biblical gift and quite necessary. It's translated in the *Amplified Bible* as "He who gives aid and superintends, [let him do it] with zeal and singleness of mind." The *King James* version says, "with diligence."

The gift of leadership or ruling is a managing approach. Men like this. The original word can mean "take the lead, to superintend, preside over." But sometimes there's a conflict in a marriage if both husband and wife have this gift. Hopefully they will soon learn not only the importance of delegating, but also of give and take. A parent with this gift orchestrates the household and organizes the life of each child and often each pet! They are good jugglers and can balance many things at once. Managers and executives who don't have this gift often wish they did. If this is your situation, find someone who does and follow their lead as much as possible. It could be your wife.

A man with the gift of administration can usually determine abilities of other people and channel them in the proper direction. He helps them make the best use of what they are capable of doing. But keep in mind that the way this gift is manifested is crucial. Some become controllers, unbending and rigid. A loving tone of voice that gives suggestions rather than directives is a must.

Men with this gift value reliability and responsibility. *Tenacious* is a word to describe them because they remain firm and steadfast even when problems arise.

If you have this gift, you need the gifts of others to bring a balance into the tight ship you run. You want your gift to be seen as a plus, a benefit, an asset, not a liability. At this point in time, is your gift of leadership helping or hindering others?[22]

"Whoever claims to live in him must walk as Jesus did" (1 John 2:6).

S ome men walk through life burdened by a load of baggage. Sometimes it's in the form of a label that's been slapped on them such as "slow," "inept," "stupid," "irresponsible," "loser," etc. It's as if someone wrote this word on a tag, attached it to their chests, and now it determines what happens to them for the rest of their lives.

During the Vietnam War a mobile army surgical hospital (M.A.S.H.) would prepare for the incoming helicopters with their load of wounded and dying soldiers. A system of triage was used to categorize the wounded by the severity of their injuries. One color tag was placed on the dying to indicate they could not be saved. They were hopeless. They would not recover. A second color tag was used for those with superficial wounds. They would receive medical attention and would recover. The last color tag was placed on those who were critical but could make it with medical care. They might recover.

A critically wounded man was brought to one mobile hospital, and after examination he was tagged with "critical—will not recover." He was given a painkiller and left to die. But a nurse came by, saw he was conscious, and began to talk with him. After a while she felt he could probably make it. So she reached down, took off the tag, and replaced it with one that read "salvageable." Because she changed the tag, he's alive today.

Are you walking through your life with the wrong tag? How do you see yourself? Critical and unsalvageable, or do you have hope for your recovery?

If you have a tag on you, who placed it there? Could you have been the one to put the tag there?

The tag God puts on you has just one word—"salvageable." Let him work on any wounds you have and give you full recovery.[23]

NOVEMBER 28

"Be like-minded, live in peace" (2 Corinthians 13:11, NASB).

What's the status of your bank account? Is there a surplus or are you running in the red? One of the metaphors used to describe a couple's interaction is that of a bank account. There are variations of this, but one is called a Relational Bank Account.

As is true of any bank account, the balance in the Relational Bank is in flux because of deposits and withdrawals. Relationship deposits vary in size just like our monetary deposits. They could be a kind word or action or a very large gift of love. Withdrawals also vary. A minor disagreement could be a small withdrawal, but a major offense could drain the account. Zingers are definitely a withdrawal, and so is defensiveness.

When you begin thinking of your relationship in this way, you can be more aware of deposits and attempted deposits as well as what constitutes a withdrawal. Naturally, the larger the balance, the healthier the relationship. And just like a monetary account, it's best to have sufficient reserves in your Relational Bank Account. Unfortunately, many couples live with their balances at a debit level.

There are two types of currencies in relational accounts—his and hers. Each may have a different valuation and could fluctuate from day to day. One major difference in this type of bank account is that the "teller" or receiving person sets the value of a deposit or withdrawal.

If there is a large balance in the account, a few small withdrawals don't impact the account that much. But if the balance is relatively small or hovers around zero, a small withdrawal is definitely felt. The ideal is to keep the deposits high and the withdrawals low.

Each partner needs to be enlightened by the other as to what he or she perceives as a deposit or a withdrawal.

What is a deposit for you? For your wife? What is a withdrawal for you? For your wife? It may help you to discuss this concept for clarification.[24]

"My grace is sufficient for you, for my Power is made perfect in weakness" (2 Corinthians 12:9).

My only son was handicapped—the diagnosis was "profound mental retardation." When he died at age twenty-two, he had never progressed mentally to more than eighteen months old. Through Matthew I learned about life. He taught me to experience my emotions, to listen with my eyes, to appreciate each small step of progress. But why shouldn't he have taught me this? He was a gift. His name means "gift from God." He was and still is.

You too can learn from the disabled, the handicapped. Hear the words of R. Scott Sullender:

> Handicapped persons teach us that life is more than a body. They demonstrate the truth of all of the great religions that the things that make us truly human and truly divine are not physical qualities. They are qualities of spirit. The qualities that save us do not include the shape of our bodies.
>
> Handicapped persons also can teach us how to suffer and how to rise above bodily limitations. Sometimes pain cannot be fixed, nor can all limitations be conquered. Most of us will have to deal with pain and limitations, at first in minor ways and later in major ways. We will learn new meanings for the word "courage." Either we will rise above our limitations and learn to live with them or we shall sink to new lows of despair, bitterness, and helplessness. The choice depends largely on the strength of our courage.
>
> In a sense, then, a handicap or a loss of health can become a gift. It never starts out that way. Initially it is a horrible loss. If through the loss, however, we can learn to nurture our spiritual qualities and learn the art of suffering well, then we will have transformed our loss into a gain. We will have grown in and through our loss. We will have risen above our loss precisely by not letting it defeat us, but by letting it propel us forward into a more advanced stage of human existence. Admittedly, not everyone makes such a major leap forward. Neither have some human beings made it past a Sunday school theology. Yet, the loss of health in later life, as horrible as it seems, can be the opportunity for growing toward an even greater level of spiritual maturity.[25]

*"But God chose the foolish things of the world to shame the wise;
God chose the weak things of the world to shame the strong" (1
Corin-thians 1:27).*

There are times in every man's life when he feels ordinary, perhaps
even useless. Such times can be very discouraging, especially when
you try to turn your life around. Moses went through the same experience.

When Moses did finally take his first baby steps toward maturity, his
performance wasn't warmly received. He didn't get a standing ovation.
His first attempts were responded to with rejection and sneers rather
than success. He was still young. He still had a lot to learn.

His impulsivity, immaturity, and inability to handle his anger led to
forty years in the wilderness. When I was younger, I viewed those as
"wasted" years. But the Almighty God used that time to refine Moses
and transform him into a strong leader. When Moses finally returned
to Egypt from the obscurity of the wilderness, he was a changed man.

When Moses chose to learn from his mistakes, God was able to use
him in mighty ways. But Moses also learned the high cost of not learning. From an early age, he had struggled with his anger. Remember,
that's what had gotten him into trouble in the first place. While he
gained some control over it, he never allowed God to help him master
it. Eventually his inability to learn from his repeated failures cost him a
trip into the Promised Land.

In Philippians 3:10, Paul expressed his desire to know Christ and
the power of his resurrection and the fellowship of sharing in his sufferings. Through the struggle and suffering that come from those big
and little failures, however, we're reminded of who we are and who he
is.

If you ever feel weak, powerless, discouraged, frustrated, limited...
if you feel ordinary... you are prime material for God to use. Time and
again, the Bible clearly tells us that our God *deliberately* seeks out the
weak and the despised things, because it's from them that he can
receive the greatest glory.[26]

DECEMBER 1

"Come to me, all you who are weary and burdened, and I will give you rest" (Matthew 11:28).

Busy, busy, busy. It seems to be a characteristic of our lives. And if we're real accomplishers, those around us reinforce it by saying, "I don't know how you do all you do. It's just amazing!" And we beam with pride.

You may be busy, but are you exhausted?

You may be busy, but are you enjoying what you do?

You may be busy, but what is it costing you?

These are hard but necessary questions.

Most busy people struggle with weariness, too. And if this continues over a period of time, work suffers, the desire to continue diminishes, tempers flare, patience becomes nonexistent, and soon we give up. We get tired of being tired all the time. It's not a new problem. Over fifty years ago the author of *Springs in the Valley* shared this interesting tale from African colonial history:

> In the deep jungles of Africa, a traveler was making a long trek. Coolies had been engaged from a tribe to carry the loads. The first day they marched rapidly and went far. The traveler had high hopes of a speedy journey. But the second morning these jungle tribesmen refused to move. For some strange reason they just sat and rested. On inquiry as to the reason for this strange behavior, the traveler was informed that they had gone too fast the first day, and that *they were now waiting for their souls to catch up with their bodies.*

The author concludes with this penetrating exhortation:

> This whirling, rushing life which so many of us live does for us what that first march did for those poor jungle tribesmen. The difference: *they knew* what they needed to restore life's balance; too often *we do not.*[1]

Let's hope we do!

DECEMBER 2

"Dear friends, do not be surprised at the painful trial you are suffering, as though something strange were happening to you. But rejoice that you participate in the sufferings of Christ, so that you may be overjoyed when his glory is revealed" (1 Peter 4:12-13).

Suffering—none of us like it. We all try to avoid it.

Often we beg and plead with God to remove it. We question his sense of fairness and try to convince him there's a better way. Then we compare our life with the lives of others. We think we've done more. We're better than others, deserve better, or perhaps even wish we were someone else. We see the easy life of others and wish we had it that good. But remember Psalm 49:16-17, "Do not be overawed when a man grows rich, when the splendor of his house increases: for he will take nothing with him when he dies, his splendor will not descend with him."

When we suffer, some of us move into the self-pity phase. Discouragement sets in and our favorite passage of Scripture becomes Psalm 73:12-14: "This is what the wicked are like—always carefree, they increase in wealth. Surely in vain have I kept my heart pure; in vain have I washed my hands in innocence."

Then we get angry—at ourselves? No—at God. It's his fault. "Why? Why? Why?" If this continues we begin to doubt God. How can he allow this to happen and stay absent? Discouragement overwhelms us because we are trying to figure out everything ourselves.

These thoughts and feelings are normal reactions. But to get back on track, we must go to the Word for the answers. "So do not fear, for I am with you; do not be dismayed, for I am your God. I will strengthen you and help you; I will uphold you with my righteous right hand" (Is 41:10).

The solution to our suffering is not to get it over with, but to learn how to enjoy the fellowship of sharing in Christ's suffering—to not falter in times of trouble, to be anxious for nothing, to endure patiently, and to walk in the power of the Holy Spirit.[2]

DECEMBER 3

Have you had a good crisis lately—you know, when a whirlwind sweeps through your life, throws you around, and disrupts all of your best-laid plans? Those crises make us feel like we're in a barrel rolling downhill, being thrown all about. All of us will have crises come into our lives. But except for adrenaline addicts, not too many of us really like to have our lives invaded by crises. Before crises come, it's important to burn into your memory the fact that you will have an opportunity for more spiritual growth during a crisis than at most other times. It is during a time of crisis that God wants to do something in your life.

The promise of today's passage is that no matter where you are, God will lead you. In Isaiah 43, the Lord declares that he will be with you through your times of crisis. Turn to that chapter right now and read it aloud before you proceed.

Did you notice the number of times God said "I will"? It appears more than ten times. Go back and notice what the "I will" statements apply to in this passage. A comforting thought is that he will not remember our sins. That is encouraging, since for some of us there's a lot for God to forget!

Many people feel that one of the most comforting "I wills" is in verse two: "I will be with you." Will you remember that when you are discouraged? Will you remember it when you are faced with a difficult ethical dilemma at work? Will you remember it when you feel that you have nothing left to give in your marital relationship? Will you remember it when you feel that you're all alone and no one else cares? These are words of comfort that can lift us at any time.

"Come to me, all you who are weary and burdened, and I will give you rest. Take my yoke upon you and learn from me, for I am gentle and humble in heart, and you will find rest for your souls. For my yoke is easy and my burden is light" (Matthew 11:28-30).

Look at your calendar. What's it saying to you? Is there any white space available or is every hour filled in? Some men's calendars are like that day after day, week after week. They'd like a calendar that has sixty days in a month and forty-eight-hour days because they're trying to cram too much into their lives. The problem is, their new calendar would soon be overfilled, too. The problem isn't the calendar, it's who's in charge of it. Perhaps you feel your hectic life is described in this poem:

> This is the age
> Of the half-read page
> And the mad dash
> With the nerves tight
> The plane hop
> With the brief stop
> The lamp tan
> In a short span
> The Big Shot
> In a good spot
> And the brain strain
> And the heart pain
> And the cat naps
> Till the spring snaps
> And the fun's done.

It's interesting, I think, that this poem was written in 1949 and appeared in the *Saturday Evening Post.* I wonder what the author, Virginia Brasier, would have written about our lifestyle today if she were still writing.

The calendar isn't the enemy, we are. We wear ourselves out. Jesus had some words for you about the hecticness of life. Read the verses from Matthew again, then consider what you'll do with them.[3]

DECEMBER 5

"For the lips of a prostitute are as sweet as honey, and smooth flattery is her stock in trade. But afterwards only a bitter conscience is left to you, sharp as a double edged sword. She leads you down to death and hell. For she does not know the path to life. She staggers down a crooked trail, and doesn't even realize where it leads" (Proverbs 5:3-6, TLB).

Solomon doesn't mince any words. He shoots from the hip. He needs to because it's a dangerous world out there. You see, many women today don't know the first thing about boundaries, nor do they even care about them. If they see a man and want him, they go after him. A lot of men are this way, too, when they see a desirable woman. There's no respect any more for wedding rings.

Let's be blunt. Anyone can commit adultery. Every one of us is one step away from adultery. It doesn't take any character to commit it. In fact a person who does commit adultery is showing a lack of character. It takes character *not* to.

The cost of adultery is terribly high. The consequences are devastating. And it will be found out. In fact, it's immediately known by you and God.

Are there safeguards to protect you? You bet there are.

First, remember your fantasy life belongs to your wife. Don't play around with any woman in your mind. Second, if you're attracted to a woman other than your wife, avoid contact with her. That may take some effort on your part, especially if you work with her. Third, if there is a problem with another woman, never be alone with her. Orchestrate it so that another man is present. Better yet, bring your wife. Fourth, be aware of the danger signals. If you are thinking of different excuses to call her or waiting around to see her, you've got one foot in quicksand. Get out now. Finally, go to some other men and ask for their help. You need them. They've probably been there too. Let them walk you through this problem.

> Therefore confess your sins to each other and pray for each other so that you may be healed. The prayer of a righteous man is powerful and effective.
> **James 5:16**

You can avoid adultery. Many men have. Let Jesus Christ stand guard over your mind and heart.

"Do not conform any longer to the pattern of this world, but be transformed by the renewing of your mind. Then you will be able to test and approve what God's will is—his good, pleasing, and perfect will" (Romans 12:2).

Do you "go along" in order to "get along"? Strange question? Sure, but it needs to be asked. Many people play to the crowd in order to get what they want. They conform. Jesus gives us permission to be nonconformists. Just look at what a nonconformist he was. He went counter to what people believed. He lived differently. You know how others saw him. They thought he was a heretic because he refused to join the self-righteous hypocrite club of the religious leaders of his day.

Other people tried to entice him to sell out and compromise, but he didn't. Satan really went after him just like he does us. Satan said, "Look, be practical. Turn these stones into bread. Doesn't everyone love a man who can give out free bread?" Satan said, "Let's join forces. Be a negotiator. And together we can rule the world. After all, isn't it the deal makers who get ahead in life?" Satan said, "What you need to do is be sensational and get everyone's attention by jumping off the top of the temple. When you're sensational everyone wants to follow you."

Everything Jesus was asked to do went back to conformity. Play to the crowd, go along to get what you want. It's a temptation we all face. The best response is the one Jesus gave. It was short. It was simple. It was definite. It was "No!"

"Therefore encourage one another and build each other up, just as in fact you are doing" (1 Thessalonians 5:11).

Perhaps you've heard the story of Johnny Lingo, a man who lived in the South Pacific. The islanders all spoke highly of him. He was strong, good-looking, and very intelligent. But when it came time for him to find a wife the people shook their heads in disbelief. The woman Johnny Lingo chose was plain, skinny, and walked with her shoulders hunched and her head down. She was very hesitant and shy. She was also a bit older than the other unmarried women in the village, which did nothing for her value. But this man loved her.

What surprised everyone most was Johnny's offer. In order to obtain a wife you paid for her by giving her father cows. Four to six cows was considered a high price. The other villagers thought he might pay two or even three cows at the most. But he gave eight cows for her! Everyone chuckled about it, since they believed his father-in-law put one over on him. Some thought it was a mistake.

Several months after the wedding, a visitor from the United States came to the Islands to trade and heard the story about Johnny Lingo and his eight-cow wife. Upon meeting Johnny and his wife the visitor was totally taken back, since this wasn't a shy, plain, and hesitant woman but one who was beautiful, poised, and confident. The visitor asked about the transformation, and Johnny Lingo's response was very simple. "I wanted an eight-cow woman, and when I paid that for her and treated her in that fashion, she began to believe that she was an eight-cow woman. She discovered she was worth more than any other woman in the islands. And what matters most is what a woman thinks about herself."

When you value others around you, something amazing happens. You increase their value and they value themselves more. I guess that's what God did for us, didn't he?

DECEMBER 8

"...perseverance, character; and character, hope" (Romans 5:4).

Did you ever wonder how a person's character is formed? Are we born with it, do we inherit it, or does it develop in some strange way? First, let's define what we mean by character. It's a combination of features and traits that forms the nature of a person. It can include qualities such as honesty or courage. It also includes reputation, ethical standards, and principles. It's what makes you distinctive. Believers in Jesus Christ are called to be people who stand out, who are different in a positive way.

So... how does character develop? In the book *Just So Stories* Rudyard Kipling tells the story of how the camel got its hump. This animal had a disposition that wasn't too nice. It had an *attitude!* It wouldn't cooperate with the other animals. When asked to do so, all it said was "Humph!" The animals complained to a genie who appealed to the camel to cooperate. But all it said was "Humph!" Finally, after hearing this again and again, that's what the genie gave him a— "humph" on his back.

When you say something or do something long enough, it becomes a habit. It could be a good habit or a negative one. And that's what makes up our character. Plutarch said character is simply habit long continued. We can end up carrying our habits around the rest of our life... like a camel.

One of the great evangelists of the past century, Dwight L. Moody, had an interesting thought about character. He said that character is what you are in the dark.

What makes up your character?[4]

DECEMBER 9

"Then I saw a new heaven and a new earth, for the first heaven and the first earth had passed away, and there was no longer any sea" (Revelation 21:1).

Everyone seems to be interested in either knowing what's going to happen in the future or predicting the future. Some use computers, astrology, or psychics to try to figure out what may happen.

In 1960, the Rand Corporation, a scientific think tank, made some predictions in a magazine article. They made some wild speculations such as manned space flight; photos of Mars and Venus by 1978; direct energy laser weapons by 1980; drugs that bring about major personality changes by 1983; regional weather control by 1990; synthetic protein foods that can be commercially created by 1990; and so forth. Perhaps the years are off, but some of these have become realities and others are in process.

The world of science seems to be expanding and we're able to create more and more. In some ways we've become scientific giants. In other ways we've become ethical and moral infants. New ways are being created to take life, such as abortion and euthanasia, rather than sustain it. Something is wrong somewhere and we wonder where it will all end. We'd like a preview.

Perhaps what we need to do is what we do when reading an intense, exciting novel. When you can't wait to see how it turns out, what do you do? Turn to the last chapter and read it.

You can if you want to. It's all right. You'll find an ending you like; it's in the Book of Revelation.[5]

"Lord, who may go and find refuge and shelter in your tabernacle up on your holy hill?" (Psalms 15:1, TLB).

If you think the above verse asks a great question, wait until you see the answer. In fact, you may want to read the entire psalm before you proceed. Better yet, memorize it. Quoting it each morning as you go to work makes the entire day go better.

David answers the question with eleven characteristics of a godly person. Open your Bible to this psalm and let's have a look.

1. Vs. 2: A person of integrity is solid and wholesome and blameless. It's who you are as well as where you go. You live the truth.

2. A person of rightness keeps his nose clean. He's honest and doesn't compromise.

3. Vs. 2: When you speak truth in your heart, it's also how you think. Your attitudes and reactions reflect truth.

4. Vs. 3: Slander is not part of a righteous man's life. Verbal poison and sharing or listening to gossip are inappropriate. If you ever have to say, "Well, I probably shouldn't be saying this, but …," just don't say it. You'll be a better man for it.

5. Vs. 3: He doesn't do in his neighbor. He doesn't create problems for him.

6. Vs. 4: He doesn't say sharp and cutting things about his friends.

7. Vs. 4: He doesn't cultivate a close association with someone who is disinterested in spiritual matters. This one is a real challenge in today's world.

8. Vs. 4: He honors those who follow the Lord. These are the people to spend time with and build close relationships with.

9. Vs. 5: He's a man of his word. Regardless of the outcome to him, when he makes a promise he keeps it. You can trust him.

10. Vs. 5: If a believer needs money, he doesn't charge interest. Be discerning about money, and if you loan it, do so out of concern and compassion.

11. Vs. 5: He doesn't take a bribe against the innocent. This speaks for itself.

So, on a scale of 0-10 on each one, where are you? Remember the promise, "Such a man shall stand firm forever" (vs. 5, TLB).[6]

DECEMBER 11

"Why am I depressed?" This is a common question asked in the counseling office by both men and women. There are reasons for anyone's depression. Here are a few that men have identified.

- Men get depressed when they continue to work at a job they hate.
- Men get depressed when they see their bodies change.
- Men get depressed when they realize they cannot accomplish the goals they have set for themselves or that another person has set for them.
- Men get depressed when their marriages fail to meet their deepest needs.
- Men get depressed when they realize their children see them only as a meal ticket.
- Men get depressed when their friends move away or die.

Do any of those statements hit home? There are other reasons for depression. Knowing what they are may help you help yourself or a family member when depression hits. Depression comes because of past deprivations, inadequate food and rest, reactions to medication, chemical imbalance, guilt over sin, self-pity, low self-esteem, and a pattern of negative thinking.

There are two other causes that also need to be considered. One cause is repressed anger. When you bottle up your anger or turn it back upon yourself, there has to be a displacement of that energy. Depression is one of the outcomes.

A second major cause of depression for any of us is loss. The loss could be tangible, imagined, abstract, or an impending or threatened loss. Too much change at one time or a personal crisis will throw us into depression. To keep ahead of depression every loss needs to be faced and admitted.

What about you? Is there any loss in your life that you've never fully grieved over? If so, this may be the time to do so. Take it to Jesus in prayer and share it with a trusted Christian friend.

Losses can be resolved. Look to God's Word to heal the pain. "Cast your cares on the Lord and he will sustain you; he will never let the righteous fall" (Ps 55:22).[7]

DECEMBER 12

"I the Lord do not change" (Malachi 3:6).

One of God's characteristics is his immutability: He doesn't change. He is consistent and constant.

We need to pray in harmony with his character. Let's consider some of God's character traits and how they should affect the way we pray.

God is holy, so we must never pray for anything that would compromise his holiness or cause us to be unholy (see Psalms 99:9; Isaiah 6:3; Revelation 15:4).

God is love, and our prayers should both invoke the love of God for others and reflect the love of God in our own attitudes (see Jeremiah 31:3; John 3:16; Romans 5:8).

God is good, and the results of our prayers must bring goodness into the lives of all concerned (see Psalms 25:8; 33:5; 34:8; Nahum 1:7; Matthew 19:17; Romans 2:4).

God is merciful, and our prayers should reflect that we have received his mercy and are willing to be merciful ourselves (see Psalms 108:4; Lamentations 3:22; Joel 2:13).

God is jealous, and we dare not ask for something that would take first place in our hearts over God (see Exodus 20:5; Deuteronomy 4:24; 1 Corinthians 10:22).

God is just, and we cannot expect him to grant a request that would be unjust or unfair to anyone (see Psalms 103:6; Zephaniah 3:5; John 5:30; Romans 2:2).

God is long-suffering, and neither our prayers nor our waiting for answers should show impatience toward him who is so patient with us (see Isaiah 48:9; Romans 9:22; 1 Peter 3:20).

God is truth, and our prayers must never seek to change or disguise truth (see Deuteronomy 32:4; Romans 3:4; Hebrews 6:18).[8]

DECEMBER 13

"Therefore, as God's chosen people, holy and dearly loved, clothe yourselves with compassion, kindness, humility, gentleness and patience" (Colossians 3:12).

Here's another story from the book *Becoming Soul Mates* by Les and Leslie Parrott.

Heidi and I realized early in our marriage that a prerequisite to intimacy of any kind was a foundation of respect for each other and for our relationship. As a result we've tried to build and maintain what I've since referred to as a "Wall of Tenderness" designed to keep out destructive attitudes, while keeping us close to each other. This wall entails:

- Not discussing problems in harsh, angry tones, but in attentive conversation, while working toward solutions that genuinely satisfy both of us.
- Not joking cuttingly about each other, especially in front of others.
- Never kidding about divorce.
- Saving constructive criticism for when we're alone and in a receptive frame of mind.
- Being willing to give in to each other's preferences, and developing a language for conveying when that is really needed. Some friends encouraged us to reserve the simple phrase "this is really important to me" for those times when we most need to be heard and respected.
- Regularly giving verbal and nonverbal encouragement to each other for who we are as well as for what we do. This includes doing things that make the other person feel treasured, including dinner dates, gifts, massages, prayers, and time alone together without distractions.
- Fostering an attitude that says, in effect, "I'd rather die than hurt or bring shame on you. You're the one precious person to whom I've committed my love for the rest of my life."

These actions and attitudes have helped us to build a strong foundation for our marriage. We're thankful to say that after almost twelve years together, we're still in love, still laughing together, still learning and growing together. And we're looking forward with anticipation to the next twelve years.[9]

DECEMBER 14

"Trust in the Lord with all your heart and lean not on your own understanding" (Proverbs 3:5).

The question "How do I know God's will?" has been asked by many. But before this question can be answered, another question should be asked. "Am I willing and am I ready to do God's will?" If the answer is yes, then the other question can be asked.

Remember that in order to do his will, what he has in mind for you may take you by surprise. Perhaps it's best expressed by Isaiah 55:8-9: "'For my thoughts are not your thoughts, neither are your ways my ways,' declares the Lord. 'As the heavens are higher than the earth, so are my ways higher than your ways and my thoughts than your thoughts.'" In order to discover and do God's will there are three words to keep in mind. The first word is *initiative*. "Jesus gave them this answer, 'I tell you the truth, the Son can do nothing by himself; he can do only what he sees his Father doing, because whatever the Father does the Son also does'" (Jn 5:19).

Let God take the initiative and then join him in the walk. The closer you are to Jesus, the easier it will be to understand.

The second word is *timing*. "There is a time for everything, and a season for every activity under the heaven.... He has made everything beautiful in its time. He has also set eternity in the hearts of men; yet they cannot fathom what God has done from beginning to end" (Eccl 3:1, 11). God's timing is perfect. He is never too early or too late. Waiting may be the best step you can take until all the indications say, "Yes, this is the time." Praying for wisdom in timing is essential.

The last word is *submit*. "Trust in the Lord with all your heart, and lean not on your own understanding; in all your ways acknowledge him, and he will make your paths straight" (Prv 3:5-6).

To know and do God's will there can't be any power struggle; he wants our will to be submissive to him. The more we value control and power, the greater a struggle we will have. But along with God's will being dependent on his initiative and his timing, he also needs to be in charge.[10]

DECEMBER 15

"There is a time for everything, and a season for every activity under heaven" (Ecclesiastes 3:1).

S olomon had a lot to say about time, but he said it simply. His famous comparison of opposites, perhaps one of the most profound descriptions of life, says there's an appointed time for everything.

For example, consider this comparison, "There is a time to be born; a time to die." That's obvious, but what we sometimes forget is that those times are out of our hands.

Have you ever thought about when you might die? You know, how old you'll be or want to be? We avoid thinking about it, but it's already set in God's timetable. Two questions to ask ourselves, then, are, "Will I be ready to die?" and "What do I want to accomplish for him before that time comes?"

There's also "a time to plant and a time to harvest." If you put seeds in the ground at the wrong time you're throwing away your money. If you don't harvest at the right time you've lost it. We have our own timetables for making changes and achieving goals, but sometimes things don't work out. It could be that God's timetable is different from ours. Ask him about changes in your life. When your ideas match his timing, things happen for the best.

There's also "a time to weep and a time to laugh." We look forward to times of laughter and fun. We need them for our very health. But we also need times to weep. C.S. Lewis said, "Pain is God's megaphone. He whispers to us in our pleasure (when we laugh), but He shouts to us in our pain (when we weep).[11]

Another writer talks about affliction in this way:

Contrary to what might be expected, I look back on experiences that at the time seemed especially desolating and painful with particular satisfaction. Indeed, I can say with complete truthfulness that everything I have learned in my 75 years in this world, everything that has truly enhanced and enlightened my existence, has been through affliction and not through happiness, whether pursued or attained.[12]

Has this been your experience... yet? If not, it will. Fortunately, when we experience affliction we're not alone, because God is there with us. It's all part of his timing.

"Do not judge, or you too will be judged. For in the same way you judge others, you will be judged, and with the measure you use, it will be measured to you. Why do you look at the speck of sawdust in your brother's eye and pay no attention to the plank in your own eye? How can you say to your brother, Let me take the speck out of your eye, when all the time there is a plank in your own eye? You hypocrite, first take the plank out of your own eye, and then you will see clearly to remove the speck from your brother's eye" (Matthew 7:1-5).

Dear God,

Sometimes I get so bothered about other men, what they do and how they think. Politicians, those in authority, public employees, friends, and even relatives get to me at times. Lord, help me to think and feel toward them as Jesus would. Help me to act towards them in a loving way so that in some way they may begin to think about you.

Lord, before I criticize and judge others, remind me of what it feels like to be criticized and judged.

Before I find fault with others and especially my family, help me to remember what it's like to have stones thrown at me.

Help me to make the allowances for others that I want for myself. Help me to be as understanding and accepting of others as I want them to be of me. Help me to verbally and prayerfully encourage others as I want them to do for me. Help me to forgive others as I would like them to forgive me. Help me not to keep score of what others have done to me but have the ability to erase those incidents from my memory bank.

I guess, Lord, I want to live and love as Jesus did. He did good to others, he served others, and forgave even as he died on the cross.

Lord, I want to be a man full of the love of Jesus.

In his name I pray,

Amen.

DECEMBER 17

"All these people were still living by faith when they died. They did not receive the things promised; they only saw them and welcomed them from a distance. And they admitted that they were aliens and strangers on earth" (Hebrews 11:13).

A rchibald Hart shared a fascinating story about a pastor's message at the conclusion of a retreat. The sermon title was, "I pray that you will all die before you are finished." Everyone was shocked at first. But here's how the story unfolded:

As he began to unfold his understanding of God's plan, his point became perfectly clear. He was not giving a prayer for an early demise; it was a prayer for a very long and fruitful life. It was a reminder that God's plan is never finished, His work never done. The speaker reminded us that the heroes of faith in Hebrews 11 had to take God's word for it!

Of course, there was a reason why these people died before they were finished. God is not a kill-joy or a sadist who would rob us of final victory just for the fun of it. "For God wanted them to wait and share the even better rewards that were prepared for us" (v. 40, *TLB)*.

What makes us think we will finish all we want to do before we die? A neurotic need to prove something to ourselves? Some memory of rejection by a parent who said, "You'll never amount to anything"? Some uncomfortable inner drive to prove that we're perfect? A hope that people will respect us more if we are successful and powerful? I suspect that the more we want to finish before we die, the more likely we'll die before we're finished. Life is, unfortunately, a chain of incompletes.

A successful life will always be unfinished, and the more successful it is, the more will be left undone. This is how life works. It may seem sad, but the positive side to all of this is that God is with us in our incompleteness and gives us permission to stop trying to accomplish everything in one brief period of existence. It is liberating to realize that we don't have to finish. All we have to be is faithful.[13]

"Be strong and courageous. Do not be afraid or terrified because of them, for the Lord your God goes with you; he will never leave you nor forsake you" (Deuteronomy 31:6).

In his book *Today Can Be Different*, Harold Sala offers some wise words about trials:

> Trials are not an indication that God has singled you out for special punishment, or proof that you're not a victorious believer. Trials happen, and God promises to be with you when they do.
>
> Here are some observations about the deep waters through which you may pass:
>
> 1. Trials never leave you where they find you. Like a whirlwind that picks something up, when you finally hit the ground you are not in the same place; you're not even the same person.
> 2. Trials will cause you to grow better or bitter, depending on what you're made of. Hopefully, you'll learn the lesson the trial has to offer without having to take the test all over again. A certain fellow saw an ad for an ocean cruise at a phenomenally low price, so he promptly bought the adventure. But, immediately upon boarding the liner, the floor opened and he tumbled down a chute, finding himself in a little rowboat out on the ocean all by himself. Toward evening, another individual came by in a little rowboat just like the one he was in. He called out, "Do they serve meals on this cruise?" The other replied, "They didn't last year!"
> 3. Trials produce growth and maturity.
> 4. Trials are of limited duration. No matter how deep the water, eventually God leads us to the other side.
> 5. Trials cause you to know His presence and power you otherwise would never experience. A Chinese friend, who spent nine months in total darkness in a Communist prison, wrote after he left China for the West: "What I miss more than all else are the intense, quiet moments with Christ that I have not known since the anguish of the days while I was in solitary confinement!"

Don't curse your trials: realize God is with you through them. His presence will make a difference.[14]

"Do not conform any longer to the pattern of this world, but be transformed by the renewing of your mind. Then you will be able to test and approve what God's will is—his good, pleasing and perfect will" (Romans 12:2).

Where are you going? What are you going to do? What will you accomplish? Has anyone asked you those questions recently? If not, ask them of yourself.

Some years ago Lawrence Appley, chairman of the board of The American Management Association, spoke at a large convention. After his presentation, he took questions from the audience. A young student asked him, "What are your ten-year goals?" The speaker looked at him and said, "Do you know how old I am? I'm seventy-five!!" The student said, "Yes, I knew that. What are your ten-year goals?" He made his point to the speaker and the audience. We are never too old to dream.

Some men react to this idea of setting goals. They say, "I like my freedom. I'm a spontaneous man. I don't want to be limited." Well, who said setting goals limits you? It's just the opposite. You need to have some thought for the future. We weren't created to drift or to bounce around off the walls of life.

God has a plan for your life, and he wants you to experience the fullness he has for you. Perhaps you never thought about goals before, but consider these questions. What are your personal goals for the next three months? Six months? The next year? The next five years? The next ten years? In that time where will you be in accomplishing the specific things you and no other person was born to do?[15]

Consider Lloyd Ogilvie's words:

There are few things which give life more verve than knowing "what is that good and acceptable and perfect will of God" (Romans 12:2) in the short- and long-range goals for our lives. We know where we are headed and can react with spontaneity to everything which brings us closer to our destiny and destination as persons. And the Holy Spirit will guide us each step of the way![16]

"Do not conform any longer to the pattern of this world, but be transformed by the renewing of your mind. Then you will be able to test and approve what God's will is—his good, pleasing and perfect will" (Romans 12:2).

Do you remember the movie *The Elephant Man*? It's the story of a deformed man who eventually achieves dignity. Although his body stayed the same, he changed, gaining a sense of personal worthiness, of purpose.

There are many men today who aren't deformed in the physical sense, but they are in other ways. Some have deformed attitudes that are basically negative and pessimistic. This deformation is curable. Some have habits that have been deformed into addictions. This deformation is also curable.

There is one deformity that mars every person alive. It's called sin. It's a spiritual deformation, distorting our values and our minds. It can even cripple our abilities. You may not be able to see it from the outside, but it's there. The worst part is that the image of God, in which we were created, has been marred by sin. Look around you, read the paper, watch the news. You'll see the results of sin's deformity.

But, praise God, he intervened to change this deformity. It wasn't an external patch job either. It's called *regeneration,* being born again, which gives us a brand-new life in Christ.

The word used to describe this change is *transformation,* which means "changing." This is not anything we can bring about, it's the Holy Spirit bringing about a major *renovation.*

So, here are the key words for today:

Deformation: In what area do you still feel deformed?

Regeneration: When did you experience this step in your life?

Transformation: What area of your life needs this?

Renovation: In what way would you like to be renovated?[17]

DECEMBER 21

"For to me, to live is Christ and to die is gain" (Philippians 1:21).

The question, "Why, God?" is as old as humanity itself. From the beginning people have been trying to reconcile the basic goodness of God with some of the calamities that befall us.

A lot of sincere, trusting individuals pondered the answer to that question when Paul Little died as the result of injuries sustained in an automobile accident. Little, age forty-seven, was the director of InterVarsity Christian Fellowship, a student organization with a worldwide impact.

Then, there was the untimely death of Dawson Trotman, founder of the Navigators—an organization emphasizing the study of God's Word that has touched millions of lives. When Trotman drowned, many asked why. The list of lives cut short includes Willis Shank, missionary pilot and Christian statesman whose plane went down in the Arctic; Dr. Paul Carlson, medical doctor who gave his life in the Congo rebellion; Nate Saint, Jim Elliot, and Ed McCully, who died on a sandy landing strip of a river in Ecuador; Clate Risley, evangelical leader and Christian educator who was murdered; Chet Bitterman, whose bullet-riddled body was found wrapped in a revolutionary flag in Colombia; Don Bowers, essential radio engineer and technician in Saipan who drowned; and many more who gave their lives in service to the Lord.

Of these people several things should be said by way of summation. First, each would immediately endorse the words of Paul, who wrote that his desire was that Christ should be glorified in his body, whether by life or by death (see Philippians 1:20). Then, it should be pointed out that God can use the untimely death of one of his servants to speak to the hearts of many others, who will then step out from the ranks to follow in Christian service. Third, our faith in Christ by no means makes us immune to disasters, but it does, without question, give the believer the assurance that death only opens the door to eternal life: "[For] to be absent from the body, and to be present with the Lord" (2 Cor 5:8, KJV).[18]

"I thought in my heart, 'Come now, I will test you with pleasure'"
(Ecclesiastes 2:1).

Where do your thoughts come from? You know, what portion of your body do you use when you think? Your head, of course—your mind is involved.

"I thought in my heart." Interesting concept. For that's where it all begins—in our hearts. It's the source of our attitudes and beliefs. We look into a person's heart to see who and what he or she really is.

Solomon went back to look at his heart, and he made a discovery. Perhaps what he discovered can help us avoid some pitfalls. Listen to Solomon.

I wanted to see what was worthwhile for men to do under heaven during the few days of their lives.

I undertook great projects: I built houses for myself and planted vineyards. I made gardens and parks and planted all kinds of fruit trees in them. I made reservoirs to water groves of flourishing trees. I bought male and female slaves and had other slaves who were born in my house. I also owned more herds and flocks than anyone in Jerusalem before me. I amassed silver and gold for myself, and the treasure of kings and provinces. I acquired men and women singers, and a harem as well—the delights of the heart of man. I became greater by far than anyone in Jerusalem before me. In all this my wisdom stayed with me.

I denied myself nothing my eyes desired;

I refused my heart no pleasure.

My heart took delight in all my work, and this was the reward for all my labor.

Yet when I surveyed all that my hands had done and what I had toiled to achieve, everything was meaningless, a chasing after the wind; nothing was gained under the sun.

Then I turned my thoughts to consider wisdom, and also madness and folly.

What more can the king's successor do than what has already been done?

I saw that wisdom is better than folly, just as light is better than darkness; but I came to realize that the same fate overtakes them both.

Then I thought in my heart, "The fate of the fool will overtake me also. What then do I gain by being wise?" I said in my heart, "This is too meaningless."

Ecclesiastes 2:3-15

DECEMBER 23

"This is how the birth of Jesus Christ came about: His mother Mary was pledged to be married to Joseph, but before they came together, she was found to be with child through the Holy Spirit.... 'She will give birth to a son, and you are to give him the name Jesus, because he will save his people from their sins'" (Matthew 1:18, 21).

Have you ever wondered what it was like for Mary to rear Jesus? Max Lucado, in his book *God Came Near*, raises twenty-five questions for Mary that will make you think.

What was it like watching him pray?

How did he respond when he saw other kids giggling during the service at the synagogue?

When he saw a rainbow, did he ever mention a flood?

Did you ever feel awkward teaching him how he created the world?

When he saw a lamb being led to the slaughter, did he act differently?

Did you ever see him with a distant look on his face as if he were listening to someone you couldn't hear?

How did he act at funerals?

Did the thought ever occur to you that the God to whom you were praying was asleep under your own roof?

Did you ever try to count the stars with him... and succeed?

Did he ever come home with a black eye?

How did he act when he got his first haircut?

Did he have any friends by the name of Judas?

Did he do well in school?

Did you ever scold him?

Did he ever have to ask a question about Scripture?

What do you think he thought when he saw a prostitute offering to the highest bidder the body he made?

Did he ever get angry when someone was dishonest with him?

Did you ever catch him pensively looking at the flesh on his own arm while holding a clod of dirt?

continued on page 370

Did he ever wake up afraid?

Who was his best friend?

When someone referred to Satan, how did he act?

Did you ever accidentally call him Father?

What did he and his cousin John talk about as kids?

Did his other brothers and sisters understand what was happening?

Did you ever think, *That's God eating my soup?*[19]

DECEMBER 24

"[Now when] Jesus was born in Bethlehem of Judea ..." (Matthew 2:1a).

Christmas each year weaves its magic spell upon our hearts. Carols float on the air and there is a surge of love and kindliness not felt at any other time of the year. Crêches appear reminding us of the miracle in the manger. In that feeding trough in lowly Bethlehem, a cry from that infant's throat broke the centuries of silence. For the first time God's voice could be heard coming from human vocal cords. C.S. Lewis called that event—the coming of Christ at Christmas—"the greatest rescue mission of history."

During each Christmas season the words of Micah resonate throughout the world. For he was inspired to give the prophecy that named the very birthplace of the Messiah: *But you, Bethlehem Ephrathah, though you are small among the clans of Judah, out of you will come for Me one who will be ruler over Israel, whose origins are from of old, from ancient times* (2:5).

Micah was telling those who were proud and powerful and rich and self-righteous that God's great ruler would not come from their stately and royal environs. He would come forth from the nondescript hamlet of Bethlehem. When over seven hundred years later the wise men came searching for Him, the scribes had to brush off the dust from the Book of Micah to direct them to the very location where he would be born.

The One who would come is One *whose origins are from of old, from ancient times* (v. 2). This literally means "from days of eternity." It speaks of the eternal existence of Christ. His providence and preeminence are also prophesied as one who *will stand and shepherd His flock and His greatness will reach to the ends of the earth. And He will be their peace* (vv. 4-5). What beautiful and precious promises are ours from this plowman who became God's mighty penman.[20]

"...and she gave birth to her firstborn, a son. She wrapped him in strips of cloth and placed him in a manger, because there was no room for him in the inn" (Luke 2:7).

O God, our Father, we remember at this Christmas time how the eternal Word became flesh and dwelt among us.

We thank you that Jesus took our human body upon him, so that we can never again dare to despise or neglect or misuse the body, since you made it your dwelling-place.

We thank you that Jesus did a day's work like any working man, that he knew the problem of living together in a family, that he knew the frustration and irritation of serving the public, that he had to earn a living, and to face all the wearing routine of everyday work and life and living, and so clothed each common task with glory.

We thank you that he shared in all happy social occasions, that he was at home at weddings and at dinners and at festivals in the homes of simple ordinary people like ourselves. Grant that we may ever remember that in his unseen risen presence he is a guest in every home.

We thank you that he too had to bear unfair criticism, prejudiced opposition, malicious and deliberate misunderstanding.

We thank you that whatever happens to us, he has been there before, and that, because he himself has gone through things, he is able to help those who are going through them.

Help us never to forget that he knows life, because he lived life, and that he is with us at all times to enable us to live victoriously.
This we ask for your love's sake. Amen.[21]

DECEMBER 26

"Jesus said, 'Follow me'" (Matthew 4:19).

Do you follow Jesus? There are many good reasons to do so.

Christ said to follow Him because following anyone or anything else gets us lost.

Christ said to know who we look like because drawing our self-image from any other source but God poisons our souls and spirits.

Christ said to love our neighbor as ourselves because we grow the most when committed to fostering another's growth, not just our own.

Christ said to clean the inside of the cup because that is the only way to develop true character and avoid a shallow existence.

Christ said to stop fitting in with our culture because our culture is sick, and adapting to it will make us sick, too.

Christ said to get real because wearing masks makes our lives empty and our relationships unfulfilling.

Christ said to stop blaming others because taking responsibility for our own problems is essential for true maturity and health.

Christ said to forgive others because unforgiveness is arrogant and hurts others as well as ourselves.

Christ said to live like an heir because to live like an orphan leads to settling for far too little in life.

Christ said to solve paradoxes because it is often that which seems contrary to common sense that is the healthiest route of all.

Christ said to stop worrying because worry only drains us of the energy we need to work on the things that we can do something about.

Christ said to persevere because the fruit of our labor won't ever show up if we grow tired of doing what it takes to bear it.

Everything Christ tells us is in our best interest, and it is critically important to understand that. His counsel wasn't designed to burden us, but to set us free. When he gave his counsel to us, it was aimed at meeting our deepest needs and it will if we follow it.[22]

DECEMBER 27

"Isn't this the carpenter?" (Mark 6:3).

Most of us don't spend much time thinking about Jesus as a carpenter. It doesn't seem very significant. And yet, maybe it does at that. A carpenter is one who fashions and creates. Jesus did this both in the expression of his divinity and in his humanity. He created the universe. "Through Him all things were made: without him nothing was made that has been made" (Jn 1:3).

But he also fashioned simple pieces of furniture for people. If anyone knew about hard work it was Jesus. This was not a "Home Improvement" set with drills, electric saws, and the latest gadgetry. It was muscle-pushing rough tools that were very basic and produced callouses. His hands were probably bruised with numerous cuts from handling the wood and the crude saw or hammer. You would not believe the amount of time and energy spent then to make a simple chair or table.

But what does Jesus being a carpenter have to do with us? Consider these thoughts from one of the officers of the Salvation Army.

> As the Carpenter, Christ forever sanctified human toil. We are all members of the corporate society. As we derive many benefits, so must we be contributive to the community. Our tasks are given dignity by the One who worked amid the wood shavings at the carpenter's bench for the greater part of His life. His labor enabled the oxen to plow without being chafed by their yokes, children to take delight in the hand-carved toys, families to live in the comfort of a home built by the Carpenter.
>
> Today, the Carpenter of Nazareth, who once smoothed yokes in His skillful hands, would take a life that is yielded to Him and fashion it into a beautiful and useful instrument of God's eternal kingdom.[23]

All your effort and toil as a parent also has purpose and merit even though you wonder at times if it's worth it. As Jesus is fashioning your life, let him work through you to fashion your child's life.

> Carpenter of Nazareth, take my life and smooth the coarseness of its grain, work out the flaws and imperfections, make me a worthwhile and useful instrument of the kingdom.[24]

"For though we live in the world, we do not wage war as the world does. The weapons we fight with are not the weapons of the world. On the contrary, they have divine power to demolish strongholds. We demolish arguments and every pretension that sets itself up against the knowledge of God, and we take captive every thought to make it obedient to Christ" (2 Corinthians 10:3-5).

Problems—we've all got them. They come in all sizes. How you solve them is based not so much on what you do with them but how you think about them. Dr. William Mitchell, in his helpful book *Winning in the Land of Giants,* gave five possible ways of thinking about our problems:

Curse the problem. This, in essence, means adding a negative opinion to the negative facts of the situation—in other words, compounding the negativity.

Nurse the problem—focusing time and attention on the problem itself rather than on its solution.

Rehearse the problem—replaying the problem until the person is actually thinking about very little other than the problem.

Disperse it. A technique used in tackling scientific problems is to break a problem down into its component parts and then to work at each part until an answer is reached. As the component problems are solved, the big problem is also solved. This principle holds true for all of life. One of the most effective things a person can do about what seems to be an overwhelming problem is to attempt to break it down into its smaller component problems and then to deal with the smaller issues one at a time.

Reverse it. Seek out the positive. No situation or circumstance is 100 percent bad. There is always some glimmer of hope, some ray of light. Recognize negativity for what it is—a distraction from a positive solution. Dismiss the negativity. Of course, you do not ignore the problem in hopes that it will go away. To the contrary! Disposing of the negative thought means facing the problem *and* facing your negative response, making a conscious decision that the negative response is going to do nothing to solve the problem, and in that light, refusing to dwell on the negative and turning instead to the positive. Only you can reverse the way you feel about a problem.[25]

"For he guards the course of the just and protects the way of his faithful ones" (Proverbs 2:8).

Years ago when Prince Charles was four years old, his mother Queen Elizabeth decided to rear him as a normal child. And the little boy thought all the kids were just like him and every child's mother was a queen! Was he ever mistaken! But in spite of his mother wanting him to be like any other boy he had to make some major adjustments as he reached adulthood. You see, life doesn't always turn out the way you think it will.

Did Joseph of the Old Testament dream of being a ruler in Egypt? Not likely. He probably had visions of settling down with a local girl and owning a few head of cattle. When Jeremiah was a young man, do you think he wanted to end up being a doom-and-gloom prophet? No, but both Joseph and Jeremiah made the shift.

Think of some others who made major changes in their lives—such as Martin Luther. He was encouraged to be a lawyer. Can you imagine his reaction if he had known what was coming: "Me, be a monk and lead the Protestant Reformation?" But it happened, because he adjusted.

Herbert Hoover was raised a Quaker and went to Stanford University to be a minister. Can you imagine his response if someone had said, "Hey, Herb, how would you like to be president of this country someday?" It happened. He adjusted.

How well do you adjust to changes, to new plans? They're going to happen whether you want them to or not. It could be your profession. We live in a changing world. Those who make the adjustments are those willing to change.

It could be that God wants you retrained for something. Wonder what it is? Just wait on him. You'll see soon enough.[26]

DECEMBER 30

"For there are six things the Lord hates—no, seven; Haughtiness, Lying, Murdering, Plotting evil, Eagerness to do wrong, A false witness, Sowing discord among brothers" (Proverbs 6:16-19, TLB).

Interesting, isn't it? Several of the things the Lord hates in this passage are the misuse of words.

Your words have tremendous power, even just one word. "Those who love to talk will suffer the consequences" (Prv 18:21, TLB). One well-placed word with the proper tone of voice and a look can have more impact than an entire sermon. The way something is said can be a source of healing or hurt. It can cure or cripple. Did you know that in face-to-face conversation the way your words are packaged can make all the difference in the world? Your words make up 7 percent of the message, your tone 38 percent, and your nonverbal 55 percent! Do you listen to your tone or ever notice how you look? It's convicting!

Our words can lacerate a person's feelings. "Some people like to make cutting remarks" (Prv 12:18, TLB). But "telling the truth gives a man great satisfaction, and hard work returns many blessings to him" (Prv 12:14, TLB).

Our words can lift people and even give them health. "Anxious hearts are very heavy but a word of encouragement does wonders!" (Prv 12:25, TLB). "Kind words are like honey—enjoyable and healthful" (Prv 16:24, TLB).

But it's possible to damage someone's self-esteem by flattering them.

> Flattery is a trap; evil men are caught in it, but good men stay away and sing for joy.   **Proverbs 29:5-6, TLB**

The good news is this: Your words can be so productive that what you say not only comes back to benefit you but others as well. That's not a bad proposition.

> Gentle words cause life and health; griping brings discouragement.
> **Proverbs 15:4, TLB**

Often we hear the phrase, "They're known by their words." What do your words tell others?[27]

"For no one can lay any foundation other than the one already laid, which is Jesus Christ. If any man builds on this foundation using gold, silver, costly stones, wood, hay or straw, his work will be shown for what it is, because the day will bring it to light. It will be revealed with fire, and the fire will test the quality of each man's work. If what he has built survives, he will receive his reward. If it is burned up, he will suffer loss; he himself will be saved, but only as one escaping through the flames" (1 Corinthians 3:11-15).

Someday you will retire, perhaps sooner than you think. But what's it going to be like? Exciting and fulfilling or empty and dull? Many men find what they're doing right now fulfilling. There are business deals to make, mergers to arrange, golf lessons to take to lower that handicap, children to raise and marry off, meetings to attend—the list goes on. Life is full... for now. But when you retire, where are the mergers and business deals? Will those muscles stand up to eighteen rounds of golf or a softball game? What if the kids live three thousand miles away? Or worse yet, what if your divorced daughter and your three grandchildren come home to live?

Much may be going on now... but how about later? Can you continue your activities into your retirement?

A number of athletes have been heard to say that for years their lives were consumed by their sport. One of the greatest baseball players of all time made the statement, "You know, for years I ate baseball, I slept baseball, I talked baseball, I thought it and lived it. One day it was over. I found out then when you get beyond those years, you can't live on baseball!" Many men live their lives as though what they do will be extended until they die. But it won't.

There *is* one thing we can do now and all our days. It's called living the Christian life. It's here now, and it will stay with you!

ACKNOWLEDGMENTS

The publisher wishes to thank those who granted permission to reprint excerpts from the following works in *With All My Strength*.

* * *

Excerpt taken from *Daily in Christ* by Neil and Joanne Anderson. Copyright ©1993 by Harvest House Publishers, Eugene, Oregon. Used by permission.

Excerpts from *How to Get What You Pray For* by Bill Austin are reprinted by permission granted by Bill Austin.

Excerpts taken from *A Barclay Prayer Book* by William Barclay, © 1990. Published by SCM Press. Permission for rights in the U.S. granted by Trinity Press International.

Excerpts from *Battle Fatigue* by Joe E. Brown (Nashville: Broadman and Holman Publishers 1995), 51-51. All rights reserved. Used by permission.

Excerpts taken from *Father Memories* by Randy Carlson, © 1992. Moody Bible Institute of Chicago. Moody Press. Used by permission.

Excerpts reprinted from *Quotable Quotations* by Lloyd Cory, published by Victor Books, 1985, SP Publications, Inc. Wheaton, IL 60187.

Excerpts from *Regaining Control of Your Life* by Judson Edwards © 1989, reprinted by permission of Bethany House Publishers.

Excerpt taken from *Approaching God* by Paul Enns, copyright ©1991, Moody Bible Institute of Chicago. Moody Press. Used by permission.

Excerpts reprinted from *Portraits of Christ* by Henry Gariepy, published by Victor Books, © 1987, SP Publications, Inc., Wheaton, IL 60187.

Excerpts reprinted from *Light in a Dark Place* by Henry Gariepy, published by Victor Books, 1995, SP Publications, Inc., Wheaton, IL 60187.

Excerpt from *Incredible Moments with the Savior* by Ken Gire, © 1990 by Ken Gire. Reprinted by permission of Zondervan Publishing House.

Excerpt from *When I Relax I Feel Guilty* by Tim Hansel, © 1979. Used by permission of Chariot FAMILY Publishing.

NOTES

JANUARY

1. R. Kent Hughes, *Disciplines of a Godly Man* (Wheaton, Ill.: Crossway, 1991), 15-16, adapted.
2. Hughes, 17, adapted.
3. Hughes, 29-31, adapted.
4. David W. Smith, *Men Without Friends* (Nashville, Tenn.: Thomas Nelson, 1990), 79-80, adapted.
5. Max Lucado, *A Gentle Thunder* (Dallas: Word, 1995), 80-81.
6. David Stoop, *Seeking Christ* (Nashville, Tenn.: Thomas Nelson, 1994), 2-3, adapted.
7. Hughes, 53-56, adapted.
8. *Webster's New World Dictionary* (New York: Prentice Hall, 1994), 1393.
9. Judson Edwards, *Regaining Control of Your Life* (Minneapolis, Minn.: Bethany, 1989), 157, adapted.
10. James Johnson, *What Every Woman Should Know About A Man* (Grand Rapids, Mich.: Zondervan, 1981), 104-5.
11. Charles R. Swindoll, *The Finishing Touch* (Dallas: Word, 1994), 72, adapted.
12. Carol Kent, *Tame Your Fears* (Colorado Springs: NavPress, 1993), 28-29. Also taken from H. Norman Wright, *Quiet Times for Parents* (Eugene, Ore.: Harvest House, 1995), September 19, adapted.
13. Bill McCartney, ed., *What Makes a Man* (Colorado Springs: NavPress, 1992). From an article by Steve Farrar, 58-59.
14. Lloyd John Ogilvie, *God's Best for My Life* (Eugene, Ore.: Harvest House, 1981), January 16.
15. Ken Olsen, *Hey Man! Open Up and Live* (New York: Fawcett, 1978), 147-48.
16. Douglas E. Rosenau, *A Celebration of Sex* (Nashville, Tenn.: Thomas Nelson, 1994), 21.
17. John Trent and Rick Hicks, *Seeking Solid Ground* (Colorado Springs: Focus on the Family, 1995), 58-60, adapted.
18. Charles Swindoll, *Growing Strong in the Seasons of Life* (Portland, Ore.: Multnomah, 1983), 27-28, adapted.
19. Lloyd John Ogilvie, *Silent Strength for My Life* (Eugene, Ore.: Harvest House, 1990), 308.
20. Gary J. Oliver, *Real Men Have Feelings, Too* (Chicago: Moody, 1993), 60-61.
21. Gordon MacDonald, *Restoring Your Spiritual Passion* (Nashville, Tenn.: Thomas Nelson, 1986), 59-60, adapted.

FEBRUARY

1. Swindoll, *The Finishing Touch*, 64-65, adapted.
2. Elton Trueblood, as quoted in Swindoll, *The Finishing Touch*, 65.
3. *Webster's New World Dictionary*, Third College Edition (New York: Simon & Schuster, 1994), 1424.
4. R.C. Sproul, *Before the Face of God, Book 3* (Grand Rapids, Mich.: Baker, 1994), 242-43, adapted.
5. Lucado, *A Gentle Thunder*, 68-69, adapted.
6. Henry Gariepy, *100 Portraits of Christ* (Wheaton, Ill.: Victor, 1987), 95-96, adapted.
7. Gariepy, 96.
8. H. Norman Wright, *Quiet Times for Parents* (Eugene, Ore.: Harvest House, 1995), September 13, adapted.
9. Mike Mason, *The Mystery of Marriage* (Portland, Ore.: Multnomah, 1985), 91, 97-98.
10. As quoted in Dean Merrill, *Wait Quietly* (Wheaton, Ill.: Tyndale, 1994), 49.
11. Trent and Hicks, 79, adapted.
12. Jim Smoke, *Facing 50* (Nashville, Tenn.: Thomas Nelson, 1994), 40-41.
13. H. Norman Wright, *How to Really Love Your Wife* (Ann Arbor, Mich.: Servant, 1995), selections.
14. William Barclay, *A Barclay Prayer Book* (London: SCM Press Ltd., 1963), 8-9.
15. Hughes, 35-36.
16. MacDonald, 96-104, adapted.
17. Harry Hollis, Jr., *Thank God for Sex* (Nashville, Tenn.: Broadman, 1975), 109-10.
18. Lloyd John Ogilvie, *Enjoying God* (Dallas: Word, 1989), 22-24, adapted.
19. Ogilvie, *God's Best for My Life*, August 27.
20. Dwight Small, *After You've Said I Do* (Grand Rapids, Mich.: Revell, 1968), 243-44.
21. Neil Anderson with Joanne Anderson, *Daily in Christ* (Eugene, Ore.: Harvest House, 1993), July 31, adapted.
22. *New World Webster Dictionary of the American Language*, Second College Edition (New York: Simon and Schuster, 1980).
23. Gordon Dalbey, *Fight Like a Man* (Wheaton, Ill.: Tyndale, 1995), 2-3, adapted.
24. Martyn Lloyd-Jones, *Spiritual Depression* (Grand Rapids, Mich.: Eerdmans, 1965), 142.

MARCH

1. Oliver, 160-61.
2. Richard Selzer, *Mortal Lessons: Notes on the Art of Surgery* (New York: Simon & Schuster, 1976), 45-46.
3. Hughes, 40-41, adapted.
4. Hughes, 42.

5. Edwards, 78-79, adapted.
6. John F. MacArthur, *Drawing Near* (Wheaton, Ill.: Crossway, 1993), January 22, adapted.
7. Gary Rosberg, *Guard Your Heart* (Portland, Ore.: Multnomah, 1994), 15-17, adapted.
8. Swindoll, *The Finishing Touch,* 281.
9. Rosenau, 8-9.
10. Les and Leslie Parrot, *Becoming Soul Mates* (Grand Rapids, Mich.: Zondervan, 1995), 144, adapted.
11. Oliver, 138.
12. Trent and Hicks, 80-84, adapted.
13. W.T. Purkiser, "Five Ways to Have a Nervous Breakdown," *Herald of Holiness,* October 9, 1974, as quoted in Jon Johnson, *Walls or Bridges* (Grand Rapids, Mich.: Baker, 1988), 176-77.
14. As quoted in Rosberg, 134-35.
15. Rosberg, 138-40.
16. Original source unknown.
17. Trent and Hicks, 20, adapted.
18. Lloyd John Ogilvie, *Climbing the Rainbow* (Dallas: Word, 1993), 114-19, adapted. H. Norman Wright, *Quiet Times for Parents,* May 21, adapted.
19. William James, *Quotable Quotations,* Lloyd Cory, ed. (Wheaton, Ill.: Victor, 1985), 181.
20. H. Norman Wright, *Secrets of a Lasting Marriage* (Ventura, Calif.: Regal, 1995), 52-53.
21. Harold Ivan Smith, *Changing Answers to Depression* (Eugene, Ore.: Harvest House, 1978), 95, adapted.
22. Peter F. Drucker, *The Effective Executive* (New York: Harper & Row, 1966), 111, adapted.

APRIL

1. Tim Hansel, *When I Relax I Feel Guilty* (Elgin, Ill.: David C. Cook, 1979), 51.
2. Hansel, 53-54.
3. Hansel, 55.
4. Ogilvie, *God's Best for My Life,* May 8, adapted.
5. Swindoll, *The Finishing Touch,* 60-61, adapted.
6. Edwards, 47-48.
7. John Sanderson, "The Fruit of the Spirit," as quoted in Tim Rites, *Deep Down* (Wheaton, Ill.: Tyndale, 1995), 59.
8. Rites, 52.
9. Paul Walker, *How to Keep Your Joy* (Nashville, Tenn.: Thomas Nelson, 1987), 17.
10. Lloyd John Ogilvie, *The Loose Ends* (Dallas, Tex.: Word, 1991), 43-47, adapted. Also Wright, *Quiet Times for Parents,* May 24.

11. Ken Gire, *Incredible Moments with the Savior* (Grand Rapids, Mich.: Zondervan, 1990), 96-97.

12. Gary J. Oliver, *How to Get It Right When You've Gotten It Wrong* (Wheaton, Ill.: Victor, 1995), 171.

13. John F. MacArthur, *Drawing Near* (Wheaton, Ill.: Crossway, 1993), January 23, adapted.

14. Charles R. Swindoll, *Improving Your Serve* (Waco, Tex.: Word, 1981), 105.

15. Patrick Morley, *Seven Seasons of a Man's Life* (Nashville, Tenn.: Thomas Nelson, 1990), 90-91, adapted.

16. As quoted in Dean Merrill, *Wait Quietly* (Wheaton, Ill.: Tyndale, 1994), 63.

17. Merrill, 62-63, adapted.

18. Charlie and Martha Shedd, *How to Start and Keep It Going*, cited by Fritz Ridenour in *The Marriage Collection*, "Praying Together" (Grand Rapids, Mich.: Zondervan, 1989), 442-43.

19. Billy Sunday, *Standing on the Rocks*, as quoted in Les and Leslie Parrott, *Becoming Soul Mates*, 111-12.

MAY

1. Merrill, 13-15, adapted.

2. Joe E. Brown, *Battle Fatigue* (Nashville, Tenn.: Broadman & Holman, 1995), 30-36, adapted.

3. Lloyd John Ogilvie, *The Heart of God* (Ventura, Calif.: Regal, 1994), 202.

4. Hughes, 62-65, adapted.

5. Sproul, *Before the Face of God*, 446-47, adapted.

6. Ogilvie, *God's Best for My Life*, May 9.

7. Brown, 116-17.

8. Parrott, 17.

9. Neva Coyle and Zane Anderson, *Living By Chance or By Choice* (Minneapolis, Minn.: Bethany House, 1995), 95-97, adapted.

10. Barclay, 28-29, adapted.

11. Ogilvie, *Enjoying God*, 4-5, adapted.

12. Ogilvie, *God's Best for My Life*, January 27.

13. Oliver, *Real Men Have Feelings, Too*, 72, adapted.

14. James S. Bell and Stan Campbell, *A Return to Virtue* (Chicago: Northfield, 1995), 97, adapted.

15. G.W. Target, "The Window," in *The Window and Other Essays* (Mountain View, Calif.: Pacific Press, 1973), 5-7, adapted.

16. Ogilvie, *Silent Strength for My Life*, 275.

17. A. Cohen, ed., *Proverbs, Soncino Books of the Bible* (London: Soncino Press, 1946), 2.

18. Robert Hicks, *In Search of Wisdom* (Colorado Springs: NavPress, 1995), 35-41, adapted.

19. Patrick Morley, *The Man in the Mirror* (Brentwood, Tenn.: Wolgemuth & Hyatt, 1989), 130.

20. John C. Maxwell, *Developing the Leader within You* (Nashville, Tenn.: Nelson, 1993), 119-20, adapted.
21. Swindoll, *Growing Strong in the Seasons of Life*, 82.

JUNE

1. *Webster's New World Dictionary, Third College Edition* (New York: Prentice Hall, 1994), 1140.
2. Rites, 52, adapted.
3. Sproul, 220, *Before the Face of God*, adapted.
4. Randy Carlson, *Father Memories* (Chicago: Moody, 1992), 13, 62.
5. Paul Ennis, *Approaching God* (Chicago: Moody, 1991), August 15, adapted. Wright, *Quiet Times for Parents*, December 20, adapted.
6. Max Lucado, *On the Anvil* (Wheaton, Ill.: Tyndale, 1985), 69-70. Used by permission.
7. Parrott, 178, adapted.
8. Hansel, 146-47.
9. Rudolph F. Norden, *Each Day with Jesus* (St. Louis, Mo.: Concordia, 1994), 216, adapted.
10. Dan Allender and Tremper Longman, III, *The Cry of the Soul* (Colorado Springs: NavPress, 1994), 250-51, adapted.
11. Barclay, 14-15, adapted.
12. R.C. Sproul, *Pleasing God* (Wheaton, Ill.: Tyndale, 1988), 79.
13. Ennis, January 5, adapted.
14. J.I. Packer, *Knowing God* (Downers Grove, Ill.: InterVarsity, 1973), 68-73, adapted.
15. Cited in *National Geographic*, December 1978, 858-82.
16. Oliver, *How to Get It Right When You've Gotten It Wrong*, 27.
17. Sproul, *Before the Face of God, Book 3*, 284-85, adapted.
18. Lucado, *A Gentle Thunder*, 69-70.
19. David Stoop, *Making Peace with Your Father* (Wheaton, Ill.: Tyndale, 1991), 60-61.
20. Stoop, *Making Peace with Your Father*, 55-76, adapted.
21. Lloyd John Ogilvie, *Praying with Power* (Ventura, Calif.: Regal, 1987), 25-26.
22. H. Norman Wright, *Holding on to Romance* (Ventura, Calif.: Regal, 1987), 178-80, adapted.
23. Ogilvie, *God's Best for My Life*, March 14.
24. John Mark Templeton, *Discovering the Laws of Life* (New York: Continuum, 1994), 247-48, adapted.
25. Joseph Cooke, *Free for the Taking* (Old Tappan, N.J.: Revell, 1975), 29.

JULY

1. Brown, 51-52.
2. Sproul, *Before the Face of God, Book 3*, 148, 149, adapted.
3. Morley, *Seven Seasons of a Man's Life*, 270, adapted.
4. William Mitchell, *Winning in the Land of Giants* (Nashville, Tenn.: Thomas Nelson, 1995), 20-21, adapted.
5. Wright, *Quiet Times for Parents*, March 25, adapted.
6. Smith, 75-76, adapted.
7. Ogilvie, *Enjoying God*, 198-201, adapted.
8. Harold Sala, *Today Can Be Different* (Ventura, Calif.: Regal, 1988), July 10, adapted.
9. As quoted in Neil Anderson with Joanne Anderson, *Daily in Christ* (Eugene, Ore.: Harvest House, 1993), May 31. Author unknown.
10. "Seven Steps to Stagnation," Robert H. Franbe Association, Chicago, Ill.
11. Lloyd John Ogilvie, *Life As It Was Meant to Be* (Ventura, Calif.: Regal, 1980), 91-92, adapted.
12. Mitchell, *Winning in the Land of Giants*, 36, 49, 50, adapted.
13. Charles R. Swindoll, *Living Beyond the Daily Grind* (Dallas: Word, 1988), 39-41, adapted.
14. Kent Hughes, *Disciplines of Grace* (Wheaton, Ill.: Crossway, 1993), 15-18, adapted.
15. G. Campbell Morgan, *The Ten Commandments* (New York: Revell, 1901), 18-19.
16. Hughes, *Disciplines of Grace*, 34-39.
17. Packer, 39, adapted.
18. Hughes, *Disciplines of a Godly Man*, (Wheaton, Ill.: Crossway, 1991), 93-94.
19. Hughes, *Disciplines of a Godly Man*, 98-104, adapted.
20. Hughes, *Disciplines of a Godly Man*, 116-20, adapted.
21. James Patterson and Peter Kim, *The Day America Told the Truth* (New York: Prentice Hall, 1991), 155.
22. Hughes, *Disciplines of a Godly Man*, 142-47, adapted.
23. Patterson and Kim, 45, 49, adapted.
24. Hughes, *Disciplines of a Godly Man*, 172-81, adapted.
25. Hughes, *Disciplines of a Godly Man*, 187-88.

AUGUST

1. Swindoll, *Living Beyond the Daily Grind*, 110-11, adapted.
2. Swindoll, *Growing Strong in the Seasons of Life*, 108-10, adapted.
3. Edwards, 124-25, adapted.
4. Dalbey, 31, adapted.
5. Allender and Longman, 254-55, adapted.
6. Parrot, 92.
7. Sala, June 27, adapted.
8. Norman Vincent Peale, *Power of the Plus Factor* (New York: Fawcett, 1988).

9. Maxwell, 101-102, adapted.
10. Maxwell, 32, adapted.
11. Ogilvie, *God's Best for My Life,* August 15.
12. Wright, *Quiet Times for Couples,* May 8, adapted.
13. Rosenau, *A Celebration of Sex,* 26-27.
14. John Baillie, *A Diary of Private Prayer* (Toronto: Oxford University Press, 1979), 33, adapted.
15. Larry Crabb, *The Silence of Adam* (Grand Rapids, Mich.: Zondervan, 1995), 79-85, adapted.
16. Ennis, January 12, adapted.
17. A.W. Tozer, *The Knowledge of the Holy* (New York: Harper Brothers, 1961), 61-62, adapted.
18. Ennis, January 14, adapted.
19. Tozer, 79-82, adapted.
20. Ennis, January 15, adapted.
21. Ennis, January 16, adapted.
22. R. Scott Sullender, *Losses in Later Life* (New York: Integration Books/Paulist, 1989), 142-43.
23. Ogilvie, *Enjoying God,* 64-65.
24. Maxwell, 30, adapted.
25. Ogilvie, *Praying with Power,* 40-45, adapted.

SEPTEMBER

1. Harold Ivan Smith, 66-68, adapted.
2. Oliver, *How to Get It Right When You've Gotten It Wrong,* 66-78, adapted.
3. Edwards, 48, adapted.
4. Wright, *Secrets of a Lasting Marriage,* 87, adapted.
5. Bell and Campbell, 133, adapted.
6. Sala, June 30, adapted.
7. *Webster's Ninth Collegiate Dictionary* (New York: Simon & Schuster, 1991).
8. Ogilvie, *Life As It Was Meant to Be,* 108, adapted.
9. Ogilvie, *The Heart of God* , 240-43, adapted.
10. Derek Kinder, *The Proverbs* (Downers Grove, Ill.: InterVarsity, 1964), 41, adapted.
11. Hicks, *In Search of Wisdom,* 194-200, adapted.
12. Baillie, 47, adapted.
13. Brown, 117-18, adapted.
14. Wright, *Quiet Times for Couples,* May 22, adapted.
15. Hicks, *In Search of Wisdom,* 45-54, adapted.
16. Hicks, *In Search of Wisdom,* 56-58, adapted.
17. MacArthur, *Drawing Near,* March 17, adapted.
18. Morley, *The Man in the Mirror,* 58-59.
19. H. Norman Wright, *Chosen for Blessing* (Eugene, Ore.: Harvest House, 1992), 40-43, adapted.
20. Parrott, 190.

OCTOBER

1. W.P. Moody, *The Life of Dwight L. Moody* (Westwood: Barbour & Co., 1985), 122.
2. Morley, *Seven Seasons of a Man's Life*, 274-75.
3. Harold Ivan Smith, *Changing Answers to Depression*, 37 and 133, adapted.
4. Ennis, May 18, adapted.
5. Ennis, May 19, adapted.
6. J.I. Packer and Sangwoo Youtong Chee, "A Bad Trip," *Christianity Today*, March 7, 1986, 12. Wright, *Quiet Times for Parents*, April 20, adapted.
7. Sala, August 29, adapted.
8. Swindoll, *The Finishing Touch*, 148.
9. Sala, August 24, adapted.
10. Hicks, *In Search of Wisdom*, 62-64, adapted.
11. Barclay, 248-49, adapted.
12. John Roberts Clarke, *The Importance of Being Imperfect* (New York: David McKay, 1981), 11.
13. Sproul, *Before the Face of God*, 424-25, adapted.
14. *Webster's New Riverside University Dictionary, 2nd edition*.
15. Oliver, *How to Get It Right When You've Gotten It Wrong*, 17.
16. Ronnie W. Floyd, *Choices* (Nashville, Tenn.: Broadman & Holman, 1994), 54-59, adapted.
17. Sproul, *Before the Face of God, Book 3*, 218-19, adapted.
18. Sala, August 30, adapted.
19. Ogilvie, *The Heart of God*, 232.

NOVEMBER

1. Paul W. Coleman, *The Forgiving Marriage* (Chicago: Contemporary Books, 1989), 47 and 52, adapted.
2. John C. Maxwell, *The People Person* (Wheaton, Ill.: Victor Books, 1989), 53-54, adapted.
3. Lloyd John Ogilvie, *Why Not Accept Christ's Healing and Wholeness* (Old Tappan, N.J.: Revell, 1985), 153-55, adapted.
4. Floyd, 38-41, adapted.
5. Trent and Hicks, 111-14, adapted.
6. Hicks, *In Search of Wisdom*, 82-87, adapted.
7. Hollis, 12-13.
8. Brown, 32-33.
9. Barclay, 254-55, adapted.
10. Swindoll, *Living Beyond the Daily Grind*, 71.
11. Bell and Campbell, 93, adapted.
12. Swindoll, *Growing Strong in the Seasons of Life*, 366.
13. Pat Hershey Owen, *Seven Styles of Parenting* (Wheaton, Ill.: Tyndale, 1983), 15, 27, 28, adapted; Wright, *Quiet Times for Parents*, January 27, adapted.
14. *Webster's New Twentieth Century Dictionary, Unabridged*.
15. Owen, 82-89, adapted. Wright, *Quiet Times for Parents*, September 5, adapted.

16. Owen, 69-77, adapted. Wright, *Quiet Times for Parents*, November 13, adapted.
17. *Webster's New Twentieth Century Dictionary, Unabridged*.
18. Owen, 48-49, adapted. Wright, *Quiet Times for Parents*, February 4, adapted.
19. Owen, 108-115, adapted. Wright, *Quiet Times for Parents*, April 24, adapted.
20. *Webster's New World Dictionary*, adapted from p. 1218.
21. Owen, 59-60, adapted. Wright, *Quiet Times for Parents*, March 30, adapted.
22. Owen, 93-99, adapted. Wright, *Quiet Times for Parents*, July 6, adapted.
23. Brown, 14-15, adapted.
24. Clifford Notarius and Howard Markman, *We Can Work It Out* (New York: G.P. Putnam Sons, 1993), 70-73, adapted.
25. R. Scott Sullender, *Losses in Later Life*.
26. Oliver, *How to Get It Right When You've Gotten It Wrong*, 20-21.

DECEMBER

1. Lettie Cowman, *Springs in the Valley* (Grand Rapids, Mich.: Zondervan, 1939), 196-97.
2. Morley, *The Man in the Mirror*, 240-41, adapted.
3. Edwards, 75-76, adapted.
4. Bell and Campbell, 15, adapted.
5. Sala, January 6, adapted.
6. Swindoll, *Living Beyond the Daily Grind*, 51-54, adapted.
7. Smith, *Changing Answers to Depression*, 134, adapted.
8. Bill Austin, *How to Get What You Pray For*, (Wheaton, Ill.: Tyndale, 1984), 63.
9. Parrott, 25.
10. Floyd, 112-14, adapted.
11. C.S. Lewis, *The Problem of Pain* (London: Collins, 1962), 93.
12. Malcolm Muggeridge, *A Twentieth-Century Testimony* (Nashville, Tenn.: Thomas Nelson, 1978), 18.
13. Archibald Hart. Original source unknown.
14. Sala, July 11, adapted.
15. Ogilvie, *Life As It Was Meant to Be*, 100-103, adapted.
16. Ogilvie, *Life As It Was Meant to Be*, 103.
17. Rudolph F. Norden, *Each Day with Jesus* (St. Louis, Mo.: Concordia, 1994), 304, adapted.
18. Sala, July 20, adapted.
19. Max Lucado, *God Came Near*, (Multnomah, Questar Publishers, 1987), 43-44.
20. Henry Gariepy, *Light in a Dark Place* (Wheaton, Ill.: Victor, 1995), 250-51.
21. Barclay, 16-17.
22. Dr. Chris Thurman, *If Christ Were Your Counselor* (Nashville, Tenn.: Thomas Nelson, 1993), 134.
23. Gariepy, *100 Portraits of Christ*, 78-79.
24. Gariepy, *100 Portraits of Christ*, 78-79.

25. Mitchell, *Winning in the Land of Giants*, 27-28.
26. Norden, 256, adapted.
27. Kinder, *The Proverbs*, 46-47, adapted.